A Gentle Rain of Compassion

A Gentle Rain of Compassion is published under Voyage, a sectionalized division under Di Angelo Publications, Inc.

VOYAGE

Voyage is an imprint of Di Angelo Publications.
Copyright 2022.
All rights reserved.
Printed in the United States of America.

Di Angelo Publications
4265 San Felipe #1100
Houston, Texas 77027

Library of Congress
A Gentle Rain of Compassion
Hardback and Paperback
ISBN: 978-1-942549-73-4 / 978-1-955690-33-1

Words: David R. Shlim, MD
Cover Artwork: Eva Van Dam
Cover Design: Savina Deianova
Interior Design: Kimberly James
Editors: Elizabeth Geeslin Zinn, Cody Wootton, Ashley Crantas, Willy Rowberry

Downloadable via Kindle, iBooks, NOOK, and Google Play.

For educational, business, and bulk orders,
contact sales@diangelopublications.com.

1. Biography & Autobiography --- Medical
2. Travel --- Special Interest --- Adventure
3. Philosophy --- Buddhist

A Gentle Rain of Compassion

David R. Shlim, M.D.

Foreword by Chokyi Nyima Rinpoche

Like a dream dreamt by a mute
An inexpressible experience arose

From *The Grand Songs of Lord Marpa*

FOREWORD

By Chokyi Nyima Rinpoche

Dr. David Shlim and I are very close friends. He loves me and I love him. He's very expert in medicine, and he really wants to serve others genuinely from his heart. We met when he offered to provide free medical care for all our monks and nuns, which he continued to do for fourteen years while he was living in Nepal. We met often, and he really learned a lot about Buddhist philosophy and meditation. He became one of my earliest students, back in a time when I wasn't nearly as busy as I am today. We've now been close friends for more than thirty-seven years.

Dr. Shlim really thinks there's a value to cultivating loving kindness and compassion. So, he wanted to share what he learned with other health professionals, in how to train in compassion, how to cultivate patience and tolerance, and how to be kind to one another.

Many years ago, he asked me if I would give a talk to Western doctors and nurses about compassion. At first, I thought that maybe I wasn't the right person to talk to doctors about this. Maybe they would not be receptive to how I look and talk. But he really wanted to do this, so of course, I agreed in the end. I went to Jackson Hole, and I taught the course. I wanted to try to avoid religious teachings, and just talk about compassion and logic and kindness, but the doctors were smart. They asked me, "How can we cultivate more compassion? How can we train in this?" So, I taught them about meditation and the relationship between cultivating a calm mind along with the desire to relieve suffering. The doctors were really touched by this; some even cried. They wanted to know more than just the theory; they wanted to gain some of the inner beauty, to be more loving, caring, tolerant, and patient. Dr. Shlim transcribed the teachings into a book called *Medicine and Compassion*. Since then, he has worked for more than twenty years to try to share the idea that compassion can be trained, can be made more stable, vast, and effortless. He has been a unique bridge between Tibetan Buddhist teachings on compassion and Western medical care.

In his memoir, Dr. Shlim really wanted to tell the story of our friendship, and how he learned Tibetan Buddhist philosophy step by step, and how valuable it has been to him. Having a close relationship with a teacher is very important and Dr. Shlim was very fortunate. Not only have we been very close, but he was very close to my father, Tulku Urgyen Rinpoche, who was one of the greatest meditation teachers of his generation. He was my father's personal doctor for eleven years, and he received very valuable meditation teachings from him. Not only that, but Dr. Shlim was able to meet and learn from many other great lamas. Even lamas have medical problems, and Dr. Shlim was always willing to help. He refused to take any money from them, but he always asked them if they had any advice for him and his practice. In this way, he gained a lot.

Tibetan Buddhism is very logical and very valuable. However, some people think of the teachings as something only "spiritual," or simply based on what you believe. Dr. Shlim approached his study of Buddhism like his study of medicine. He wanted to know what was true, what was of value, and what could be proven and experienced. The teachings on compassion were directly valuable in his medical practice, and he thought, "If these teachings are valuable to me, maybe they can help many other doctors in the same way." I think that when people read about a doctor who learned Buddhism and genuinely experienced its value, they may take more interest in learning for themselves. I think that anyone who reads this book will develop an interest in learning about how we can train in compassion and loving kindness.

Dr. Shlim's life was filled with many challenges and many successes, both medically and personally. He tells these stories very well. I hope that many people will read his book and come away thinking about how they can investigate what he is talking about. The message is ultimately simple: if you cultivate a calm mind, you will automatically feel more kind. If you feel kind, you will also have a clear mind for solving problems. What our world needs right now is more people with calm, kind, and clear minds. If each person can work in this way, the whole world will benefit. I deeply appreciate that Dr. Shlim has shared his story of his education in Buddhist philosophy and how it can be of benefit to the world.

- Chokyi Nyima Rinpoche

PROLOGUE

I couldn't breathe.

Actually, I could breathe. It just wasn't doing me any good. I was breathing sixty times a minute, trying to get some oxygen into my blood. It was as if I was standing on the summit of Mt. Everest. Except I wasn't. I was standing on a mountain pass at 9,000 feet near Jackson Hole, Wyoming. I was so exhausted by my efforts to breathe that I no longer had the strength to stand up, and I simply fell over in the snow, lying alone in a foot of fresh powder in subzero temperatures, a mile and a half from the nearest road.

I looked up as two people slowly skied right past me on the low-angle trail. They asked me if I was okay. I raised my left hand reflexively, gave them a thumbs-up, and said, "I'm good." It was a nuts reaction, given that I was completely helpless and stranded.

I wasn't meant to be alone at that moment. I had headed out from the trailhead with my wife, Jane, and our friend John. I had slowly developed chest pain and shortness of breath—without saying anything—until I fell far enough behind that I could no longer see them around the ridge.

I reached for my cell phone. Hopefully Jane still had hers turned on.

She answered.

"I'm not feeling very well," I told her.

"Okay, I'll come back and give you the car keys, and we can meet you at the bottom."

I hesitated. "I'm really not okay." Saying it out loud for the first time made me realize it was true.

"I'll be right there," she said.

But when Jane and John reached me a few minutes later, they didn't know what to do, and they deferred to me—the doctor—to decide our next move. *Maybe I could ski out*, I thought. But to try that, I had to take off my skins, the coverings on my skis that had allowed me to climb up the trail. I struggled to my feet and managed to stand on one leg long enough for Jane to peel off one skin, but then I fell over again, completely spent.

We probably would have stayed like that for a while, but a voice of reason suddenly arrived in the form of another skier: a physician's assistant whom I knew casually. He asked what was going on, and when I told him, he said, "It looks like you're having a heart attack. We need to get you out of here. Jane, call nine-one-one." His voice was so calm and reassuring that it seemed like this must happen to him every time he went skiing.

Jane got through to 911 and within a minute she ended the call and announced, "They're sending a helicopter." A third skier arrived. Hearing the words "heart attack," he started rummaging through his pack. "I just took a wilderness first responder's course," he said. "I have an aspirin!" He reached toward my mouth, but by then I had been lying on the snow for about twenty minutes, and my jaws were clenched involuntarily from shivering. I tried hard to relax and allow him to put the aspirin under my tongue without biting him. Aspirin is the number one first aid for a heart attack. A single aspirin improves the survival rate by 25 percent. Everyone should carry one either for themselves or for someone else. But I never had. It never occurred to me, even at age sixty-three, that I might have a heart attack.

I heard the *thwump, thwump, thwump* of the rotors as the helicopter arrived overhead, but I couldn't see it. I was cocooned in a tubular space blanket stuffed with spare jackets, surrounded by volunteer rescuers who had all stopped to help when they heard someone was in trouble. I heard a rescuer say they should stamp out a platform in the snow where they could do CPR if I had a cardiac arrest—followed immediately by a quick "Shhhh" from someone else. When I heard them mention CPR, I thought how distasteful it would be to have people blowing in my mouth and pushing on my chest.

And that's when it hit me. If I was having a heart attack, I could die any second from a cardiac arrest. My heart would stop, and that would be it. I wouldn't have to worry about people blowing in my mouth and pushing on my chest. I wouldn't be there anymore. And that made me think: *If my time has actually come, what should I be doing?*

Pheriche

ONE

I wanted to be a doctor my whole life—following in my father's footsteps—but my path in medicine was not smooth. I dropped out of medical school after my first quarter, unable to focus on education while my emotions were reeling from four years of Vietnam-era college rebellion and significant romantic difficulties. I floundered in uncertainty for eight months, during which the woman I had been living with at medical school ran off to Europe with her old boyfriend, came back psychotic, and had to be hospitalized. I helped her through that episode, but finally managed to flee back to medical school. Not only was I distracting myself from that pain, but I had always thought of myself as a doctor and felt I had to complete that training before giving up on the concept. That's fairly weak motivation to engage in medical training, but I managed to stay on track, largely due to a single, life-changing lecture—about altitude illness, of all things.

I was primed for this lecture by my adolescent fascination with mountaineering expeditions to the Himalayas. I read the accounts of the first British attempts to summit Mt. Everest in the 1920s with the mystery of Mallory and Irvine's disappearance near the top. I learned about Sherpas and Nepal from reading about the successful first ascent by Edmund Hillary and Tenzing Norgay in 1953. The book that had the most profound effect on me was Jack Olsen's *The Climb Up to Hell*; it depicted the horrifying struggles of climbers trapped on the north face of the Eiger in Switzerland, in full view of tourists looking through telescopes at the lodge near the base of the peak. The Swiss authorities, having announced that they would no longer provide emergency response to the deadly face, stood by while mountain guides from around Europe arrived to attempt a rescue.

I was determined to learn to climb and took a climbing course at age thirteen from an Oregon mountaineering club called the Mazamas. My mother was against it, but to her credit she let me persist, even after she made the mistake of staying to watch the film *Mountains Don't Care*, which expounded all the ways you can die while climbing. The course culminated with a summit climb on Mt. Hood, the highest point in Oregon at 11,243 feet. As chance would have it, I summited Mt. Hood the same week that the American Everest Expedition summited Mt. Everest for the first time in 1963.

The life-changing lecture was a grand rounds talk at Rush Medical College in Chicago, where I was going to school. The year was 1974. Drummond Rennie, one of the few world experts on altitude illness, had gone on an expedition to Mt. Dhaulagiri in Nepal, the seventh highest mountain in the world. He was tall, with curly gray hair, steel-rimmed glasses, a British accent, and a lean, lanky look. He showed slides from the climb; the porters with heavy baskets of supplies hanging from their foreheads, the long-haired climbers smiling ruggedly at base camp, then inching their way, ant-like, up the massive white walls. He described the challenges of climbing to extreme altitudes. Most notably he described the perils of altitude illness, a strange syndrome that, in its more severe forms, could kill unwary climbers who ascended to high altitude faster than their bodies could adjust. Little was known about this condition and the only way to study it was to venture into the high mountains.

That suits me, I decided. I could sense most of the other members of the audience were disinterested, probably wondering why they were listening to a lecture about niche disease that only occurs at high altitude; my life changed precisely because it *was* a disease that only occurs at high altitude. I made up my mind to travel to places where altitude illness was a risk, where I could combine medicine and mountaineering.

I followed Dr. Rennie around like a puppy for the next two years, angling to sit with him in the hospital cafeteria if I could, to talk about climbing, Nepal, and altitude. I don't know what he thought of my persistence, but I'm grateful that he tolerated my enthusiasm. I was miserable in Chicago, lonely, with few friends. On weekends I would go to the one mountaineering store in the city and look for the latest edition of *Mountain Magazine*, a British publication that reported on expeditions around the world. Then I would often get stoned and go to a movie by myself.

I had not managed to pursue mountain climbing through high school and college, but between my third and fourth year of medical school, during a trip to Europe with my closest college friend, I went off by myself to take a rock-climbing course from Dougal Haston in Leysin, Switzerland. I had read the books that Dougal had written about his life and climbs. Tall, lean, and long-haired like a rock star, a Scottish hard man, Dougal was one of the world's greatest climbers. He made the first ascent of the massive south face of Annapurna in Nepal and completed the first direct ascent of the north face of the Eiger in a grueling weeks-long winter effort. I got to climb with him and a young British man for five days, getting tutored in rock climbing, anchors, rescue, and ice climbing. At night I socialized in the notorious bar at the Club Vagabond where I was staying, trying to match the drinking prowess of professional climbing guides.

I finished medical school without knowing what I wanted to do in medicine. Unable to choose a specialty, I did a one-year flexible residency back in Portland, Oregon, rotating through different specialties to gain experience. This allowed me to get my medical license, and I went into general practice in Fortuna, a tiny town in northern California. I started working in emergency rooms as well.

During this time, I attended the first mountaineering medicine course at the Palisades School of Mountaineering in Bishop, California. There I met Gil Roberts, the doctor on the 1963 American Everest expedition who had become a role model by being both a doctor and a hardcore climber. I also reconnected with Drummond Rennie at this meeting. When I managed to climb a short, steep rock face that Drummond was unable to complete, he said, "If I'd known you could climb when you were in medical school, I would have paid more attention to you."

More importantly, I met Peter Hackett at this meeting, who was in charge of staffing the high-altitude rescue post in Pheriche, near the base of Mt. Everest. The Pheriche Clinic was at 14,000 feet, an altitude where the numerous trekkers on their way to Everest Base Camp might begin to experience serious altitude illness. It was the best place in the world to see and treat the disorder and to experience what it's like to work in a remote setting with few resources. A stint there was considered a stepping stone to a career as a mountaineering doctor. Peter appointed me to work there in the spring of 1979.

My life up until then had lacked focus and direction, but I suddenly had both. I had barely made it through medical school and managed only one year of residency training. I still didn't know what I wanted to do with my life. However, at that moment I knew I was going to quit my job, travel to

Nepal, and work at the Pheriche Aid Post. Nothing else mattered. Eighteen months after finishing my training, I was on my way to Nepal.

Back in 1979, not that many people had been to Nepal, and there were very few books about it. I had only the vaguest ideas of what life there would be like. It was almost dark when our plane started its approach into Kathmandu. I pressed my face against the window, trying to get a first glimpse of the country that had so captured my imagination. I saw rugged, forested hills, with a few narrow tracks—walking trails—and no roads. Scattered on the ridgelines were clusters of thatch-roofed round houses that looked like they belonged in a fairytale. When we landed, I made my way to the Panorama Hotel that a friend had told me about. It was mid-winter, and I was the only guest in the hotel. When I ventured out into the streets, I didn't see another foreigner.

The next morning, I headed out and discovered, by chance, the Thamel district with a handful of hotels that catered to tourists, and I met some other travelers. I moved to the Kathmandu Guest House, and suddenly felt like I was connected to a unique club of adventurers. Waking up early in the foggy mornings to remarkably loud bird sounds, I would go for coffee, oatmeal, and fresh fried Tibetan bread at a small restaurant in front of the hotel. I lingered over a pot of tea and wrote in my journal as I prepared to head into the Everest region.

Due to a shortage of food in the region, I had to bring my own supplies to the aid post. However, I had no idea how to shop for supplies, so the Himalayan Rescue Association (HRA) secretary arranged for a Sherpa to go shopping with me. He spoke no English. The shops were low storefronts set behind ancient, carved wooden pillars where the shop owners sat cross-legged behind their few goods. He first took me to buy cloth. I didn't need any cloth, as far as I could tell, so I wondered if the Sherpa was shopping for himself. He bought dozens of meters of a white cotton material about a meter wide. I thought, *Okay, now let's go buy some stuff for me.*

Next, he took the material to a tailor, a man sitting behind a foot-powered sewing machine. What was this—clothing for his family? I grew impatient. The tailor cut and folded the cloth, sewed it along two edges, and then I finally figured out what was happening. He was making bags. I abruptly realized that there were no bags at the shops; to carry supplies, we needed to bring our own and there did not seem to be shops that sold bags of any kind. I began to understand how much we take for granted in our privileged lives back home. This was twenty years before anyone thought to bring their own bags to a grocery store in the U.S.

Laden with flour and rice and sugar and garlic and onions and lentils and candles and more, we took two bicycle rickshaws back to the Kathmandu Guest House. I now had eight porter loads of gear, and my intention was to walk to the aid post from Kathmandu—a two-week journey. However, I suddenly strained my lower back by moving some of my supplies around. My back muscles were constantly spasming and I could barely walk. I would need at least a week to recover. So, I reluctantly sent the porters on ahead, hoping to meet up with them in a week by flying to Lukla, a tiny airstrip at the entrance to the Everest region.

The porters had already made it to the main Sherpa village of Namche Bazaar when I landed. I found a porter to carry my personal duffle bags to Namche; he had a narrow face and prominent ears, and a delightful ten-year-old daughter who traipsed ahead of us on the trail in a long black wrap-around Sherpa dress. Whenever the porter met someone on the trail, the two of them would talk surprisingly loudly. I figured that Sherpas were just more boisterous than I had imagined. It took two days to get to Namche. When I got there, I asked the owner of my hotel why Sherpas speak so loudly. He was initially puzzled by the question, but when I mentioned that my porter had spoken at such a volume with friends, he laughed. "Oh, your porter, Ang Tharkay, he's deaf."

With two nights in Namche to acclimatize, I took the opportunity to meet up with the park ranger from New Zealand, Bruce Jeffries, who was helping to create Sagarmatha National Park. I went up to Kunde—a village on a sheltered plateau about an hour's walk above Namche—to introduce myself to the New Zealand doctor who worked at the hospital that had been founded by Sir Edmund Hillary. I spent the night as his guest and started learning about medical care in the Khumbu Valley. Just as I arrived, some Sherpas brought in a Nepalese porter who was suffering from severe shortness of breath after flying back from Kathmandu that day. We made the diagnosis of re-entry high altitude pulmonary edema, a form of altitude illness that occurs in people who live at altitude and then go down to lower elevation for a while. When traveling back rapidly, they develop altitude illness. This form of altitude illness had never been documented in the Khumbu before that night. He recovered with supplemental oxygen and rest.

From Kunde, it was a day's walk to Thyangboche, the site of a beautiful Tibetan Buddhist monastery set on a ridge beneath the towering peak of Ama Dablam. In front of the monastery, the massive Lhotse-Nuptse wall hides all but the upper reaches of Everest.

I was dazzled by the scenery and culture at every turn—the blue-white-red-green-yellow sequences of prayer flags strung across enormous gaps; long-haired yaks with intimidating horns lumbering along the trail with bells around their necks, carrying heavy bags strapped to wooden saddles on their backs; barefoot porters in shorts with cable-muscled legs laboring under crushing loads that weighed between 100 and 200 pounds. I passed giant rocks carved with hundreds of repetitions of "Om mani padme hung" in Tibetan script across their faces. It is the Tibetan Buddhist mantra of compassion.

The Khumbu Valley is the gateway to Mt. Everest and is thought by the local people to be a sacred hideaway from the world, a kind of Shangri-La, although the local word for this is *beyul*. Years later I was surprised to learn from Tom Hornbein—the first person to climb the West Ridge of Everest in 1963—that he had made a conscious decision never to return to the Khumbu, fearing that the present-day version would not live up to his memories of the virtually untouched region. My father had a similar feeling about returning to the highlands of New Guinea, where he had been stationed for almost a year during World War II. He had been posted to that part of central New Guinea less than ten years after the people there had first made contact with the outside world; it was so novel that the army sent a Hollywood cinematographer to document the medical work he was doing there. Although my father often told me about his wartime experiences in Mt. Hagen, I couldn't get him to take me there. "It wouldn't be the same," he said.

Hornbein's visit to the Khumbu was, in fact, only thirteen years after the first Westerners trekked there in 1950. I arrived sixteen years after Hornbein and there were still only primitive teahouses, one-room lodges and perhaps a single outhouse per village. Local food was the only choice: boiled potatoes served in their skins with salt and chili, or rice served with lentil soup and vegetables. For seven days I walked by myself, trying to absorb every new sight.

It was late winter, before the trekking season, and there were few other Westerners on the trail. From Kunde, I had to descend 1,500 feet to cross the Dudh Kosi River and then ascend 1,500 feet through a forest of pine and rhododendron trees to the Thyangboche Monastery. I emerged from the forest and found my way to a small teahouse behind the monastery, where I would spend the night. The next day, I planned to walk four hours further up the valley and take up my duties at the Pheriche Aid Post, at 14,000 feet. I would stay there for three months.

That afternoon, I walked over to the monastery, standing on the porch of the main prayer hall in front of massive black wooden doors that proved to be locked. I was in one of the most beautiful places I had ever been; indeed, one of the most beautiful places that there is. In spite of that, I started to feel uneasy, a restless disquiet that I couldn't pin down. I hadn't felt it before I approached the monastery. It finally dawned on me that my nervousness had a strange cause. I realized that I wanted to be noticed. I wanted to be singled out as a worthy person and invited in to meet the head lama—even though I had no idea who he was. I could see us sitting around a low table, a pot of steaming tea between us. The head lama reached over and poured me a cup and asked if I had any questions. At that moment I somehow knew that he had some answers for me, something that could change my life.

Regardless of my fantasies, I didn't get to find out. Even though I spotted a few monks walking around, no one took notice of me. I lingered on the porch; the sun sank behind the mountains to the west. It started to get cold, and I slowly retreated to the teahouse. I tried to understand how I could feel so disappointed. I hadn't given a thought to visiting the monastery until I was standing outside it. Having now had the vision, I felt a strange sense of longing and regret. But longing and regret for what? It was tantalizing to think there was something that I could learn, but it remained in my mind as a mystery. Was there some ancient knowledge in there that could benefit me? How would I ever find out? And most mysterious of all, why did I think it really mattered?

"Are you the Pheriche doctor?"

The question caught me off guard as I returned to the teahouse. A young Sherpa man posed the question, and I realized that I was (or would be the next day). He told me that his grandfather had fallen down the stairs and had a cut on his head and asked if I would be able to go see him. His house was two hours' walk further up the valley, but that didn't matter at the moment, as I had not brought any instruments for sewing up a wound. However, I knew I could borrow them from the Kunde Hospital, which I had left just that morning to come to Thyangboche. I wrote a note to the Kunde doctor and asked the Sherpa man to walk the four hours to the hospital and bring the instruments back the next morning.

At eight o'clock the next morning, he found me at the teahouse and handed me a small metal box filled with instruments, local anesthetic, and suture. We headed off together down the meadow in front of the monastery, through a forest of twisted rhododendron trees draped with lace-like moss. We arrived at a terrifying cable bridge across a two-hundred-foot-deep ravine over a roaring river. Broken boards were lashed irregularly to two cables, forming the walkway of the bridge. Some boards were missing. Two other cables formed low railings. The bridge swayed in the wind as I swallowed hard and headed across. I think my rock-climbing background gave me the mental discipline to avoid the panic that was fighting to get out. From there I climbed a ridge and descended into Pangboche.

The old man that I had come to treat was, in fact, old. At eighty-four, he was lying motionless on the floor of his house, wrapped up in blankets, the top of his head hidden by a thick, bloody cloth. The house had few windows, and the upstairs floor where he lay was both dark and cold. In order to have light and heat, I needed to move him outdoors.

The Sherpas carried him outside. The instruments needed to be sterilized. At the far end of the room, a woman was squatting next to a small clay hearth, and I dropped the instruments into some water in an aluminum pot. She placed a few small pieces of wood into the coals and blew on them until a fire was going. Once the instruments were boiled, I had to wait for the water to cool off, so I began unwrapping the cloth on the patient's head. It was stiff with clotted blood. The Sherpa man had been silent until then, but now he moaned and began muttering.

"What is he saying?" I asked the grandson.

"'Leave me alone. I want to die.'"

"How did this happen?" I asked.

"He fell down the stairs. He was drunk."

The cloth came away in my hands. A massive flap of scalp had been carved away from the man's skull, splitting his right eyebrow and making a huge arc across the top of his head to the back of his neck. It was the biggest scalp laceration I had ever seen.

What would an expert do? Who, in fact, were the experts in sewing people up on the ground, and why had I never talked to them? This was before there was any hint of a Wilderness Medical Society, or an International Society of Travel Medicine. All my training had been in hospitals, where the emphasis was constantly on the fact that the least violation of sterile technique could result in a wound infection. Now I had a patient lying in the dirt; no gloves, no clean place to put my instruments down, and no sterile cloth to keep the trailing length of suture thread from dragging across the patient's unwashed skin. The question was no longer what was ideal, but what could I safely get away with?

I had also been taught that a wound must be sewed up within a few hours of infliction, or else left open for a few days to decrease the chance of infection. This wound was now more than twenty-four hours old, but it was far too large to leave open. The skin edges would lose their blood supply and start to shrink, the muscle underneath would dry up and start to die, and the man's skull would be perpetually exposed. Leaving it open was not an option.

I squirted some betadine antiseptic into the boiled water and left the instruments in the pot. I drew the anesthetic into a syringe and began injecting the edges of the wound. The man stirred and moaned but didn't try to push me away. Since I had no gloves, I would have to do the whole repair barehanded. I saw that if I set the instruments back down in the antiseptic water after each time that I used them, they would stay clean—and my hands would get disinfected as well when I picked them up.

I used some of the boiled water to wash out the wound and began to sew it up, starting in front to make sure I got his eyebrow straight. Squatting next to him on the ground, I worked my way across his forehead and over the top of his head—sometimes using two or even three layers of suture to close the deeper tissues. It took an hour or so. At the end, I wrapped a large, clean bandage around his head, and told his family to change the bandage after three days.

The patient recovered with no wound infection and regained his interest in living. The techniques that I invented on the spot ended up being useful for the next twenty years of sewing up people in the field, none of whom ever got infected.

Two hours later, I crested the final ridge and looked down into the Pheriche Valley. The chill February wind whipped past me. I stopped to catch my breath, the thin air much more noticeable at 14,000 feet. The valley floor was flat and treeless, with scattered patches of old snow. The Dudh Kosi River snaked through the middle, carrying the melted ice from Mt. Everest. Two peaks—Tawoche and Cholatse—dominated the left side of the valley, rising almost vertically to over 24,000 feet. Nestled at the base of a low ridge on the opposite side of the valley was Pheriche itself, a tiny village of five or six stone houses that, before the advent of trekking, had only been used as yak herding huts in the summer.

The day had clouded up. The air was cold, and the sky was the color of slate, making the bare valley appear remarkably desolate. I still had a half-hour walk to get to the aid post, but as I stood looking at the valley, despite the bleak impression, a warm feeling of having arrived home suddenly and unexpectedly washed over me. I usually didn't feel at home in new places, but as I walked, I was already relishing the fact that I would get to stay here for the next three months.

The trekking seasons in Nepal were in the spring and the fall, and the aid post was only staffed during those times. Summertime was the monsoon season with heavy rains and dense clouds hanging over the mountains. Wintertime is too cold for most trekkers, and the teahouses shut down. It was late February, and I would stay until mid-May.

After I descended the hill, I crossed a short wooden bridge over the river. Below the bridge, carved on a large rock, is "In Memoriam Dino de Riso 1975." The bridge had been built—I later learned—by the family of an Italian man who had died of altitude illness in the Pheriche Valley four years earlier, at a time when people with altitude illness thought they had the flu, or a chest infection, and failed to descend in time to save their lives. I was there to educate trekkers and try to save their lives from a disease I had just seen for the first time in Kunde. How hard could it be?

TWO

At two in the afternoon on my third day at Pheriche, I was called outside to meet a New Zealander trekker who had been carried down on the back of a yak from Lobuche, a village 2,000 feet higher, on the way to Everest. Walking out to greet her, I felt the frisson of cool at the recognition that I was finally taking care of patients who arrived by yak. That cool feeling lasted about an hour and a half.

Freckled, with reddish blond hair, Barbara was a twenty-six-year-old intensive care unit nurse who had been sick for two days. That morning she had tried to walk down, but ultimately couldn't keep going, which is how she ended up being ferried on the yak. When I helped her down from the wooden saddle, she was able to walk inside and sit on a bench near the wood stove. I asked her how she felt, and she said, "Tired." She didn't have a headache and didn't feel any shortness of breath. From what I'd read about altitude illness, she didn't seem to have it. On the other hand, I had only ever seen one case of altitude illness, and it was nothing like this, so how would I know?

My Sherpa assistant, Ang Rita, brewed some tea, and Barbara managed to take a few sips before she laid down on the bench and fell asleep. I watched her sleep and wondered what was making her ill. Her face looked a little puffy, like she was retaining fluid, and her skin had a faint bluish tinge, suggesting that she was low on oxygen. Was she getting worse while she was lying there? But worse with what? If she had altitude illness, she should be getting better with the descent. If she was just tired, I should let her rest. Why wake her up needlessly? This went on for over an hour before I finally felt like I had to wake her up.

I shook her gently by the shoulder. She didn't respond. I shook her a little harder. She stirred but still didn't wake up. She was unconscious! It didn't make sense. It didn't fit what I had read about altitude illness. On the other hand, it's pretty rare for anyone to just slip into a coma without a reason, and the best reason was still that her brain was swelling from not being able to adapt to the altitude. I decided she had to have high-altitude cerebral edema.

Barbara had been trekking with her best friend, Anne, in an organized trekking group. Anne was also a nurse, and as we warmed our hands over the wood stove, we discussed our options. I had two small bottles of oxygen that had been purchased from an Everest expedition, and a storeroom full of unsorted leftover drugs from those expeditions. The right drugs would buy some time, but the only way to save her life was to get her to a lower altitude. The question was how.

The trail from Pheriche down to Thyangboche is relatively flat. Barbara could no longer sit up, so riding farther down on the yak was out of the question. We didn't have a stretcher, and even if we could fashion one to carry her, it would take many hours of awkward maneuvering in freezing temperatures down a narrow trail to get her down a thousand feet in altitude. That amount of descent was not going to be enough to make a difference.

What I needed was a helicopter to evacuate her to Kathmandu, which would accomplish 10,000 feet of descent in an hour. The aid post didn't have a telephone or a radio, so my only way of requesting a rescue was to send a written note to the ranger station in Namche Bazaar. Namche was a one- or two-day walk back down the valley for most Westerners, but a Sherpa, genetically adapted to the altitude and mythically strong in the mountains, can make the trip in four hours. My note would not reach Namche until after dark, so the best I could hope for was that a helicopter would arrive the next morning.

With the note written and sent, Anne and I turned to take care of Barbara. Ang Rita brought out an oxygen bottle and we strapped the mask over her nose and mouth. I started an intravenous line and gave her some dexamethasone, a drug that decreases brain swelling. Barbara was still stirring at times, turning her head with her eyes open, but not responding to us verbally in any way. An hour later, she suddenly jerked violently in bed and vomited all over herself. As I stared at the nauseating brown mess, it hit me that, as a doctor, I had never been asked to clean up a patient before. While I stood feeling helpless and slightly queasy, Anne got a towel and some water from Ang Rita and cleaned her up.

Unconsciousness is actually a broad concept, and the degree of unconsciousness is measured by the Glascow Coma Scale, a fifteen-point ranking system that ranges from mildly confused to unresponsive to deep pain. Since her arrival, Barbara had been sliding steadily down the scale. She no longer stirred spontaneously. Then, an hour later, her legs suddenly stiffened at the knees with her feet pointed down like a ballet dancer *en pointe*. Her arms locked straight at the elbows with her hands bent at right angles at the wrist and twisted behind her. Her body was contorted as if possessed in a horror movie, but I knew it was a complication of coma called decerebrate posturing.

Two hours later, her decerebrate posturing relaxed, but further examination showed that she was actually worse, not better—she had gone *beyond* being decerebrate. The swelling of her brain had continued to push her down the scale from twelve to three in a matter of hours. Three was the lowest possible score; if she went any lower, she would die.

Anne was as calm as someone taking care of her dying best friend could be, and her presence was an invaluable comfort, but the decision-making on how to care for Barbara had fallen to me. The doubts that had quietly surfaced when I had to figure out how to sew up the scalp wound were now waving their hands and shouting out questions like reporters at a press conference. *Is there anything else you could be doing? Does she actually have high altitude cerebral edema? Are you missing the real diagnosis? Do you really know enough to be up here all alone?*

I was undertrained as a physician. I had done a one-year internship, whereas these days the minimum post-graduate training for licensure is three years. I didn't know what kind of doctor I wanted to be, so I was unable to choose a residency. I figured I'd go back when I knew what I wanted to do. The only work I was qualified to do was family practice or emergency medicine, and a lot of my time was spent learning on the job. With no way of contacting anyone for help, I had to go with what I had.

Even if I'd had more training, I was suddenly discovering that caring for an unconscious patient in an isolated outpost was far more intimate and unrelenting than anything I had ever experienced in a hospital, where there is always someone around to run a thought by, to commiserate with. The sicker the patient, the more they are surrounded by glowing electric lights and machines that beep reassuringly, monitoring all the vital output from the body at the same time. We monitored Barbara's desperate struggle by the dim, flickering light of three candles.

By 3:00 a.m. I realized that I hadn't emotionally anticipated the implications of heading off into the mountains by myself to take care of sick or injured people. In all my medical training and practice, I had never been *all alone* (professionally) with a critically ill patient. Despite my efforts, Barbara's life was slipping away. As far as I could tell, her only hope was that the helicopter would arrive in time to save her.

When I faced up to that fact, I was overcome by a totally unexpected wave of dread. I realized that I was not emotionally prepared to watch her die, which didn't make rational sense to me. I had been involved in the care of hundreds of patients who had died. Some died suddenly, some after a long-wasting illness. In the emergency room, life and death situations were a nightly occurrence. In the ER, we could take action. We were not forced to sit and just watch and wait and hope that forces beyond our control would allow someone to live.

I knew how to take action. I once dragged a one-hundred-seventy-pound woman out of the back of a car—where she had just suffered a cardiac arrest—lifted her onto a gurney, pushed the stretcher into the emergency room, intubated her, and shocked her heart back to life. The idea of facing a life and death crisis was sobering to me, but not usually intimidating.

Barbara was just three years younger than me. In all the times I had fantasized about working in the Himalayas, I hadn't thought about being forced to sit helplessly while someone died. There was another twist as well: I had been told that if she died, we would not be able to fly her body out of the mountains. Nepali pilots would not fly dead people in their helicopters. I would have to arrange for her to be cremated, a raw event that I couldn't imagine organizing, let alone having to watch.

I stepped outside under a moonless sky full of stars to take some deep breaths and calm myself down. Anne had taken a nap earlier, and I laid down at 4:00 a.m. for two hours of restless sleep. When I woke up, it was light. Yet as I looked out the window, I realized that all I could see was white. A violent storm was blowing snow sideways up the valley, completely obscuring the mountains. Whatever hope we had of getting a helicopter had vanished. I went to check on Barbara—she was still deeply comatose.

At 10:00 a.m. a Sherpa arrived at the clinic, having hiked up through the driving snow for two hours from Thyangboche. He ran the National Park Teahouse, where I had stayed just a few days earlier. He pulled a bright yellow portable radio out of his backpack and helped me set it up so that I could talk to Bruce Jefferies, the Kiwi park ranger I had met in Namche Bazaar.

When Bruce came on the radio, I told him about the desperate condition of the patient and my concerns about the weather. He gave me his own grim news. He hadn't yet been able to contact Kathmandu; the park officials who were supposed to man the radio were not answering. He had just sent a runner up the hill above Namche to a weather station that had the only other radio in the region, to see if they could reach *their* base in Kathmandu and ask them to send someone over to the national park office to tell them to turn their radio on. My heart sank as I realized that the rescue request had not yet even reached Kathmandu.

An hour later, Bruce radioed to tell me that he had reached the national park office, but things had stalled again. When he requested a helicopter rescue from the army, the contact at the army told him that someone would have to pay for the helicopter in advance or they wouldn't fly. The army official had called the trekking company in Kathmandu to guarantee the $2,000 payment, but—remarkably and inexplicably—they had refused. Bruce told them that he would personally pay for the helicopter flight. The army accepted the financial guarantee, but then told him that, unfortunately, the phone lines had just gone dead in Kathmandu. They had no way to reach the pilot, who had already gone home for the day. Bit by bit, as fluid continued to leak into Barbara's brain, the obstacles to getting a helicopter continued to mount.

Bruce called me back at 1:00 p.m. "Maybe it would be best if we just tried to organize the helicopter for tomorrow morning."

Barbara was corpse-like, barely breathing. She no longer responded to pain at all. She was breathing only four times per minute, a feeble effort that could cease at any time.

"If the helicopter doesn't come this afternoon, there'll be no point in sending it tomorrow," I replied. "She'll be dead."

"Got that."

We finally got a break. Bruce's assistant park ranger, also a New Zealander, happened to be in Kathmandu, and had wandered into the national park office, unaware of the drama taking place. He immediately took the initiative to have someone go by car to find the helicopter pilot. We waited by the radio for another two hours. It had stopped snowing, but the wind still blew waves of clouds up the valley. Bruce came on the radio.

"Pheriche, Pheriche, Pheriche," he said. "The helicopter has landed at Namche to offload fuel. The pilot wants the patient ready to go. Do you read me?"

I felt a chill run from the back of my skull to down my spine. Barbara might survive! We bundled her up in her sleeping bag for the journey, and then I stepped outside into the bitterly cold wind and gazed down the valley. For a while, all I could hear was the noise of the wind. Then the helicopter, white like the clouds, rounded a corner a hundred feet off the ground.

Roaring past the clinic, the pilot made a sharp turn and circled back, landing in a cloud of dust and dry, powdery snow in an empty potato field. The pilot stayed in the helicopter with the engines on, gesturing to us impatiently. We carried Barbara to the helicopter and slid her onto the floor behind the pilots. Anne got in with her, and the pilot took off, flying low over the ground past the clinic, disappearing into the clouds.

Drained, I stood there, indifferent to the cold wind lashing me. After the agonizing wait, Barbara had magically been plucked out of my hands moments before she would have died. We didn't find out what happened to her for three days, when I finally got a message relayed via the Namche ranger station. Despite being within minutes of dying, Barbara's condition responded dramatically to the ten-thousand-foot descent. On arrival at the Shanta Bhawan Mission Hospital in Kathmandu, she was breathing normally and responding to pain. By the next day, she was awake and sitting up in bed, eating, an almost impossibly rapid recovery from such a severe brain injury.

All of our efforts had probably kept her alive for a couple of extra hours, just enough to allow all the obstacles to be overcome and the helicopter to finally arrive. If the aid post hadn't been open, she would have certainly become another altitude illness casualty. Through this case, I came to understand that high-altitude cerebral edema is unique in that it can be reversed so remarkably. It meant that one should never give up on a HACE patient if they are still breathing on their own and can be transported to a lower altitude.

When I finally stepped back into the clinic, I noticed I was holding a package that the pilot had handed me as we packed Barbara into the helicopter. I tore open the wrapping to find a can of Foster's beer, sent up by Bruce. I popped the top, and beer sprayed me in the face. Ang Rita laughed, and I laughed with him. Some other trekkers had stopped by to help, and we drank the beer and then bought a small bottle of Nepali whiskey at a teahouse.

That night, the wind that had been blowing all day kicked up a few notches into a massive windstorm, flattening tents up and down the valley. I lay in my sleeping bag, listening to the wind howling through the small cracks in my window. I played back the last twenty-four hours in my mind, over and over again. I felt confident that I had done everything that was possible, under the circumstances, to save Barbara. I was incredibly relieved that the helicopter had arrived in time. Barbara had been saved, but I was still trying to come to grips with how fearful I had been that she might die. As I said, I was used to life and death situations. Or I thought I was. There was something about the inescapable intimacy of caring for her in that remote setting that had changed the rules; that, and the fact that my treatment options had been so limited. The fear that she would die was a new emotion for me, and I couldn't understand why I felt that way. Plus, I had learned that if I failed to save a patient's life, I would need to cremate them. That fact hung over me as a peculiar added pressure to my time in the mountains.

THREE

I was back in Portland, attempting to settle back into my normal life. I had taken my time getting home, traveling down through Thailand, Malaysia, Bali, and Fiji for two months before moving back into my small house on one of the highest hills in Portland. At night, when I was in Pheriche, I would share some warmth around our woodstove with some travelers and listen to their stories of traveling through Southeast Asia. I stayed in a grass shack on a beach in Bali, traveled by motorbike across the whole island, and snorkeled the elaborate reefs and crystalline water in Fiji—I was able to hold my breath underwater for deliciously long minutes and swim among the massive coral formations, a result of the high hemoglobin level I gained living for three months above 14,000 feet. My body was thin and fit and tan. There had not been much food up at the aid post, and I had lost twenty pounds.

I went to work part-time in two emergency rooms. Working mostly twelve-hour night shifts, I felt jet-lagged a lot of the time, lying on my couch at two in the morning, choosing from the three broadcast channels that existed in the pre-cable era. I remember a particularly obnoxious home furnishings salesman who would pretend to knock loudly on the inside glass of the TV screen, shouting, "Wake up! Wake up!" which was often effective.

I went rock climbing as much as I could. In support of the rock climbing, I started taking ballet classes. My brother Larry had started taking ballet classes, and after watching one of his classes, I decided to sign up. I took an adult beginners' class and found the mental discipline and physical effort required were both addictive. One of the main things I learned from ballet is how to keep your body completely still while moving one limb to a very specific point. This is identical to what is required in many of the moves of rock climbing. Plus, it takes incredible core strength to do that. I often rushed from a twelve-hour emergency room shift to take an hour-and-a-half class.

Beyond these activities, I had only a few friends in Portland, and even fewer who could relate to my experience in Nepal. Most people in Portland, it turned out, didn't know where Nepal was. I spent a lot of time thinking about the Khumbu, the slow way of life, the friendliness and openness of the Sherpas, their phenomenal competence and fitness and effortless sense of time. They were never in a hurry, and yet they never appeared to be wasting time. They just did what needed to be done without a fuss. I envied the ease with which they accomplished their daily tasks. Doing the dishes was not a chore; it just needed to be done, so they did it. I wanted to be like them, but I didn't know how to change.

The Sherpa that I had become closest to was Ang Rita. He was my main assistant at the aid post, doing the shopping, cooking, cleaning, and assisting with medical procedures. He wore his hair long and had crooked teeth, which made him look vaguely like an English rock-and-roll star. Born in the upper Khumbu, there had been no opportunity to go to school. He had taught himself to write in English, and his spoken English was adequate. He translated for me when I saw local patients. He could speak Nepali, Hindi, Tibetan, and Sherpa. He had an instinct for what was happening all around him. When we got word that a patient was coming, he always knew how long it would be before they got there, or how serious it sounded. He helped me with everything—making tea for visitors or the people who had brought in a sick patient; helping set up for minor surgery; cooking all my meals; starting the small fire that we allowed ourselves each evening at dinner time to warm up our main room before we shuffled off to our small unheated bedrooms. He had a native curiosity and asked perceptive questions. I enjoyed his company and his competence to such an extent that later in life I often went trekking in other parts of Nepal, with him as my sole companion.

At Pheriche, the mornings dawned sunny almost every day, but it was cold, and we were in a deep valley. I would often stay in my sleeping bag and watch as the sun worked its way down the slopes of Tawoche, to the valley floor, and finally across the narrow strip of land to our aid post. Only then would I brave getting out of my sleeping bag, put on layers of clothing, and move out into the warming sun.

Our patients would arrive in waves. Those who had spent the night in Pheriche and woke up feeling unwell would come see us in the morning. Later we saw ill and injured people who had walked up to Pheriche that day, arriving in the mid to late afternoon, if they had a problem. In between, we would see those who were descending from higher up the valley.

Every afternoon I gave a lecture to the newly arrived trekkers about altitude illness and how to avoid dying. This was unique to a rescue post— we were trying hard not to have to rescue people. And it worked. As far as I know, in all the years that we ran the rescue posts, no one who attended a lecture had ever died of altitude illness.

My last night in Pheriche, the Sherpas threw a going-away party for me. The whole village crammed together in the main room of our aid post. They formed a circle around the small wood stove, the men together on one side, and the women on the other, arms around each other's shoulders. Then they sang, starting slowly, and danced, stepping forward and back until the music went faster and faster and it became impossible to match their footwork. After a while, it didn't matter, because a profoundly innocent-looking grandmother with long silver braids and sweet smile made her rounds in the middle of the circle with a teapot full of a potent distilled rice brew called *rakshi*. She was impossible to resist. She handed me a full drinking glass of the clear brew, and then gestured for me to drink it right then, saying, "*Shey shey shey*." In Sherpa culture, when you are offered something to eat or drink, it is polite to initially refuse. Then the host encourages you, and if you want to be more polite, you continue to pretend to refuse. Finally, you give in. The cleverness of this system is that there is no actual way to refuse. They just think you are being extra polite. That seductiveness, combined with my desire to show off a little bit, led to a delightfully hazy evening of warmth and friendship. At one point, the lodge owner from down the street leaned over to me to translate a melodic slow song: "When I look around me, all I see are mountains, and when I see these mountains, I know that I will have to come back again."

When I left Pheriche after the first season, I knew that I would go back again. That's why, in the fall of 1980, I once again found myself n the Khumbu.

I walked into Pheriche for my second season from near Kathmandu. It was a ten-day trek to Namche, and I had a duty to fulfill en route. Friends of mine from Bishop, California, were leading an expedition to Baruntse, a 23,000-foot mountain near Pheriche. The climbers had gone in a month earlier to teach the first Sherpa climbing school. Although Sherpas had accompanied Westerners to the highest summits in the Himalayas, no one had ever thought to teach them solid climbing techniques. They were so strong and practical that they picked up what they needed to know, but it left them a notch below the Western climbers. This climbing school was an attempt to start changing that paradigm.

However, all climbing expeditions in Nepal are required to have a Nepal government liaison officer stay at their base camp. The liaison officer (LO) needs to be accompanied to base camp by the leader or deputy leader of the expedition. Since I was headed into the Khumbu at the right time, I had been designated the deputy leader of an American Baruntse expedition.

The LO was an overweight bureaucrat from Kathmandu, but he proved able to walk without problems and wasn't bad company. It was August, and full-on monsoon season, with daily rain showers, clouds, drizzle, and a few hours of sunshine per day. Walking across the grain of the Himalayas means climbing and descending thousands of feet per day. There were no real lodges—it was a time when local people just took trekkers into their homes and had them sleep on the floor. Fortunately, two young American men from New Jersey started the trek at the same time, and we formed a small group. The LO was able to translate for us, which made arranging lodging and ordering food much easier.

The twelve-day trek proved to be one of my more memorable experiences, a feeling of traversing a wondrous land of emerald-green rice paddies and eerie cloud-draped forests. The rains were often incessant, but we learned to walk through the hot weather in shorts and t-shirts with an umbrella to keep the rain off our faces. At times it felt like we were being hounded by leeches, two-to-three-inch blood-sucking worms that rose from the grass and dropped from the trees, sneaking into our socks, and drinking from our feet. We usually didn't feel them, but when we went to change our socks, they were blood-soaked. Sometimes I would pause to catch my breath and see masses of heat-seeking leeches rising up in the grass and moving rapidly toward my shoes, forcing me to take temporary refuge on top of a rock and then having to move on as the leeches crawled onto the rock, even though I had no rest.

This trek was the beginning of my learning that one's best travel stories come from both the highest and lowest points of one's adventures.

When I arrived at Thyangboche, the rains were ending, and I had dried out. I found a place to stay at the National Park Teahouse and then walked over to the monastery. Once again that nervous feeling arose in my stomach. I was alert, standing near the front doors, hoping to get noticed. A few red-robed monks walked past. One of them, maybe eighteen years old, looked at me and gestured for me to come. Like a guy in a bar who can't believe that a woman is gesturing to him and looks behind to see who she is really interested in, I initially didn't pay attention. But he walked up to me and gestured with his hands that I should follow him. He led me around the prayer hall, through a wooden arch, and down a covered walkway to a door. I was inside the monastery. It was happening! They were taking me in. He unlocked the door and gestured me inside. I stepped into a cluttered room that was filled with jackets, robes, food items, dirty dishes, statues, books, and a couple of large wooden trunks. The bed was the only place to sit, and he swept some things off its surface to make room for me.

He went over to a trunk and opened it up. He removed some rolled-up papers—ancient scrolls?—and brought them over to the bed. Were these the secret teachings? Is this how they shared their secret knowledge? My heart was pounding. He unrolled them and I saw the outline of Buddhist deities, primitively drawn. In crayon. I couldn't recognize who they were.

He looked at the paintings, and then at me, and said, "You want to buy?"

Ugh. It was an especially deflating kind of disappointment that I felt. Mortifying, actually. I wasn't special. I was just a tourist who might be willing to part with a few rupees to give him spending money. My uncertain but high expectations shattered in an instant, as if a director yelled, "Cut!" and the characters suddenly became mere actors. Flustered, I paid him for a few of his drawings and retreated once again to my teahouse with that frustrated sense of loss.

I had arrived in Pheriche before the trekking season started, so I spent time at Baruntse Base Camp, and then attempted a hard route on Island Peak, which I wasn't able to complete due to dangerous snow conditions. The rest of the season was fairly routine, with a few serious altitude illness cases that improved with descent, and some frostbite cases that had to be evacuated by yak to Lukla Airport. My love of living in this wild valley was undiminished, but I was becoming accustomed to the grandeur. In my whole first season, I could never step outside without being stunned by the scenery once again. This year, I could look up and just quietly smile and carry on.

FOUR

When you start training as a physician, you often find yourself on the edge of what you can handle emotionally. There's no limit to what you can be forced to confront, whether it's spurting blood and protruding bones, the dark queasy tension of suspected child abuse cases, the numb horror of rape victims, or people wasting away from incurable disease. Or having to go out into the waiting area—with no prior training or advice—and find the wife of the man who just came in off the tennis court with a cardiac arrest, and tell her that he didn't survive. The main commitment that you make when you choose to become a doctor is that you will be willing to take it—that you won't run away, and that you will somehow find a way to handle whatever comes. That willingness to do whatever is necessary is the unspoken bond that joins medical practitioners together and, to some extent, separates doctors from non-doctors. Until my third season at Pheriche, I had always been able to take it.

I wasn't supposed to have a third season in Pheriche. I had planned for months to go on a mountain climbing expedition to Dolpo, in west Nepal, a region that one could visit only with a special permit from the Ministry of Tourism, which was rarely granted. The expedition leader was Gordon Wiltsie, a mountain climber and photographer who I met through the Palisades School of Mountaineering courses, and who had been on the Baruntse Expedition eighteen months earlier. Dolpo was a sparsely inhabited, Tibet-like high mountain region of Nepal that George Schaller and Peter Matthiessen explored in the mid-1970s, a journey described in Matthiessen's book, *The Snow Leopard*. That book was widely popular, and in my experience, Matthiessen was one of the first visitors to Nepal to confess a secret spiritual agenda: to meet a reincarnate Tibetan Buddhist lama and gain some wisdom.

The expedition to Dolpo seemed like the logical next step in my career as a mountaineering doctor, serving as a doctor on an expedition to a remote Himalayan peak. I spent months planning and preparing my gear, my climbing harness, pack, clothing, sleeping bag, tent, and so on, but at the last minute, just weeks before we were to leave, our permit was not granted. Since I had the time off and was planning to go to Nepal anyway, I decided to go back to Pheriche for the season.

For the first time, I would have a partner. Jon Rosen and his girlfriend, Helen, were also going to be there that season. Since I was supposed to be off climbing a mountain in West Nepal, Peter Hackett had appointed Jon to be the doctor at Pheriche. However, the clinic had gotten busy enough in the recent past to justify having two doctors; with two doctors, the clinic would always be open, even if one doctor went off trekking or climbing briefly. Jon had just completed his residency in internal medicine. He had high energy, curly hair, a good sense of humor, and keen judgment. Helen was not medically trained, but willing to help in whatever way she could.

The season went smoothly for a while. Then, we faced a major crisis at the Mani Rimdu Festival at Thyangboche Monastery at the end of October—a major Buddhist celebration, with exotic lama dancing playing out mythological stories, and a fire *puja*, in which blessed objects are burnt as offerings. A French woman in her early fifties, traveling alone, became psychotic the day before the festival started and began attacking people. She threw a pan of heated oil on a young Sherpa girl, then ran outside and began tearing down tents with the occupants still in them. Fortunately, the pan of oil had not been on the fire long enough to heat up to a dangerous temperature, and the girl was okay. After a tense twenty-four-hour period where we tried sedating her with narcotics to no avail, we finally had to tie her up and sit on her in a tent through a long night, during which she continually screamed, "*Au secours*" into the cold night air. Finally, by the following afternoon, we obtained some antipsychotic medication from Kunde Hospital, and she recovered enough to walk out of the mountains. It had been a fraught time, with a very uncertain outcome, and we were still digesting it two weeks later when something happened to eclipse that particular event.

We were sitting around the woodstove, savoring the warmth and our camaraderie before we went to bed. Around eight o'clock we heard a knock at the door, and a Sherpa woman came in with a three-year-old boy in her arms. She had just carried him for two hours in the dark, down from Lobuche, where she worked at one of the two lodges. The baby had been suffering from a cold for three days, but the day before he started having a rasping, seal-like cough—almost a bark. When the baby coughed in the clinic, I recognized it immediately as croup.

Croup is a viral infection of the breathing tube that causes the tissue to swell. In an adult, the swollen tissue produces an irritating cough, but in a young child, the same amount of swelling narrows the breathing space so that it can become extremely difficult to breathe. In a trachea the diameter of a soda straw, a millimeter or two of swelling can spell the difference between being unable to breathe at all and recovering completely.

As the mother held the child in her arms, he exploded into a rapid series of painful-sounding yelps. The child was about the size of an American eighteen-month-old. He had a full head of dark hair and a beautiful face with sun-burnished red cheeks, glowing even more with a slight fever.

There is no specific treatment for croup. Antibiotics don't help, but given our remote location, I started the child on an antibiotic just in case there was something else going on. Croup almost always goes away by itself after one or two nights. For unknown reasons, the symptoms are always worse at night. The November night was already cold: the thermometer read 18° F. The treatment at that time was to provide heated, humidified air that would soothe the inflamed tissue and help ease breathing. When the morning came, it was likely that the breathing would improve on its own. We just had to help him make it through the night.

However, heated air—let alone humidified air—is difficult to come by at 14,000 feet in the Himalayas. The Pheriche Aid Post was made of chiseled, stacked rocks with no mortar. There was a wood stove in the main room, but the whole building was so poorly insulated that a pan on the stove would not create any significant moisture in the air. We decided to set up a tent outside with a stove and a pot of water, then put the mother and baby inside the humidified environment.

Ang Rita set up the tent and got a kerosene stove roaring. The boiling pot of water filled the tent with steam, which condensed on the cold nylon walls into droplets that ran down and pooled on the floor. The same happened when the steam reached our clothing. Soon we were all soaking wet. The baby hadn't improved. After an hour or so, we abandoned the experiment.

Back inside the aid post, we continued to boil water, but the wisps of steam that were generated did not venture far from the surface of the pot.

The mother continued to hold the child and sway gently back and forth, while the child showed increasing signs of breathing difficulty. His small chest muscles strained with exertion, showing his ribs on each breath.

I knew that, theoretically, the child could die from croup. I had never seen it happen, and I had treated dozens of children at night in a hospital emergency room who were just as sick as this child was. We usually gave some advice and sent them home. Rarely, a child was admitted to the hospital and given supplemental oxygen.

We had a few bottles of oxygen that had been purchased from an Everest expedition. I decided to use one of the bottles at a low flow, through a mask over the baby's face. If he was having trouble getting air, at least I could enrich the air he *was* getting.

The next step, if he took a turn for the worse, would be problematic. If the child's airway became too narrow to allow him to breathe, we would have to insert a breathing tube down his throat past the obstruction. To insert the tube, I could use a pediatric laryngoscope, which is basically a flashlight with a metal blade attached that allows one to pry open the patient's mouth and light up the back of the throat. The problem was that I didn't have a pediatric laryngoscope, which actually didn't matter because I had no pediatric-sized breathing tube.

I did have an adult-sized laryngoscope, but the blade was massive compared to the child's small mouth. Searching for something I could use as a small breathing tube, I eyed the green, plastic oxygen tubing running from the oxygen bottle to the mask. A child's trachea is about the same diameter as their little finger; the oxygen tubing about matched the boy's pinkie. A piece of that hose could possibly work as an endotracheal tube, but how would I get it in? Even if I could somehow utilize the adult laryngoscope, I needed a flexible piece of metal that I could insert inside the plastic tube so that I could direct it into the larynx. Once the tube was in, I would pull the metal out. But I didn't have any metal the right size in the aid post.

The child continued to struggle to breathe. The mother held him snugly across her left breast. The decision to attempt to put a tube down his throat could not be made lightly. Even if we just tried to look at the back of his throat to put the tube in, it might cause a spasm in the throat muscles, or make the swelling worse, and suddenly his airway would shut off completely, essentially killing him on the spot. I looked at my watch: 3:00 a.m. Maybe we could hold out for a few more hours until dawn, still hoping that we would see the morning improvement that happens with so many croup cases for reasons that weren't clear to me. I was grateful that Jon was there and we continuously talked over each decision, but we couldn't decide whether doing something or doing nothing was the better choice.

I sat in front of the mother, observing not only the faintly blue toddler struggling for air, but the mother's heartbreaking struggle to will her child to live. We wrestled with the decision as to whether to decisively intervene, despite the risk, or just hope for the best. The father of the baby had walked all the way down from where he was working at Everest Base Camp as soon as he heard that the baby was in trouble. He now paced restlessly around the clinic in large, red, plastic climbing boots.

The first signs of dawn gave me hope that we would see the usual spontaneous improvement, but instead, the child was still getting worse. He was less arousable, and his efforts to breathe were starting to slacken. The muscles in his chest were wearing out from the effort of sucking air through the narrow opening in his throat. I didn't know what to do and neither did Jon, who had been up all night as well.

At ten o'clock, the baby made its last feeble effort to breathe, then stopped. I grabbed the baby from the mother and laid him down on a desk, his head towards me. There was no longer any risk from trying to fit the giant laryngoscope blade into his mouth. Unless I could get a breathing tube inserted in his trachea in the next minute or so, he would die. Since the child was completely unresponsive, I was able to fit the big laryngoscope into his mouth. I scanned the back of his throat for the opening to his trachea. All I could see was pink swollen flesh, like freshly ground hamburger. I took the oxygen tubing with a beveled end that I had fashioned during the night into a makeshift breathing tube and tried to shove it through the middle of the pile of meat, but without a metal insert, it simply bounced off. I pulled out the laryngoscope and stuck a needle in the front of his throat to try to get some air past the obstruction. We couldn't find any air—the entire trachea was swollen with tissue. There was no use trying CPR—there was no airway, and no hope of creating one.

With a groan of despair, the mother took the child back and put her mouth over the baby's mouth, trying to blow life back into him. I knew the effort was futile. The father stomped around the room, moaning in agony. Jon and I left the grieving parents, retreating to the kitchen, and sat on a wooden bench, emotionally drained. The image of the mother unable to keep her baby alive in her own arms was heartbreaking—literally intolerable. All night long we had counted on the baby getting better in the morning. I started to cry, not just a few tears but gut-wrenching sobs that tore at my insides. Jon started crying as well, the two of us sitting there, our arms wrapped around each other. I had never cried over the death of a patient before, and now I couldn't stop.

Finally, drained of our tears, our throats raw, we took some deep breaths, wiped our faces on our sleeves, and went back into the room with the mother and the baby. We had a nagging doubt, knowing that the baby could have been saved if he had been in a hospital in America. I kept replaying the choices we made during the night, wondering if we could have done something different.

Other Sherpas from the village came to help. They laid the baby down on a bed and covered him with a white cloth. By that time, the mother and father had calmed down. In fact, the parents were handling the death better than Jon and me. That got my attention. How could they be so accepting of a tragedy so irredeemably horrible? How could the loss of your child be anything other than unbearable?

A lama had been summoned from the monastery at upper Pangboche. He sat next to the bed, chanting prayers and periodically ringing a bell. The sense of confidence that the lama exhibited eased the helplessness that I felt—the fact he knew how to respond in a situation such as this was reassuring. On the second day after the death, the lama determined that it was the appropriate time to take the child for cremation. They wrapped up the body and placed it in a three-foot square cardboard box left over from an expedition, which was the only closed container we had. A Sherpa looped a strap around the box and carried it from his forehead. As he slowly walked out of the clinic and down the path, Sherpas from the village draped white scarves, called *katas*, over the makeshift casket. The family and friends walked up the valley towards Mt. Everest. Some carried firewood for the pyre.

I was torn. I wanted to be able to go with them and support them through the cremation, but I truly felt like I wouldn't be able to stand it. I couldn't face the prospect of having to watch the baby's body burn on a pile of wood.

A few hours later, I looked up the valley to the base of a rocky peak and saw a few wisps of smoke that lingered in the still, cold air, as if the child's spirit were reluctant to leave, having so recently arrived in the world. Up to this point in my career, despite having to witness the aftermath of terrible drunk-driving tragedies, gunshot wounds, knife attacks, domestic violence, hate crimes, and child abuse, I had never experienced anything as raw as this. The poignancy of a mother's love, unable to keep her baby alive in the safety of her loving arms, was more than I could bear.

Yet at the same time, the Sherpas had managed to go from "How can this possibly be happening?" to "This happened," in a remarkably short time. How could they do that? The level of acceptance in the family and the village astonished me. I assumed that they drew support from their Buddhist beliefs, but virtually none of them spoke English, and I could only guess what they were thinking. All I knew was that I admired their fortitude in the face of disaster, and I wished I could find the same strength within myself. It was a good example of how to handle life, but the example wasn't enough. I needed to know how to get there.

FIVE

When I finished what was to be my last season at Pheriche, I had to face the fact that I still didn't know what to do with my career. I began to realize that I couldn't just keep coming to volunteer in Nepal, but if I didn't have Nepal to look forward to, what would I do? I had not enjoyed general practice in a small town, and emergency medicine was already beginning to wear on me. I started to think that maybe I wasn't meant to be a doctor. It was time to leave the aid post, but I wasn't at all sure what my future was going to hold.

We were supposed to start hiking out on December 1, but both Jon and I had awakened with a fever and cough and aches and pains. Ang Rita and Helen remained well and were able to help care for us. We spent the day in bed, reading, drinking fluids, and hoping to be better by the next day so that we would feel strong enough to begin our four-day trek to Lukla.

I had finally gotten to sleep when I was awakened at eleven o'clock by a soft but persistent knocking on the door of the clinic. I crawled out of my sleeping bag and put on some pants and a jacket. I opened the door to find a Sherpa man who didn't speak any English. Ang Rita came from down the hall and translated for me. The man said that his wife was in labor, but the baby had not come out after sixteen hours. Could we help?

My spirits sank. I still felt achy and had a fever. But the main reason I was dismayed was that this was one of my worst nightmares. I didn't know much about delivering babies, but I knew enough to know that I had precious little to offer in this situation. If the baby was truly stuck in the birth canal, it could lead to disaster—as it often did in village births throughout Nepal. It could be a prolonged nightmare of pain, infection, and ultimately death—for the baby and the mother.

The woman was in a tent high above the village of Pangboche, which was a two-hour walk back down the valley. They had been staying in the tent while grazing their yaks. However, there was no way that we could refuse to go. We had to try.

Just before midnight, we set out: Jon, Helen, Ang Rita, and I, led by the Sherpa husband. It was a full moon night, the light so bright that it cast shadows. We didn't need headlamps to see the trail. Jon and I were still sick. We walked a short way, then started coughing, then had to stop, hands on our knees, trying to catch our breaths. We had to climb the hill out of Pheriche, then down the valley a way before veering straight up a steep switchback trail on a ridge for more than a thousand feet. I felt an intense sense of dread during the whole walk. What could we offer? We were both still raw from the death of the Sherpa boy. How was this going to end?

Finally, we reached a small, flat area and approached a large yak hair tent. A kerosene lantern cast a light through the flap of the tent. I stepped inside. The tent was tall enough for me to stand. Three older women sat cross-legged on the ground. The expectant mother was lying under covers on some padding off to my right. I glanced at their faces, trying to get a feeling for how things were going. They all seemed remarkably calm. I approached the mother and knelt by her bedside, my heart pounding. She looked up at me and shyly pulled back her covers, revealing a healthy baby girl with a full head of dark hair nursing at her breast. I nearly fainted with relief. Ang Rita pulled out the thermos of hot tea he had made for the trip and shared it all around, and by 2:30 a.m. we headed back down the trail.

With the crisis passed, I somehow didn't feel as ill. I could appreciate the beauty of the moonlit peaks, the black sky, the bright stars that shone without blinking at this high altitude, and the wonderful sense of purposeful camaraderie that we could share. Even though we hadn't done anything medically, we had been willing to go and face whatever we had to face.

By five in the morning, we were back in our sleeping bags for a few hours. When we woke up, we felt well enough to head down the valley, retracing some of our steps from the night before. We walked for four days to get to Lukla, and then sat there for eight more days waiting for a flight. Bad weather had prevented flights for several days. An average of three flights a day came in and out of Lukla. Under the system they had set up, if you had a reservation for a given day, and your plane came in, you could leave on that plane. However, if your plane didn't come in, the people who had reservations for the next day got priority, and you were suddenly on standby. Since the seventeen-seat planes were usually completely full, this could mean being stuck for a number of days, waiting to be allowed onto a flight.

This backlog at Lukla was common and often led trekkers to behave badly. They banded together in vocal protests. They threatened the ticket agent with ice axes. They demanded that extra planes be sent. They wondered why they'd been told the planes couldn't fly because of bad weather when the weather above us was crystal clear. Each day, the trekkers weighed the rigors of the ten-day walk back to Kathmandu versus the chance that they would get out before then by plane. We all feared heading down the trail for a few hours, and then seeing planes fly in that we could have gotten seats on.

Also waiting at Lukla was my friend Brot, who was working in Namche

Bazaar to install the first mini-hydroelectric plant and bring electricity to the Khumbu for the first time. Finally, after eight days, Brot was able to use his knowledge of Nepali and his connections to charter a flight out with the legendary Swiss pilot, Emil Wick, who had pioneered small plane transport in Nepal.

The plane had just enough room for the four of us to crowd in. Having finally made it back to Kathmandu, I still felt kind of lost. I didn't know what to do when I got back to the U.S., which was an increasingly uncomfortable feeling. General practice and emergency medicine were the only options with my current level of training. My father wanted me to train in general surgery, and then join him in practice. I had spent a year as an intern in the hospital where he worked, and I had assisted him in surgery many times. He was a natural surgeon—unflappable and deceptively fast. He knew just how to handle tissue to make progress and not cause harm. He had developed many skillful shortcuts. He had a kind, direct manner that reassured his patients. Sharing a practice with him was a tempting career choice. However, I still couldn't face up to the five or six years of residency training that would be required to pursue that path. I couldn't think of any other residency I wanted to do, so my options remained limited. My career path was becoming narrowed to the point that it was in danger of petering out altogether.

Flying halfway around the world by myself and walking for two weeks into the remote mountains to face whatever medical emergencies I encountered didn't feel like a risk to me. It felt like a need. The risk I was having trouble accepting was to enter residency training and then find out that I didn't like my life. Then what?

Three seasons in the Himalayas had taught me a lot. I could watch a trekker walk into the clinic at Pheriche and decide within minutes whether he or she had altitude sickness and had to descend or could spend another night at Pheriche. I felt like I had gotten all I needed to get from working at Pheriche. I was ready to move on but had no idea where to go.

It was in that state of mind that I went to look up David Peterson.

In Pheriche, I heard about a clinic that had just opened in Kathmandu, run by Peterson, a former expedition doctor, whom I had briefly met a few years earlier. I gave him a call and went to see him. The clinic was behind his house, on the outskirts of Kathmandu in a residential neighborhood. Peterson was tall and lanky, with unkempt balding hair and wire-rim glasses. He had been on an expedition to Everest, and, by chance, had been on the same Dhaulagiri expedition as Drummond Rennie, and the basis of the slide show that had changed my direction in life. The clinic was small but functional: two exam rooms, a waiting room, a lab, and a small office. We talked for a while, and he offered me a job, which I tentatively accepted.

As I headed back to my hotel, I realized I wasn't sure if I really wanted to move to Kathmandu. I'd never thought about living in Kathmandu. First of all, it had never been an option, as there were previously no jobs at all for foreign doctors. Secondly, the bustling chaos of the city was far different from living in a remote high valley. I wandered the city on foot, trying to picture myself living there. I walked through cobblestone streets in narrow alleys, overhung by three-story buildings with elaborately carved windows of dark-stained ancient wood. Barefoot porters plodded by carrying huge loads from straps across their foreheads, while others toiled to push heavy-timbered, wheeled carts through the streets. Bicycle rickshaw drivers offered me rides. The few cars on the streets were mostly Indian-manufactured Ambassadors, used as taxis. Any signs of modern civilization seemed tacked-on, haphazard. The electrical wires hung so low that you often had to duck, and they met on wooden or cement poles in tangled coils so dense that it seemed impossible that electricity could go in one side and emerge from the other.

Although the trappings of modern civilization sat uneasily on the ancient city, the spirituality of the people manifested in a completely integrated and natural way. Both their need to carry out spiritual offerings, and the unselfconscious grace with which they did it, balanced the chaotic infrastructure of Kathmandu.

The climate was far different as well. Kathmandu sits at only 4,300 feet in elevation, at the same latitude as Orlando, Florida. As a result, Kathmandu Valley is a lush garden, an exuberant mixture of imported trees and flowers from all over the world. Chilean pines tower over palm trees, mixed with bamboo and bougainvillea. The faint but persistent odor of stool in the alleys (most people did not have a toilet in those days and had to sneak around outside to find a place to defecate) was counteracted by the potent perfume of jasmine, honeysuckle, and gardenias. Birdcalls were ever-present in the background: the high sharp calls of kites, the laughter of mynas, shrieks of parakeets, and the flutter and buzz of thousands of birds I couldn't name at dawn and dusk. Giant fruit bats hung upside down in tall trees during the day near the Royal Palace. Rudyard Kipling, in a widely quoted poem, compared this city favorably to the eclectic botanical garden in England: "The wildest dreams of Kew, are but the facts of Kathmandu." It was wild all right, but was it home?

I thought back to what my mother had told me only a few months earlier. My parents had flown with me to Kathmandu before the start of my season. As I said goodbye to her before heading up to Pheriche, she told me, "I can see what you like about this place. Just don't come home and tell me that you want to move here."

Amid my aimless wandering, I ran into friends I had met a couple of weeks earlier at Pheriche. They told me they had discovered a hot tub at the Hotel Vajra, which was a new hotel built on a hill to the west of Kathmandu. The hot tub was in a private room, rented by the hour. This was the first hot tub in Nepal.

I took a taxi to the hotel. The time in the hot tub proved to be pivotal. As I sat immersed, relaxing in hot water for the first time since I flew to Nepal three months earlier, I gazed out over the cityscape. The low buildings of brick and plaster started turning a lush yellow-orange as the sun slipped behind a mountain ridge. I took some hits from a joint being passed around. The buildings began to look like they were melting, suffused in warm light, creating a mystical landscape of soft, dancing colors. A feeling of bliss coursed through me, coming out of nowhere. And then a thought appeared, strong and pre-formed and confident: *You need to move to Kathmandu.* It was as if the decision was being made for me, and it never faltered. Given all that was to happen to me as a result of that decision, I came to think of this as karma intervening, making sure that I didn't blow this decision that was to lead to so many great things for me. That warm vision stayed with me through two months of further travel in India and Thailand, back to Portland, where I gave notice on my emergency room job, packed up my possessions, rented out the small house I owned, and returned to Kathmandu in August of 1983.

SIX

I was back at the Hotel Vajra. A dance party was in full progress on the rooftop terrace overlooking Kathmandu Valley. Two months earlier, I had moved to Kathmandu, found a house, bought a car, hired two household staff, bought a piano, and started work at the CIWEC Clinic. CIWEC was the acronym of the Canadian aid project that had funded the clinic at the start (Canadian International Water and Energy Consultants).

Moving to Kathmandu felt like going back to college. The expatriate community was a separate, intimately connected group set against a large background of a different community, much as a small college is part of—yet separate from— the town that houses it. About 2,500 expats made their home in Kathmandu, which, at the time I moved there, had a population of about 200,000. Expats, like college students, generally stay from two to four years, and then move on, either because they are diplomats, aid workers, or they've had enough.

Some, however, are in it for the long haul, having arrived in the sixties or seventies and made Kathmandu their home. They learned Nepali, found ways to support themselves as trekking guides, art dealers, or manufacturers of goods that tourists might want, such as peanut butter. Foreigners could only get a visa for three months in a given year in those days, so they found creative ways to obtain visas that allowed them to live there for many years.

Some became noted scholars, started successful aid projects, or joined international organizations based in Nepal.

The stories from that era are legendary and worthy of their own book, but they are still closely held by the people who lived through them, and now many are no longer alive. I only know the stories from dinner parties and camping trips during which the original players shared what they had experienced. Since many of the stories involved quasi-legal activities, the participants have been reluctant to write books or share their stories with an author. The era has been dubbed "The Rock and Roll Raj," and it's my hope that we'll get to read about it someday. If only to share the story of the man who was busted in India for allegedly trying to smuggle a valuable necklace but managed to escape from jail and made it back into Nepal at a remote stretch of the border by riding an elephant across.

New expats arrive like college freshmen, not knowing how anything works, or what they need to do to get things done. Those who moved there a year or two before and learned how to solve all these problems generously took the new arrivals under their wings. Household furniture and cars are passed on from those who are leaving.

Living in Kathmandu required patience. So many things that you take for granted at home, such as continuous electricity, or running water, were no longer a given. Getting up to light a candle when the lights went out became a normal, smooth reflex. Water flowed for only an hour or two a day into an underground tank and then had to be pumped up to a rooftop tank—which needed electricity. If you forgot to pump the water, and the power was out, you would have no water for a while. Roads were often roads in name only—unpaved, deeply rutted, and a slick morass of mud during the monsoon rains. Construction or repair projects would block a road completely, without warning, often forcing a long backtrack or detour. Going to a government office to get something done was an exercise that seemed designed, like some kind of reality TV show, solely to test one's tolerance.

"The man with the key has gone home," was such a common excuse that it became the knowing refrain among expats, shorthand for the challenge of interfacing with the government.

There is a story: an expat is talking to one of his counterparts at an aid agency, having learned through experience that things are slow to get done in Nepal. He mentions to his counterpart, "In Mexico they have a word, *manana*, that means, 'we won't do it today, we'll do it tomorrow.' Is there a word like that in the Nepali language?" The Nepalese man thinks for a moment, then says, "We don't have a word like that in our language that suggests that degree of urgency."

The birds are awake in Kathmandu before most people. The sounds fill the air. The days usually dawned sunny and warm. When I looked down from my upstairs window, I could see graceful women in saris walking on the dirt track outside my compound walls. They carried silver trays filled with bright-colored powders and flowers to make offerings at the local shrines. If they looked up to see me watching, I would sometimes be rewarded with a flicker of a shy smile. Charming moments like this came one after another, and more than compensated for the sense of mild, consistent hardship that was the shared experience of the expat community. After a while, few of the obstacles were experienced as hardships; they were just the way things were in Nepal. The Nepalis recognized this fact of life as well. This recognition was built into the language: *Yo Nepal ho* translates as, "This is Nepal," but the phrase carries with it a vast nuance, reflecting frustration, senseless obstacles, official corruption, and ultimately...acceptance. When things don't work out, they simply accept it with a shrug, saying *ke garnay*, which translates literally as "what to do," but really means, "what *can* you do?" The foreigners who got this could last a long time. Those who didn't eventually weeded themselves out.

Passive forms of entertainment were nonexistent. Television had not yet arrived in Nepal, there was no internet, and the sole movie theater in the city showed only Hindi movies. The one government-run radio station had five minutes of English news in the morning and evening. The one newspaper was also printed by the government, delivered in the same vein as the daily weather report, which almost always read, "Mainly fair throughout the Kingdom."

As a result, the expats sought out each other's company far more than what would have been likely otherwise. In the early days, there was no traffic at night at all—if you saw another car after 6:00 p.m. it was likely another expat going to the same dinner party that you were headed to. Dinner parties were what we did. We all had cooks. None of us went shopping or did our own dishes. To host a dinner party, all I had to do was tell my cook, "I'm having eight people for dinner tomorrow night," and it would be taken care of. We ate, and talked, and relaxed together.

If you're talking to people who have never lived in a place like Nepal, it can be awkward to discuss having household staff, suggesting that the foreigners lived in some fancy way unavailable to local people. However, the fact was that everyone had household help—even relatively poor Nepalese families had someone poorer who helped around the house. Working for a foreigner was considered a desirable job—the salary was higher, and foreigners often proved to be less demanding than wealthy Nepalese. At a time when the average *annual* income of a Nepalese person was $157, the salary of household help in Kathmandu was about $50-100 *per month,* depending on their position.

That first night back at the Hotel Vajra, I met Elliott, an American dentist who had been in Nepal a year already, providing dental care to the expat community. Elliott proved to be the funniest guy I ever met, a person who could pretty much destroy a dinner party, inducing people to spit their food across the table with involuntary laughter. We sat on a porch, sharing a joint and looking at the lights of the city, finding out about each other. I perked up when he said he was a drummer. I had switched from piano to guitar at age fifteen when I first heard a recording of Donovan's "Catch the Wind." Ever since then, I had wanted to play in a rock-and-roll band, but it hadn't happened. Elliott knew a bass player, a Scottish aid worker, and we were joined shortly by an American lead guitarist who taught at the American school. Fear of Heights was born, the first rock-and-roll band to ever play in Nepal. I was the lead singer and rhythm guitarist.

For five years, we provided nights of drug- and alcohol-fueled extravagance for the music-starved post-hippy expatriates in Kathmandu. We rented ornate ballrooms in old Rana palaces, and the entire crowd of three hundred people danced. I led the charge towards wanton excess as best I could, sometimes drinking an entire bottle of scotch during a performance. On one memorably hot May night, the British First Attaché abandoned his sweat-soaked clothes and went home draped only in a white table cloth.

And then there was my motorcycle. Not just any motorcycle, but a 1982 BMW R80 GS, Paris Dakar model, a bike that *Outside Magazine* called "the greatest adventure motorcycle ever made." I bought it from a British man who had ridden it out from England. It was the largest bike in Nepal—at

800cc—and when I parked it, I would return to find a scrum of young Nepali men swarming over it. As I stepped near in my leather jacket, they would jump back in respect, and then jump again when I pushed the electric start button as it roared to life without my having to kick the starter, something that was unheard of on local bikes at the time.

Riding a great motorcycle was special for me. However, compared to that, flying around the Himalayas in helicopters was even more exceptional. I'd only been in Nepal a short time when I first got asked to fly on a helicopter to rescue a trekker. The helicopters were all flown by the army. I had never flown in a helicopter, and I felt giddy with excitement when the green army chopper rolled forward and launched into the sky, up and over the city and out over the rugged low mountains, while the white wall of the world's highest peaks suddenly leaped into view. It was often tricky finding the patients, as even the army didn't have detailed maps or GPS. When we landed, the sense of relief on the patient's face was intense—they felt the way that I did when the helicopter came to rescue Barbara.

SEVEN

The first New Year's Eve after I moved to Kathmandu set the tone for the rest of my time in Nepal. It was the first public performance of Fear of Heights, playing at a party in an old Rana palace that was now rented by an expatriate couple. Past New Year's Eves had not been kind to me—I had somehow never managed to be with someone I genuinely cared about on that night. Now I was at a party, and I *was* the music—I was the lead singer and guitarist. When midnight struck in Kathmandu, I played "Old Lang Syne" on a small electric keyboard, and everyone in the room, a hundred and fifty people from dozens of different countries, crossed arms, held hands, and sang verse after verse—I didn't know that there was more than one verse. Seeing such warmth and companionship in an international gathering choked me up.

It reinforced that Kathmandu was working out for me.

Before I moved to Kathmandu, I was living in Portland, Oregon. I grew up there, but was away at school for eight years before moving back for my residency. I worked in the emergency room of the hospital at which I had trained. Although I liked living in Portland, my work as an emergency room doctor kept me feeling out of sorts. I worked twelve-hour shifts, mainly at night, during which I saw a lot of things that most people are never forced to confront: fights and beatings, overdoses, child abuse, rapes, and psychotic patients. On days off I felt jet-lagged. I didn't have a girlfriend most of the time, but I wanted one. I rock climbed a lot, taking advantage of the flexible schedule of an ER doctor to drive all over the west in pursuit of new climbs. Despite these activities, however, I had the overall feeling that my life wasn't taking off, which boiled down, most of the time, to not having a girlfriend or a firm handle on my career, in that order.

I started work at the CIWEC clinic in Kathmandu within a couple of days of arrival with virtually no orientation. David Peterson used my advent as an opportunity to go on a two-month home leave. The work at the clinic was a paid job, which is what allowed me to move to Kathmandu. The salary was quite low, by Western standards, but the cost of living was low. As our practice focused on the care of foreigners in Nepal, we charged for our services.

Before long, I figured out that being a doctor in Kathmandu was in many ways more difficult than being a doctor up near Mt. Everest. Although in the mountains I had few resources to care for patients, the goal was just to keep them alive until they could be evacuated to Kathmandu for more definitive care. Now I was in Kathmandu with only slightly more resources than in the mountains, having to improvise ways to provide that definitive care. The pool of patients increased exponentially as well, from a few thousand up in the Khumbu region to 2,500 resident expatriates and over 400,000 tourists a year visiting Nepal.

One of the hard truths of medicine is that you can't diagnose something if you can't think of it. The easiest way for a doctor to go wrong is to take the existing facts of the case and try to fit them to something they already have seen, rather than recognizing the subtle differences and continuing the search for an answer. The result of all one's medical training is to store an extensive list of names of diseases that can be triggered by the right set of facts. The quickest way out of that comfort zone is to move halfway across the world and start treating infectious diseases.

The list of serious infections that one can acquire in Asia is easily over forty if you just count the obvious ones—almost all present with fever and a headache. Many of them require obscure laboratory testing that can only be done in specialized labs. I had no idea what we could expect to see.

A month after I started working in Kathmandu, I had invited one of my closest emergency room friends, Milt Cohen, to join me in David Peterson's absence. Milt was board certified in internal medicine, and I'd always admired his clinical skill. A few days after he arrived, he came into our shared office and said, "I think I have a guy with dengue fever."

I thought, *What?* I'd heard of dengue fever, vaguely, but had never seen a case. I didn't know where it was likely to be acquired, how long the incubation period was, what the symptoms might be, or what the lab work would look like. I was amazed that my friend Milt had somehow retained this knowledge from his medical training. I asked him, "What makes you think so?"

"The patient asked me, 'Could this be dengue fever?' so I looked it up, and it fit."

At CIWEC Clinic, we quickly learned that it's better to be lucky than good, a common saying among physicians who are honest with themselves. We were so often dealing in a realm of medical uncertainty that I coined a saying: "If you don't know what someone has, it's better if they are getting better instead of getting worse."

Operating with so much uncertainty and unpredictability, the staff of the clinic shared the special bond that forms under stress. Despite the pressure, medicine was far more enjoyable for me with a patient population that I could relate to, and who, in turn, greatly appreciated that we were there. Drunk and dangerously aggressive patients in the emergency room were replaced by travelers who were surprised and happy to discover a modern-looking Western medical clinic in the midst of a semi-medieval city. The faces of the patients relaxed as they stepped through the door and realized that they were finally going to receive genuine medical care that they could trust.

I found myself getting over my crisis of faith in medicine. I had patients I wanted to care for, with problems that were unique and challenging to solve. I had stumbled, against all odds, into a practice that I could believe in.

Once the CIWEC Clinic was started, tourism became safer in Nepal. In the early 1980s, medical care was very basic. A foreign tourist had very few options for seeking medical care, and if they were gravely ill or injured, their ability to get good treatment, or get evacuated, was very uncertain. However, once the clinic became aware of a patient, we could help them get evacuated from the mountains, make sure they got the best care available in Kathmandu, or help them get evacuated to Bangkok, where medical care was quite good.

Helicopter rescue requests came in from the mountains in a haphazard way. There were virtually no telephones in the countryside, and the only communication between mountain villages and Kathmandu in those days was through scattered police radio stations. A message would be written in English, often just a couple of sentences, carried on foot for four hours or more, then translated into Nepali, and back to English again before we saw it. We couldn't send a message back to ask for further information about the patient, as the actual patient was often hours away from the police post. Actual messages said, "Very sick," or, in one case, "No arms, no legs." In that latter case, the patient was a Dutchman in his twenties who had fallen from a trail and had a broken left wrist, dislocated right hip, and a fracture of his left lower leg.

When I first arrived in Nepal, helicopter rescues were only provided by the army and had to be paid for in advance with cash, which often delayed the rescue by one to three days as the patient's family was contacted in their home country and desperately tried to wire the money to a bank in Nepal. The consular officers at the various embassies were charged with organizing helicopter rescues for their citizens, but the embassy did not pay for them. If a consular officer guaranteed payment for a helicopter, and the rescued patient didn't end up paying, the consular officer would be obligated to pay out of his or her own pocket. To speed up the dispatching of helicopters, I set up a system by which all the consular officers in Kathmandu, and myself, would contribute $200 to a fund that would only be used to pay for a helicopter rescue that the patient refused to pay for. In that way, we were all only risking $200 to make the guarantee, rather than $2000 to $4000. In the end, no patient ever refused to pay for a rescue while I was there. This system dramatically speeded up rescue in Nepal for many years, until private helicopter services started to take over from the army.

Just because we were Western doctors didn't mean that we knew what we were doing. Diarrhea was the predominant problem that brought people to the clinic, accounting for thirty percent of our patient visits, but when I moved to Nepal in 1983, little was known about the causes of diarrhea in travelers.

A stool exam could give useful information in about half the cases, but definitive diagnosis would require days of culturing for bacteria, along with elaborate testing that was not available to us. When I first arrived, I assumed that someone must know what caused diarrhea in travelers, but as I pored through textbooks and journals, I found out that very few studies existed, and most of those had been done in Mexico. Almost no studies had been done in Asia. We didn't know which symptoms were more likely to be associated with various stomach bugs. Soon it dawned on me that, for the first time in my medical career, I didn't know something, not because I hadn't studied enough, but because the answer wasn't known. Trying to find a place where medicine could be satisfying for me, I had ended up in a place where few Western people had ever practiced before.

The best way to find out what was causing diarrhea in our patients would be to do our own research, but I didn't see how this could happen. I had never done any medical research; I had barely *read* any medical research, and I would have been voted least likely to succeed in research if they had such a category in medical school. I had been so marginally interested in the science of medicine—I majored in English literature in college—that the head of my internship program took me aside one day and told me that I would never be a good doctor if I didn't become more interested in science. Which didn't change anything at the time.

I would have never embarked on a research program if not for a phone call from David Taylor, an American doctor who worked at the Armed Forces Research Institute for Medical Science (AFRIMS) in Bangkok. He had heard about our clinic, and he wanted to discuss studying diarrhea in our travelers. The U.S. army had an interest in defining the disease risks that troops might face in Asia, but it was not easy to get hold of stool samples from travelers. A sick traveler would often not even try to get medical care from a local clinic, or if they did, the local clinic would not keep any record. Because thousands of patients were suddenly getting their care from one clinic in a high-risk country—the first such clinic in the world—we were in a unique position to conduct a study of the causes of diarrhea in travelers.

Finding the cause of diarrhea was an elaborate process that involved days of handling a single specimen, spreading a stool sample on an agar plate that was then incubated for one to two days before isolating colonies of bacteria and placing them in a series of test tubes for identification. The samples were then packed and shipped to Bangkok. To keep these specimens alive, we had to ship them on dry ice, which was not available in Nepal. The ice had to come up on the daily flight from Bangkok; someone had to be waiting at the airport to retrieve the ice, pack up the specimens in the hour that the flight was on the ground, and ship them to the lab in Bangkok.

The AFRIMS lab was known at the time as the best diarrhea research lab in the world, and they spared no effort in trying to identify disease-causing organisms in the stool, sometimes shipping frozen pieces to far-off labs in Finland or Japan to look for a specific newly-discovered virus. The process of finding all the potential bugs in a single specimen was so time-consuming that we could only process two samples per day.

In one year, we were able to enroll almost four hundred patients, one of the largest detailed studies of travelers with diarrhea ever conducted. We wrote up our findings and submitted the paper to the *Journal of the American Medical Association*, which was the second most prestigious journal in the U.S. at the time. It was accepted for publication—my first research paper, and David Taylor's fiftieth.

Our paper showed that the vast majority of travelers who came to our clinic with diarrhea had a bacterial pathogen, an organism that could be treated with an antibiotic. I also observed that patients with bacterial diarrhea characteristically had a sudden onset of symptoms. When I asked patients with bacterial diarrhea how they became ill, they all gave me the time of day their illness began: "Last night at eleven o'clock I got diarrhea,"

"This morning at five-thirty I got diarrhea." The history of abrupt onset of relatively severe diarrhea confirmed that they had a bacterial pathogen and thus could be treated with an antibiotic. In contrast, patients with diarrhea caused by parasitic organisms, such as *Giardia* or amoebas, had a gradual onset of low-grade gastrointestinal distress that lasted for days or weeks before they sought help.

These insights had a lasting, worldwide impact on the diagnosis and treatment of travelers' diarrhea. Until we made this observation, travelers and doctors had no idea whether diarrhea meant an infection with *Giardia*, amoebas, bacteria, viruses, food poisoning, or even worms. Just looking at the stool through a microscope seldom gave a definitive answer. By focusing on the nature of the onset of symptoms, rather than basing treatment decisions on a stool exam, we could provide correct treatment more than ninety percent of the time.

This system of diagnosing travelers' diarrhea meant that we could teach travelers how to diagnose and treat themselves. The benefit that this strategy provided was especially pronounced in a destination like Nepal. Thousands of trekkers came to attempt a trip of a lifetime, walking for one to four weeks in the remote high mountains. Many had their treks ruined by severe diarrhea, sometimes laying ill in primitive teahouses for several days, barely able to recover enough to walk out, or even having to be evacuated by helicopter. Many Himalayan climbers had their climbing ambitions thwarted by an episode of diarrhea that occurred at a key point in the climb. A microscopic speck of bacteria had undone years of planning and thousands of dollars in expense, sometimes discouraging the traveler from ever venturing from their home country again. All of this, simply because no one had been able to figure out an effective way to solve the problem.

By sending antibiotics along with each trekker with simple instructions, we saved their trips from a lot of needless suffering. This system worked so well that taking this precaution began to make sense for travelers going anywhere that reliable medical care was not available, which was virtually anywhere in the resource-poor world. Prescribing antibiotics to travelers to carry in case they got diarrhea gradually became the standard approach around the world—and it all began with our research in Kathmandu.

When I began to speak at international conferences on travel medicine, I found out that my new approach to travelers' diarrhea was not universally embraced. Many doctors still held that since travelers' diarrhea was self-limited—in that it went away within two to seven days without treatment—that antibiotics should not be used. Having seen so many travelers with diarrhea by then, more than any other doctor in the world, I had learned that patients who came to me with diarrhea *did not want to have diarrhea.* They wanted to get better. I also found that the doctors at the meeting had a high tolerance for other people's diarrhea, but when it came to themselves, they quickly took drugs. I became one of the main advocates for travelers to carry their own drugs and use them when needed.

David Taylor taught me how to design and carry out a research paper. I began to study and report on many of the diseases we were confronted with in travelers: typhoid fever, hepatitis, rabies prevention, and altitude illness. We had so many studies going that, for a while, I was publishing at a rate of five new papers a year.

At the same time, we were dealing with crisis after crisis, especially during the trekking seasons in the spring and fall. Missing trekkers, trekkers who died unexpectedly in bed, trekkers who needed helicopter rescue, psychotic tourists in jail in Kathmandu who needed to get out of jail and get sane enough to travel home, pregnancy, childbirth (only one birth in the clinic in all those years, thankfully), fractures, acute abdomens, severe malaria, and heart attacks. This was my world, my everyday world, in addition to all the other activities, teachings, and adventures that I had.

Three years after we started our research program, we discovered something remarkable. On June 26, 1989 (I still remember the exact day), our lab technician, Rama, asked me to look at some particles he had spotted in a stool exam. Looking at stool under the microscope is like looking at a lawn covered in leaves and trying to spot a particularly rare kind of leaf. Rama noticed a "leaf" he had never seen in any textbooks. Under the microscope, he pointed to a small round structure with some internal markings that vaguely resembled bicycle spokes. It appeared to be a protozoal organism, but it could also be a vegetable spore. He had seen it on and off for a few weeks and finally decided to say something. On the day he showed it to me, he saw it in the stools of six different patients.

During that same spring, I was seeing patients who had a prolonged diarrheal illness that started abruptly and violently, then lingered for weeks with daily loose stools and intermittent nausea, with a constant undercurrent of fatigue, loss of appetite, and weight loss. We couldn't find any known pathogens in their stool, despite multiple attempts, and the patients didn't respond to treatments for the usual suspects. After a prolonged period, ranging from two to twelve weeks, they would get better on their own.

I asked Rama to start recording the unknown organism on the lab slip, just writing "unknown organism" in the margin. Right away we found this organism was present in patients with the prolonged undiagnosed symptoms. The correlation was one hundred percent: all the patients who had these symptoms had the organism in their stool, and the organism was never found in patients who were well or had obvious other causes for their diarrhea. In addition, the organism disappeared from their stool exam as soon as their symptoms went away. We had reason to believe we had discovered a new disease caused by a previously unrecognized organism.

The problem was, we had no way to figure out what it was. When all you can do is look at an organism under the microscope, the only option is to formulate an opinion as to what it could be. There is no way to prove it. I headed back to the U.S. on home leave in the middle of the summer, and I carried a preserved stool sample. I sent the sample to an expert I knew in Washington, D.C. She had never seen it but agreed that it probably was a coccidia, based on its staining characteristics and size. She walked the sample across the street to the head parasitologist at the National Institutes of Health, who thought she had once seen a similar organism in a patient from Haiti. Finally, a pathologist at the CDC shared with us that he had been sent seven other specimens that appeared to have the same organism. He had a startling hypothesis: he thought these organisms were a type of cyanobacteria, a blue-green alga.

The pathologist based his opinion on electron micrographs of the organism, even though there was no precedent for a light-utilizing organism being able to inhabit, much less infect, the dark insides of intestines. Other experts at the CDC also expressed skepticism, so in the end, our first paper was published under the equivocating title, "An Alga-like Organism as a Cause of Diarrhea in Travelers."

The organism had mysteriously disappeared from all stool exams by November, along with the illness that it caused. The following spring, we were watching for the organism when it started showing up in May. We traced the whole outbreak, and this time we did a true case-control study to show that it definitely was the cause of the new disease. No treatment had proven effective, and patients who showed up with the organism were destined to feel debilitatingly tired and steadily lose five to ten pounds over the duration of the illness. Blue-green algae season started to create fear among the expatriate community. Because May to November is a low time of year for tourists, the disease mainly impacted the expats. No one had yet looked for it in Nepalese patients.

I presented our findings at the International Society of Travel Medicine meeting in Atlanta in 1991. Bradley Connor, a gastroenterologist from New York, whom I met for the first time at the meeting, decided to fly out to Nepal at his own expense to do the first upper endoscopies, and take biopsies from the upper intestines of these patients. His spontaneous decision to fly to Kathmandu with his endoscopy equipment was the start of our life-long friendship; I loved this way of doing research—no grants, no waiting for funding, just doing it to find out what was going on.

The biopsies that Brad obtained showed that the organism caused significant temporary damage to the upper intestine, which was why people felt so awful while they were sick. We still didn't know how to treat it. Finally, in the summer of 1994, I spotted a letter in *The Lancet* from a researcher in Peru (where they had also found this organism) that suggested that trimethoprim-sulfamethoxazole, also called Bactrim, had cured one person with this disease.

We used Bactrim to treat bacterial diarrhea when I first moved to Nepal, but we gradually abandoned it in the late 1980s because it had become less effective due to bacterial resistance. I realized that we had started seeing this new organism at the same time we stopped using Bactrim routinely. We may have been accidentally treating the organism when we thought we were treating bacterial diarrhea. We carried out a study that proved that Bactrim was an effective treatment against this organism, with a one hundred percent cure rate. To this day, there is no other effective treatment.

When you discover a new organism, traditionally you get to name it. I was hoping that we could do that, but to give it a name, you have to know what kind of organism it actually is, and we were still stumped. Then the Peruvian group made an accidental observation that led to their being able to identify the organism as a new species of *Cyclospora*. This dashed my hopes of being able to name the organism after our clinic, and it ended up being named after a university in Lima: *Cyclospora cayetanensis* (sadly not *Cyclospora ciwecki*).

The medical world took only scant notice of our research until the organism started showing up in outbreaks in the U.S., traced to raspberries that had been grown in Guatemala, where the organism was not previously known to exist. The outbreaks occurred at large gatherings, such as weddings, where fresh raspberries had been served. Thanks to the work that we had done in Nepal, the investigators already knew the symptoms of the disease, how to diagnose it, and what the treatment should be. Without the research from our clinic, they would have been starting from scratch. Cyclospora proved to be the first new protozoan intestinal pathogen that had been discovered in over seventy years.

As of writing this book, I've published over fifty-five papers on the medical problems of travelers. I've written more than two dozen chapters for textbooks, and I became an editor of the Centers for Disease Control's *Health Information for International Travel*, the main source of medical information for travel medicine professionals in the United States. My partner at the CIWEC Clinic, Prativa Pandey, became the first woman and the first person from Asia to be elected president of the International Society of Travel Medicine. Six years later, I was elected to the same position. Our

David R. Shlim, M.D.

tiny clinic has produced two of the most well-known travel medicine experts in the world.

It feels awkward to write about my accomplishments in this way, but I want to demonstrate that during my time in Nepal, I developed solid scientific credentials on the world stage. This stature became particularly important as I formed a strengthening connection to Tibetan Buddhism, and I began to witness and experience things that are difficult or impossible to explain in the realm of conventional science.

EIGHT

"Why don't I just go out there once a week and see whoever is sick?"

A year into living in Kathmandu, I offered to hold a free weekly medical clinic at a Tibetan Buddhist monastery just outside the city. It was a spontaneous thought that entered my head while talking to one of our receptionists, Margie, who lived near the monastery and often tried to help the monks obtain medical care. I had never been to the monastery, but I thought that since I was now working for a salary at CIWEC Clinic, it might be nice to volunteer some work that could benefit a local population.

Chokyi Nyima Rinpoche was the head of the monastery. "Rinpoche" is an honorific term that means "precious." In Tibetan Buddhism, it's a way of showing respect when addressing the reincarnated, or accomplished lamas and teachers of Buddhist philosophy. Someone with that title is usually addressed simply as "Rinpoche," in the same way that a Catholic priest might be addressed simply as "Father." When Margie told him about my offer, he said, "I want to meet that doctor." Margie brought me out there the next day. His monastery was massive compared to Thyangboche. We climbed up the stairs from the parking area to a grassy courtyard that suddenly revealed a view of the whole monastery: a massive, white square four-storied structure with two lower wings on each side for the monks' quarters. We ducked through a cement archway into a small courtyard, and then climbed four flights of cement stairs that opened onto a sunny waiting area. I had just taken off my shoes to enter his chamber when Chokyi Nyima Rinpoche suddenly burst out of the door holding a small bronze Buddha statue.

"Here, doctor. I want you to have this for helping our monks," he said in English.

I was taken aback. "But I haven't done anything yet," I replied.

"I'm happy that you have offered to help," said Rinpoche. He stood there with his arm outstretched, pushing the statue towards me. Margie made a shooing gesture with her hands to get me to take it. It felt surprisingly heavy, despite being just seven inches tall. The surface was a dark yellow bronze, mildly pockmarked with age. It was my first Buddha statue.

Rinpoche gestured me back into his chamber, a large room roughly twenty by forty feet, with a single square pillar in the middle and a dark wooden floor. To my left was a wall of glass cases filled with Buddhist statues of various sizes, from a few inches to a few feet in height, in poses whose symbolism I didn't yet understand. The opposite wall had windows that overlooked the Boudhanath Stupa, the most sacred Buddhist landmark in Nepal. At ten stories tall, it was a large white half-dome filled with precious objects, capped by a soaring gold-plated tower with the eyes of the Buddha painted on four sides. The Stupa was said to represent the mind of the Buddha, and devout Buddhists spent hours circumambulating the structure in a clockwise direction.

We sat in Western-style chairs made of hand-carved wood with yellow silk cushions as he served me some tea. Rinpoche was short and wiry, with close-cropped dark hair and a round face. He wore traditional monk's robes, a maroon skirt, a yellow shirt, and a wraparound maroon top. His mouth was slightly crooked, as if from the strain of constantly holding itself back from breaking into a smile. He laughed easily and often.

He arranged for me to take over a room in the monks' quarters to use as a clinic. I bought file folders and a large cabinet to keep them organized, and a table on which I could examine the monks. I put a poster of Galen Rowell's iconic photo of a rainbow over the Potala Palace in Lhasa on the wall. Chokyi Nyima Rinpoche appointed a young monk named Tashi to translate for me. Although I was learning Nepali and could do basic medical care in the language, most of the monks spoke Tibetan, which was new to me. Tashi was twenty-two years old and had fled the Chinese occupation of Tibet with his family when he was fifteen. China had invaded Tibet in 1950 and completed their takeover by 1959. More than a million Tibetans died during the takeover and in the twenty years after that, and hundreds of thousands escaped to exile in India. Those that remained behind found that they were living in an occupied country, trying to get on with their lives in a completely changed environment. When the oppression became too much, Tibetans, who were not permitted to travel abroad, snuck out of the country over some of the highest mountain passes in the world.

Tashi was studying English at the English Language Institute, a small school run by the American Embassy, which made him one of the only monks who could speak English.

When I came out every week, Rinpoche asked me to stop by first to have some tea, and then often asked me to come back to have lunch with him. His English in those days was quite broken, but adequate, and we would chat about the clinic where I was working, politics in Nepal, or what was going on in the world. I felt comfortable with him—he was thirty-three years old, a year younger than myself. I had a notion to ask him questions about Buddhist philosophy, but I didn't know what to ask, and he didn't bring it up.

So why was that? Given how I had felt outside of Thyangboche Monastery, with the surprising desperation to get invited in and receive teachings, I find it difficult to explain, in retrospect, why I felt so casual about having finally met the head lama of a monastery five years later. The anxious, eager feeling I'd experienced at Thyangboche had gradually faded over the years as I found myself unable to connect with any Buddhist teachers. After failing to obtain Buddhist teachings in the Everest region, I traveled down to Bodhgaya, India, the site of the Buddha's enlightenment. After two weeks there and having sat through a five-day Zen retreat at the Japanese monastery, I felt no closer to understanding Buddhist philosophy. At that point, I had pretty much quit looking.

Perhaps that attitude allowed me to start fresh, with no preconceptions. There's also another possibility: by moving to Kathmandu, my life had taken off in so many positive ways, I didn't feel as unfulfilled as I once had. My life felt like it was finally on a positive track. Except in one key area: I was still looking for the perfect woman. If I could find her, it would go a long way towards making my life feel complete.

Which begs the question as to whether it was just a coincidence that a few weeks after meeting Chokyi Nyima Rinpoche, I met a woman.

Jane was the most beautiful woman I had ever met. She was seated across from me at a small dinner party at my friend Lisa's house. She had the kind of beauty that demanded one's attention. She was tall and slender, with long, fine blond hair framing her face and falling below her shoulders, smooth skin that seemed to glow, and blue-green eyes that gave off an open, playful quality, flirtatious without being overt. She was relaxed and natural and funny, and our conversation flowed easily. She wore a green dress that draped her figure in a way that made me gasp involuntarily when she moved in certain ways. She had spent a year working at Tiger Tops, a pioneering jungle lodge that took tourists to see the exotic jungle in the lowlands of Nepal. She was at Tiger Tops the year before I moved to Kathmandu, but moved back home to Canada just before I arrived. She was just back in Nepal for a brief visit, staying with Lisa.

I soon learned that she was engaged to be married in six weeks, back in Toronto. I tried to take that into account as I sat across from her, laughing and sharing stories, relishing the easy way she made eye contact or occasionally touched my arm. Although it didn't make sense, at the end of the evening I asked her if she would like to have dinner with me the next night, not knowing how she might react. "That would be really nice," she said.

The Kathmandu of today is noisy, polluted, and congested with traffic, but at that time Kathmandu was exotic, scented, moonlit, framed by the Himalayas, and full of surprises. It was, in some ways, the perfect romantic backdrop.

I took her to the Hotel Eden, which at six stories was the tallest building in Kathmandu, and boasted the first elevator in Nepal, a metal cage that looked like it had been hand-woven from wire. A screeching noise echoed as if a brake was on for the entire ride all the way to the top, where it opened directly onto a rooftop garden restaurant.

As Jane walked over to the edge of the roof, her graceful body and loose blond hair were backlit by a wall of Himalayan peaks that were just turning yellow in the glow of the setting sun. I felt a familiar stirring of desire and made a half-hearted effort to fight it off, given that she was engaged to be married. Although this was the kind of date that I had dreamed of since moving to Kathmandu, it lacked one key element: a woman who was free to pursue a relationship with me. Taking this into account, I made up my mind to just enjoy her company and try not to think about a future that wasn't going to happen. It didn't make sense, I rationalized, *not* to have dinner with her just because I was attracted to her.

We looked down on the densely packed three- and four-story apartment buildings built above the street-level shops. Across from us were the pagoda-roofed palaces of Durbar Square.

"How did you end up coming to Nepal your first time?" I asked her.

"I'm a model," she said, unselfconsciously. "I got hired to do a fashion shoot for a Canadian fashion magazine. It was timed around the first Canadian Everest Expedition." Her gaze met mine casually as we spoke.

"But you ended up staying in Nepal."

"We went down to Tiger Tops and did some shots with elephants. I just fell in love with the place. I asked if I could work there, and I stayed for a little over a year."

I'd been to Tiger Tops several times, mostly at Lisa's invitation. The place was remote, even by Nepal standards, reached mainly by plane; at certain times of the year, only elephants could forge across the river from the airfield to the lodge. In a solution unique to the subcontinent, the wooden stairs that helped the tourists down from the airplane were then wheeled over to waiting elephants and allowed the tourists to climb up onto the wooden platforms on their backs. The fact that she had stayed at Tiger Tops for a year told me a lot about her flexibility and grit. And made her even more desirable.

She stood close to me as we watched the glow fade from the mountains. "That's Everest, there," I said. "Way over to the right." Jane leaned in as she struggled to pick out a dark triangle of rock, jutting out of a distant wall of white. A wisp of fine blond hair blew across one of her eyes and I reached, without thinking, to brush it away.

"When did you move back to Canada?"

"Last spring. I met the man I'm going to marry when he took a group to Tiger Tops. He owns a travel agency in Toronto."

"It sounds like you're getting married right before Christmas," I guessed.

"Yes. The invitations have all been sent out. I'll have a lot to do when I get back."

The peaks had receded to a shadowy outline. Temple bells rang, horns honked, dogs barked, and the occasional shouting voice rose above the general hubbub in the streets below. She had on a sleeveless denim dress over a white t-shirt, and the cool October breeze gave her goosebumps on her arms.

"Do you want to go get some dinner?" I asked.

"Pretty soon," she said, adding, "You know, I'm not sure I'm brave enough to get in that elevator again."

We walked down six flights of stairs to the street. The narrow lanes were filled with people headed home from work, stopping to buy last-minute items for dinner from the vegetable stalls in the street, haggling good-naturedly over the price. Despite the congestion, everyone appeared relaxed, and we steered through the flow of people like a kayak through a river. I had a favorite Indian restaurant, the New Kabob Corner. I had flirted with becoming a vegetarian at various times, but since discovering tandoori chicken, I felt that it would be impossible for me to ever completely give up eating meat. The waiter seated us and lit the candle in the middle of the small table.

Things started to happen. On one level, we were just talking and eating dinner. On the other, everything was heightened. Our legs brushed accidentally, and then not so accidentally, and then stayed in contact. I touched her arm as I was talking, she kept it on the table, and then at some point we were holding hands. Every time our eyes met, every time my breath caught as I felt a rush of attraction, I knew that it made no sense. She was *engaged to be married*—not in some abstract future, but *in six weeks*. How could our attraction possibly turn out okay?

Although many people are skeptical of instant love, it was the only kind I had any faith in. I was always alert to the possibility of meeting a woman unexpectedly. I never knew when it could happen. One time it was on a train, another was a meeting in a restaurant. One relationship started in a friend's sauna, and another while walking down the trail from Pheriche to Thyangboche. Each romance lasted from three months to a year or more. To me, the experiences were more than just falling in love. It was an immediate and overwhelming emotion, making me feel whole, giving my life meaning. It was a religious experience. The Dalai Lama said, "My religion is kindness." *My* religion was romance.

If romance was my religion, this was my religious practice. Having this kind of loaded experience was what I cared most about in life. It wasn't just the possibility of sex—which of course was the energy behind all the heightened sensations—but it was the fact that the combination of anticipation, joy, and charged energy could even exist! All the lonely times I spent between relationships could be redeemed and erased in moments like these. The intoxicating feeling left me helpless in its spell. Her beauty and easy manner, wry humor, and intelligent warmth were what I had dreamed of finding. The overridden, sensible voice in my head was trying to get my attention to ask me how this was going to end any other way but badly, but I managed to tell myself that even if we had no possible future, I could at least enjoy the pleasure of sitting across the table from such a beautiful, charming woman. The sensible voice retreated with disdain.

Driving back to Lisa's house, I caught a glimpse of something off to my right—the driver's side in Nepal. It was the fleeting sensation of a silvery-white object flitting past the car, a sense of motion that didn't have a definitive shape. It darted past my vision and disappeared.

"Did you see that?" I asked.

"What?"

"Kind of a white shadow flying by on the right?"

Jane looked puzzled. "A white shadow? You mean like a ghost?"

"I don't know," I said. "It kind of felt like that, but in Kathmandu, it's hard to know what's going on a lot of the time."

"That's true," she said, and let that hang. When I glanced over, she was looking straight ahead.

At Lisa's house, I asked her if she wanted to drive up to Kakani the next day.

"Sure. I'd like that." We hugged good night. She leaned against the doorframe and watched me as I walked back to my car and drove away. I felt like I was in a movie. I no longer wondered *what* I was doing, but it was still fair to ask *why* I was doing it.

The next day, Jane and I drove west out of town, over the shoulder of Nagarjuna Mountain, through the Queen's Forest. I was still feeling hopefully romantic, a tingling that Jane's manner did little to dispel. We laughed and touched, together in a world of suspended disbelief, ignoring, for now, the implications of our attraction. We felt like anything could happen. Which was when we saw the leopard.

The lithe beast was calmly sitting upright by the side of the road. It didn't react as we pulled up next to it, but just gazed calmly back at us. Behind it was a dense forest, one that I had hiked in a number of times without ever thinking that it could harbor leopards. They are common in the Terai, but I'd never heard of them venturing so close to the city or this far north. It was still sitting there when we finally drove off.

I took it as a sign that something special must be happening. I never saw a leopard again in Kathmandu.

We reached the rim of the valley and turned right, up a short, steep dirt road that led to a large Nepalese house that had been converted into a small hotel. Brick and plaster, with a red tile roof, the house was part of a complex that had been the summer home of a British resident in Kathmandu in the late 1800s. The patio in front of the house overlooked a deep valley that plunged down about three thousand feet. We ate lunch on the patio, looking across to the giant mountains, stretching east and west for a hundred miles. I never got used to seeing those mountains, no matter how long I lived in Nepal.

We came back to my house for dinner, and afterward I sat down at my piano and played a song I had written in the aftermath of a brief but incredibly intense relationship I had in my last year of medical school in Chicago. Writing songs had been the artistic, emotional outlet of my failed relationships. *The relationship didn't work out*, I would console myself, *but at least I got another song.* I told Jane about the background of that particular song.

"I went to visit a friend in Detroit by train. I sat down next to this tall, blond woman and we fell in love before the train ride finished. Her name was Peggy."

"She must have been something." Jane was sitting on a couch across the living room from where I was sitting at the piano.

"The problem was, she was living with her boyfriend when we met."

"Oh," she said. The wry smile. She paused for a beat. "How did it turn out?"

"We moved in together a week after we met. It was really great for a couple of months. But I was in medical school, and she didn't have much to do in Chicago. She didn't have any friends there. She was alone most of the time until I got home from school. When we went on a road trip over Christmas, she told me that she was going back to her old boyfriend."

"What happened to you?"

"I didn't take it very well." Putting it mildly. In fact, I had started drinking entire six-packs of Colt Malt Liquor talls, three quarts of beer a night to try to dull the pain enough to go to sleep and still get up and go to medical school the next day. Peggy had embodied what I had always imagined that falling in love would be—instant and complete, a woman in whose arms I felt whole and safe, loved, and loving. The feelings that I experienced in the right woman's arms were so fulfilling, so impossible to attain any other way, that their loss triggered profound despair, a feeling that never quite went back to neutral, but was always there as an unfulfilled longing.

Jane stood up, and we met in the middle of the room. She reached up and put her hands on my shoulders, and I put my hands on her hips.

"I hope you'll find the right woman someday," she said.

She tilted her head up and I kissed her—a tender, excruciatingly pleasant kiss. She broke the kiss and buried her head in my shoulder, and we stood there for a long time. I had no doubt I *had* found the right woman, in a completely improbable situation. What could possibly happen that would keep her from marrying her fiancé in a month and a half? I had no idea, but she was going to be in Nepal for another week or so, and I made up my mind that I would just keep seeing her until it played out somehow. Whatever that might be.

But now that I'm alone again
It's wintertime with falling rain
And time alone will ease the pain
Of Peggy on the train

Jane went down to Tiger Tops for four days. She called me when she got back, and I went to see her. She was subdued.

"Are you okay?" I asked.

"Not really. I got a telex from my fiancé. He's postponed the wedding."

An entire flood of conflicted feelings rushed through me at that instant.

"Do you know why?"

"I don't know. I can't figure it out. We've sent out invitations already. It's going to be a mess."

"Did you talk to him?"

"I was able to get through once, but it was a bad connection. I really don't know..."

I took her out to eat at the nicest restaurant in town, an Italian restaurant at the Soaltee Oberoi Hotel. As we drove back to my house, I caught another glimpse of what I had begun to call "the white phantom." This time I didn't say anything. The moon, almost full, was bright orange, hovering low above the city to the east.

We sat on a couch in my living room.

"Let's go up on the roof and have a drink," I said. The roof of my house was flat, with a low parapet around it. A metal ladder gave access to the roof from a second-floor porch.

There were no chairs on the roof, so I brought two sleeping pads and a blanket. I had a bottle of good cognac that I had bought at the duty-free store. The moonlight reflected off Jane's face and hair, and her white blouse seemed to glow. The feeling of desire that her closeness inspired was as intense as I had ever experienced, but I just kept staring at the moon. I was always very conscious of the moon in Kathmandu—the way it hung in the sky over the urban landscape, seemingly larger and brighter than in any other city I had been in. We took sips from our drinks, sitting on the pads. I lay back to look at the stars, and she lay down beside me. A lone dog barked insistently from nearby. The air was lightly perfumed with the night-blooming jasmine that grew as a vine on the wall around my compound, mingling with Jane's faint perfume. I lay there, consumed with the sense of her body so close to mine.

I sat up, saw that her glass was empty, and offered her some more cognac. She sat up and held out her glass and I put my hand over hers to steady the glass as I poured, but it was my own hand that was shaking. My chest felt tight, and I didn't know how to break the tension. She looked up into my eyes and didn't look away. I leaned forward and kissed her, taking the glass from her hand, setting it down, and pulling her back on top of me. We kissed and held each other. I was trembling with longing, but I tried to keep my emotions in check, just in case she suddenly sat up and decided to stop. But she didn't stop, and we made love in the moonlight in the scented air.

She spent the night. I lay next to her, suspended in hope and fear. We were affectionate, but a lot of unspoken words hung between us. What was there to say? We weren't free to pursue this relationship until she sorted out her current lover. There wasn't much I could do. I had become a bystander to my own life, waiting to see how things would turn out. It was an all-too-familiar feeling.

The next night was to be Jane's last night in Nepal. I picked her up after I finished work, and we ate dinner at a restaurant. I knew that she was as confused as I was about what we were doing, and it would only make things more difficult if I tried to take her home again. Instead, I drove north out of Kathmandu to the foothills at Budhanilkantha. We walked along a stream where I often went for walks with my black lab, Lhasa, who had come with us, jumping along the rocks next to the stream. The moon was even brighter than the night before, rising above the hills on the far side of the valley, truly full, suspended over the lights of Kathmandu that spread out below us. The moonlight was bright enough to cast shadows, and we could see easily as we followed a primitive path along the right side of the stream. We discovered a small shack built of rough-hewn stones and a corrugated metal roof, open on one side, a goatherd's hut to provide some shade during the day. We wandered inside, and I turned to her. I kissed her hard, all the passion and longing that I felt going into the kiss. She kissed me back and I pressed her against the wall. We stayed in the shack for a while, like desperate lovers with nowhere else to go. Which we were.

Afterward, we walked slowly back down the stream, holding hands lightly.

"I liked the feel of the rough stones on my back," she said simply. We arrived back at the road where we had parked. We were the only people out at that time of night. We were reluctant to get back in the car. It was so peaceful and beautiful. We both knew that this might be our last night together ever. I kept trying to say something, but there was nothing more to say. I had placed myself in her hands. If romance was a path to enlightenment, it was not an easy path, and not without risk.

NINE

I had driven Jane to the airport in the early evening. There was an unexplained security alert, and I could only drop her at a gate, half a mile from the terminal. A bus would take her the rest of the way. I returned to my house and went up on the roof. There were so few flights in and out of Kathmandu in those days that when I heard a jet take off, I knew it was her plane. I watched its lights until they disappeared over the western foothills. She was going to London to meet her fiancé.

Three days later I met another woman named Jane. She suddenly appeared at my office in the afternoon, ambushing me between patients.

"Are you David Shlim?" she asked. She was as cute as the other Jane had been beautiful—with freckles, bright eyes, glasses, and an easy athletic figure.

"I am."

"I'm Jane. I'm a friend of Peter Hackett's." I had remained friends with Peter ever since he had first appointed me to work at Pheriche. In 1981, as part of a medical research expedition to Mt. Everest, he had climbed to the summit of Everest alone and nearly died coming down. Jane had been trekking that year and met Peter as he was walking out from the expedition. He was now a noted expert in the field of altitude medicine.

"Peter suggested that I look you up if I got the chance," said Jane. "I'm sorry to barge in on you like this. I tried calling you, but your receptionist wouldn't put me through to you. I thought I'd take a chance and ride my bike out here to see if I could find you."

"I'm sorry about that." Our receptionists were often overly protective of our time. "What are you doing in Nepal?"

"I've been trekking in the Khumbu with my boyfriend. He had to go back early, but I decided to stay on in Kathmandu for a while."

This new Jane had an easy way about her that touched me. Raw from my longing for the first Jane, I thought I could use some enjoyable female company. "I've got the day off tomorrow," I told her. "I've been thinking of driving out to a new restaurant I heard about on the valley rim to the east, overlooking the mountains. Would you like to come?"

The next morning was sunny and crystal clear. As soon as we passed Boudhanath, we entered a rural environment of small villages and terraced, lushly green rice fields, the tops just starting to dry, ready for harvest. Jane, totally at ease, told me that she was born in Calgary, and grew up skiing in the Canadian Rockies. She'd gone west to Vancouver for university and then settled there, working as a special education teacher.

We drove through a village with two-story houses the color of red clay on the first floor and white on the second floor. Chilies hung in huge braids from the upper porches, drying a deep crimson in the sun.

"What else do you do?" I asked her.

"In the fall I help my boyfriend on his sailboat that takes clients on nature tours of the islands off the British Columbia coast. In the summers I work in Jackson Hole for the Exum Mountain Guides, in their office." Not a dull life.

The road started switch-backing as it climbed up to the valley rim. When we crested the top, a great swath of the Himalayas came into view. A short way down on the other side was the Dhulikhel Mountain Resort.

Red bougainvillea flowers bloomed bravely on thin, newly planted trunks. We sat at a table shaded by a freshly thatched roof. Thousands of feet below in the valley, the sun glinted off a river. I had gone as long as I could without talking about the first Jane.

"You know, it's funny. I just met another Canadian woman named Jane last week," I said.

I couldn't keep myself from talking to Jane about my affair with the other Jane, how it started out innocently enough, then got complicated. How I didn't have any idea what would happen next.

"Have you been in touch with her?" she asked.

"No. I'm not sure where she is. I don't have a phone number—only her mother's address. I wrote a letter."

I sipped on my drink—fresh lime juice squeezed into a glass, served with a bottle of soda water on the side. I idly watched two large vultures circling slowly on a thermal.

Jane had her own encounter to tell me about. "I met Hugh Swift yesterday," she said. Hugh was a well-known modern Himalayan explorer. He had recently completed a two-volume guidebook on the mountain regions of Nepal, India, and Tibet.

"I know him," I said.

"I saw him in a restaurant, and I recognized him from the picture in his books. I made myself go over and talk to him. He was really flattered that I wanted to meet him. He seemed a little lonely."

Hugh was a tall, bearded, painfully shy man who spent a lot of time trekking through the Himalayas alone. He was the kind of traveler I was never destined to be—totally comfortable for weeks at a time alone in areas where it's illegal to even enter. I had asked him how he got into all the off-limits parts of Tibet that he wrote about. He told me that the Chinese policemen never knew what to do with him when they caught him. Their consistent instinct was to send him back to the last place he had been. When he got caught, they asked him where he had just traveled from, and he told them the name of the next town he wanted to see. They drove him right where he wanted to go. I related this to Jane.

"But then he'd still be in jail," she said.

"It didn't seem to bother him. He would get out by writing a letter of confession and promising not to do it again."

Jane laughed. She laughed easily, and often, and her laughter allowed me to laugh along with her, a letting-go that hadn't come easily in the past week. I asked her if she wanted to have dinner at my house. After dinner, I drove her back to her hotel, and she invited me up to her room. We sat and talked for a while.

"Thanks for a lovely day," she said as I stood up to leave. We kissed goodbye, slightly prolonged, somewhere between friendly and romantic. It had been a nice day. What are the odds of going out with two blond women named Jane from Canada in the same week? In addition, for both of them, Jane was their middle name, but they used it as their first name. They were both born in Toronto. The coincidence was enough to stick in my memory for a long time. The first Jane became "the real Jane," and the second Jane became "the other Jane."

TEN

I hadn't known Chokyi Nyima Rinpoche very long. I wanted to ask him about what to do with my feelings for the first Jane. I was obsessed with her, my mind alternating between hope and fear. Maybe he would have some advice on how to deal with this situation. On the other hand, I wasn't sure if it was even okay to talk to him about her. He was a monk—did he know anything about romantic desire? However, since I couldn't stop thinking about her, and Chokyi Nyima Rinpoche struck me as a trustworthy confidante, I went to see him.

I spilled it all out to him. I told him about meeting the real Jane, getting involved, feeling like I was in love, and the fact that she had a fiancé whom she planned to marry, and how my life felt completely on hold, helplessly waiting to find out what she would decide to do.

"I can't help feeling that she's going to come back somehow," I told him.

He remained silent for a moment when I finished, then leaned forward and said, "Don't worry. She's coming back."

My mind stopped dead. "Do you know this kind of stuff?" I finally blurted out.

"I don't know everything. But a few things I can get a feeling. And in this case, I know she will come back. You can just relax."

Just relaxing seemed out of the question, but his statement gave me hope.

I had figured that, at best, he would have given me some advice on how to wait more patiently, or how to not be so obsessed. Instead, it was, "Don't worry. She's coming back." As if that would take care of it. As much as I wanted to believe he was telling the truth, maybe he just said stuff like this. At least it was better than him saying she wasn't coming back.

In the days and weeks after that, however, as far as I could tell, Jane was gone. I wrote to her, but she didn't write back. A month went by and then another. I heard from Lisa that things were difficult for Jane, but I couldn't get any details. Then, a little while later, Lisa told me that Jane's fiancé had been having an affair, which was why he had suddenly postponed the wedding. Although this gave me hope, I still hadn't heard from her.

Having waited for three months without hearing from her, I tried offering to send her a plane ticket, having convinced myself that she might want to come back but couldn't afford it. Although I wanted to believe that Chokyi Nyima Rinpoche would be proven right, it felt better, at the moment, to try to be more proactive. Using a roundabout connection through the local Pan Am office, I got a message back from her via telex. It said, "Don't send the plane ticket, I'm not coming back." This was my first communication from her in over three months. Any rational observer would admit that it didn't look good. But I was not a rational observer. I still didn't believe it. I clung to the belief that she would return. I didn't ask myself at what point hope slides into delusion.

Gilda came by in the afternoon. Gilda was the nurse practitioner in our clinic, a graceful woman with curly brown hair and a deep compassion for patients. She had been working at the clinic since before I started, and we had shared a lot of intense experiences treating patients. She was also close to Chokyi Nyima Rinpoche.

"I finally heard from Jane," I said.

"What did she say?"

"She said not to send her a plane ticket, she's not coming back."

"Oh. I'm sorry."

"Thanks," I said. "The funny thing is, I still don't believe it. I still have the feeling that she's going to come back. Pretty hard to prove right now, however."

Gilda was headed out to Boudhanath to see Chokyi Nyima Rinpoche, and she called me around 7:00 p.m. "I told Rinpoche about the message from Jane. He said, 'Don't worry—she's coming back. Please tell David that I said that. He should not send any more letters. He should just wait.'"

"Thanks. It's funny, but that's how I feel. In any case, it will be easy to follow his advice, because I don't really know what else to say to her."

Two days later, I was still in bed when the phone rang at seven in the morning. There was the faint background hiss that indicated an international call.

"Hi." It was Jane.

"Hi."

"I guess maybe you've heard how hard things have been."

"Lisa told me a little bit."

"I'm so confused. I feel like I'm going crazy. I think about you a lot."

I sat up on the edge of my bed. "Look. Don't worry about me," I said. "My feelings for you are not going to change. I love you. If you want to come back here and be with me, I would love that." My heart felt like it had stopped, but my mind was surprisingly clear. "Take your time, whatever it takes. I'll be here."

"Thank you." We said goodbye.

I got up, got dressed, ate some breakfast, and drove to the clinic. I knew now that Jane would come back. Chokyi Nyima Rinpoche was going to be right. A week later Jane phoned again.

"Do you still want me to come to Nepal?"

"More than ever."

"It will take me about three weeks to get ready and fly over."

"I'll be here."

ELEVEN

Waiting for Jane to come back to Nepal gave me time to reflect on my life since moving there. I had plenty of time, as every second of waiting seemed to last a minute, and it felt like a nearly endless amount of time until she arrived.

I thought about how I had gotten to this point. It may well have started with the mountain climbing books I devoured when I was young. I suddenly realized that I had now entered these books as a character myself, albeit a minor one. I met, and later treated, Sir Edmund Hillary when he fell sick in the mountains. I met Reinhold Messner, the greatest alpinist of his generation, when he came through Pheriche in my second season. I befriended Jeff Lowe, the great American climber, and he stayed at my house when he came through Kathmandu for his Nepal expeditions. I had great dinner conversations in Kathmandu with Galen Rowell, the preeminent climbing photographer. It made me wonder how many children there were, their heads absorbed in books, who would grow up and enter the books they once read.

I still had to go to work. I think most patients don't think about what's going on in their doctor's mind while they are being seen. The long training and the commitment to the patient's welfare teach us to always put the patients first when we are with them. But behind that façade sometimes lies an obsessed mind. What comes out of my mouth is, "How long have you been having diarrhea?" What's going on in my mind is, "You know, I'm having a really hard time concentrating on your problem right now. The love of my life is flying back to Kathmandu in twenty days, and that's all I can think about right now."

Often, my patients had their own emotional turmoil, in addition to whatever illness had brought them into the clinic. A clinic that focused on the care of travelers in the middle of their journey had never existed before, so no one had been in as good a position to witness how travelers reacted to illness while they were still traveling. Travel is often not easy; traveling in Nepal can be harder than in many places. In those early days, travelers often took off on extended journeys for months, sometimes years. If I asked them an open-ended question, "Have you been traveling long?" they might say, "Yes. A long time now. More than three weeks." Or they might say, "No, not really, just six months."

How well they could handle the journey became an issue when they got sick. Most patients were coping reasonably okay, and just wanted to get well and carry on, and we helped them do that. Others were struggling and began to think of going home. Even if your trip has gone well so far, being sick can make you want to go home. If you're already struggling, it can be the tipping point. Patients dealt with these issues in different ways, and not always very directly. I usually told them, "Look, you're just traveling for fun. If it's not fun, then of course it makes sense to go home. Right now, you're sick, and I'm sure that makes you think about going home. But now's not the time to make that decision. I can make you better. Once you're better, then you can decide if you've had enough travel for now." This soothed most patients and allowed them to regain their motivation for travel.

Then there were the travelers with P.U.T.A. Not infrequently, travelers would come in with diarrhea, or weight loss, or a persistent cold, or some combination. I would try to be encouraging and usually had suggestions that could cure them, but they'd keep deflecting the reassurance and bringing up the fact that their overall health was deteriorating. No matter how I tried to come up with a plan, they would counter it.

"Maybe it's best if you head home," I would finally offer.

"No! I don't want to go home. I need to finish my trip."

"Okay. Let's work on that."

"But I've been sick so long. I'm really losing weight."

"Then maybe you should take a break, go home and recuperate. You can always go traveling again."

"Do you really think I have to go home? For my health?" I almost never did. But after I gained some experience, I realized that they were asking to be sent home. They didn't want to admit defeat, but they had reached their limit, and being sent home by a doctor would not be as disappointing as finding out they were just having a hard time traveling.

"I'm sorry, but I do. I'm not sure you'll get better if you don't give your body some rest."

"Damn it! Oh, well. If you say so. Maybe it's for the best."

There were enough of these kinds of patients that we needed a shorthand way to describe them around the clinic. I called it P.U.T.A.: Psychologically Unfit to Travel in Asia.

To be fair, traveling in Asia, particularly in those days, was not for the faint-hearted. The biggest stressors for sensitive people were beggars and filthy outhouses. Leprosy-deformed beggars sticking out their stump-fingered hands with a pleading look made travelers uncomfortable. They wanted to help, but they didn't know how much money to give, or they didn't have small change, or, truthfully, they didn't want to touch the beggar. They walked on by, conflicted, and often dwelled on the encounter for hours. Outhouses were another matter. Local people had rarely built outhouses for themselves; they preferred to sneak around and defecate in the open air, on the ground. But tourists were not accustomed to that, and with the numbers of tourists coming through, it was impractical to have them all trying to defecate out in the open. Outhouses required people to squat to poop, and many Westerners were not flexible enough, physically or mentally, to accomplish that. As a result, an outhouse used by Western tourists had stool everywhere. Urgency, explosiveness, and lack of coordination created a messy and queasy environment, making it difficult to even step inside. Local people may have assumed that Westerners didn't know where their anus was, or at least how to aim it.

Combine these stresses with long, crowded, vomit-scented bus rides, cheap but sometimes awful accommodations, street hustlers, lack of accountability by some of the people you did business with, being jerked around by government bureaucrats, not to mention the constant threat of illness, and it was no wonder some travelers succumbed to P.U.T.A.

Successful travelers, on the other hand, learned how to be functional in the chaos of Asia. They managed to take things in stride, to be patient, to solve problems one step at a time. In Nepal, the stresses of travel can be balanced by the natural beauty, the basic good nature of the people, the chance to travel across the countryside on foot at a pace unchanged by centuries, and the appreciation of how people could be so happy yet be so poor. The ups and downs of travel, I observed, were good training for managing the ups and downs of life. They just alternated more rapidly, and with wider swings than back home.

Traveling in Nepal, in terms of one's health, was in some way like swinging on a flying trapeze without a net. Medical care for local people in Nepal was extremely basic in those days. There were three government hospitals offering bare-bones care, so bare that they had no medicines and few bandages. For a patient to receive treatment, the family had to take a prescription from the doctor in the hospital and go out to a pharmacy to buy the drugs and bandages. If the pharmacy was closed, care would have to wait until the next day. There was one mission hospital, Shanta Bawan, offering quite good care, but in a fundamental setting that could be unnerving to foreigners. There was virtually no private practice. For foreigners, obtaining medical care was extremely difficult.

Our clinic was a mixture of general practice and emergency medicine. We often started the day with only one or two patients on the schedule and would see forty or fifty people by the end of the day. One couldn't schedule an appointment for an attack of severe diarrhea.

It turns out, though, that this challenge became one of the things that made the practice so compelling. General practice in much of the U.S. involves fielding and directing serious cases to specialists. In the absence of specialists, I had to hone my thinking skills. I approached serious cases by asking myself, *What's the worst this could be, what's the best it could be, and how can I decide?* Deciding who needed to travel to get care, and whether it was safe for them to travel, required a lot of careful thought. Patients put their trust in our clinic to help them make those decisions.

Often, the decision came down to instinct. Instinct is difficult to trust in medicine. It doesn't have to be just a mystical impression, however. It's based on experience, on hearing hundreds of stories and seeing how this story matches previous ones, knowing the outcomes in past cases. As an example, a forty-five-year-old Australian man came to see me on a Saturday afternoon, just a couple of hours after arriving in Kathmandu from his long flight. He told me that he had some chest discomfort while just sitting in a chair in his hotel room, a vague pressure in his chest that lasted less than five or ten minutes. He was supposed to leave on a three-week trek to the Everest region the next morning, and just wanted to make sure he was okay.

He was thin and fit and well-muscled. He was used to running every day back home. But in the last few weeks, he had occasionally experienced similar chest pain at the start of his daily run. It lasted a minute or so, and when he kept running it went away, then he continued to feel okay. While planning this trip, he had asked his doctor about it, and the doctor reassured him that if it had been his heart, the pain would only have gotten worse when he kept running, so he cleared him to go on the trek. I did an electrocardiogram, which was normal. But chest pain at rest is an ominous sign—it can mean that he is just a few clotted platelets short of a full-blown heart attack. If it was actually heart pain.

The fact that he had chest discomfort at the start of his runs was significant. The fact that it went away when he continued running seemed to be a good sign. But somewhere along the line, I had heard that it was possible to have heart pain at the beginning of exercise that then went away as the heart and the body warmed up. We had no further tests that we could run, and there was no cardiac care available in Nepal at all—no stress tests, no monitored beds, no catheterizations, no heart surgery. There was just me and my judgment standing between his having to turn around and fly back to Australia or continuing on to head off into remote high-altitude terrain that would almost certainly kill him if he was actually having heart pain at rest.

It was the way he described his chest pain that made the difference to me. Not a sharp pain, but vague and pressure-like. And transient. I decided to talk him into going home. He was initially shocked, and reluctant—understandably. But I put it to him like this: "The question of whether you have heart disease has already been raised. That's why you came in to see me this afternoon. I'm unable to put that question to rest without further tests that are not available in Nepal. Although it's disappointing to have to turn around like this, the worst that can happen, in terms of making this decision, is that you'll get home and find out that you *don't* have any heart disease. That wouldn't be so bad, would it? If you do have heart disease, you will have made the right decision."

He flew home the next day. I put him on some medication to protect his heart, just in case. I was nervous the whole time he was in the air. There was no precedent for the decision that I had made. It was like diagnosing someone with an impending heart attack in Portland, and instead of calling an ambulance to take him to the hospital straight from my office, I told him to go to the airport the next day and fly to London and see a doctor there. If he died en route, how would I justify that? Would other doctors support that decision? And yet, I didn't see any alternative.

I held my breath for the twenty-four hours it took for him to get home. He wrote to me afterward to tell me what happened. He made it home safely. When his doctor performed an exercise stress test, it was so quickly positive they immediately took him for a heart catheterization that showed the main blood vessel supplying his heart was ninety-nine percent blocked. He was so close to having a massive heart attack that they wheeled him straight to open-heart surgery from the cath lab.

That's an example of the kind of decision-making we faced on a weekly basis.

TWELVE

Jane flew in on a Saturday morning. She emerged from the terminal in a beige linen dress, displaying a shy smile, and carrying two bags. She set down the bags, and we embraced. Months of anxiety and longing suddenly evaporated just by being able to hug her and know that she was really there.

We lay on my bed in the afternoon sun.

"It's been really hard," she said. "I wanted to write you, to call you, but I just couldn't."

"It's okay," I said.

"What were you thinking all that time?"

"It's funny, but I just couldn't shake the feeling that you were going to come back. Right after you left, I asked Chokyi Nyima Rinpoche for some advice."

"What did he say?"

"He said, 'Don't worry, she's coming back.'"

"I wish he had told *me* that."

I basked in Jane's presence for another day. I had to go back to work on Monday. In the past months I'd had difficulty concentrating at work because Jane wasn't here; now it was hard because she *was* here. But I didn't have to worry about it anymore. She was here. The clinic by then had three full-time doctors and a nurse practitioner. In order to provide seven-days-a-week coverage, we each worked an average of four days a week. On the days I was working, Jane didn't have much to do, but on my days off we explored Kathmandu. After two weeks we decided to go visit Tiger Tops for four days.

We flew down on the thirty-minute flight around noon. We landed on a grass runway, and the plane taxied back to an open-thatched shack with a corrugated tin roof. The sun was hot; the faint outline of white Himalayan peaks shimmered through the haze. Elephants waited at the side of the airstrip to carry us back to the lodge. After traversing through tall grass, crossing a river, and seeing three types of deer, a crocodile, and a rhinoceros, we arrived at the wood-and-thatched three-story hotel that formed the main lodge.

When Jane descended from the elephant, she was greeted like a princess. The staff loved her, and we were shown to the owner's private house to use as our own. We walked through the dense forest for a short way, looking up at the high canopy. Monkeys loitered in the tall branches, eyeing us like gang members on a street, waiting for an opportunity to urinate on passing tourists.

The next day we headed out with two Nepali tiger trackers on the trail of a mother with two nearly grown cubs. The soil was sandy, the footprints easy to spot. As the three tigers had approached the bank of a small stream, we saw from the tracks that they had exploded into a full run. The small hoof prints of a barking deer led the tigers over a small rise. I girded myself to see the bloodstains and the carcass, but the deer had hung a sharp right turn into tall, thick grass and escaped.

We crossed several low ridges before climbing to a much higher forested ridge. A loud, deep-throated roar from the mother tiger, somewhere in the thick jungle just below us, let us know that we had approached too close. I couldn't believe that we were stalking wild tigers, unarmed, but the guides seemed unconcerned, so I tried to *act* unconcerned. Jane didn't seem worried at all. The guides knew the behavior of tigers and how to stay out of trouble, and Jane had lived there for a year. We intersected a stream and followed it up until it opened into a magical, rock-enclosed amphitheater called Golden Pond, a seldom-visited pool fed by an overhanging waterfall at the far end. Our clothes were already sweat-stained as we changed into swimsuits and cooled off in the clear water, relaxing on rocks sprayed by the gentle mist of the waterfall. Jane was in her element, and our attraction seemed to be suspended in the timelessness of the primeval setting, with no past or future.

Afterward, we swam and waded down the river, holding our packs above our heads to keep them dry. We changed into dry clothes when we reached the riverine meadows filled with tall elephant-grass. An elephant and driver waited to take us back to the lodge. The elephant kneeled on its back legs as we used its tail to pull ourselves up onto the wooden platform on its back.

THIRTEEN

The headline in the *Bangkok Post* read, "Plane Crash Kills 11 on Board."

Jane and I were at a café on Patong Beach on Phuket Island, having flown down from Bangkok the night before—on the same plane that was now featured on the front page. As we had waited to get off the plane in Phuket, we'd chatted with a flight attendant who told us that this was the end of a big holiday weekend in Thailand, and that they were going to fly one more round trip that night from Bangkok to Phuket to pick up the extra people who were waiting to get home. I recognized her photograph on the front page as one of the eleven who had been killed.

We were late getting into Bangkok from Kathmandu to catch the connecting flight to Phuket, but two Thai Airways representatives met us at the door of our Kathmandu flight and raced us through the airport so that we boarded just as the doors were closing. We weren't that worried—if we missed that flight, we could have caught the next one. Except the next one crashed into a mountain on approach to Phuket, killing all on board.

The reason that we were late arriving in Bangkok was that our first attempt to leave Kathmandu, on a Royal Nepal Airlines plane, had run into difficulties. It had to turn around and return to Kathmandu due to a pressurization failure. Jane said she wasn't going to fly on that plane again, and I tried to change our tickets to the Thai Airlines flight, but I wasn't allowed out of the transit lounge. Jane took charge, and through some combination of guile and charm that beautiful women can assert, managed to switch our tickets, which landed us in Bangkok about thirty minutes before the Royal Nepal Airlines flight finally arrived.

The newspaper headline made it hard to know how to feel. We were glad we had missed the flight but sad for the people who were on it. I got a chill down my back when I first saw the photo of the flight attendant and realized that she had been just two hours away from her own death during our conversation. How could she have known? How do any of us know? By a twist of fate, we were alive this morning.

It was also just a twist of fate that had brought Jane and I together a few months earlier. And as we drank our coffee, I caught the first faint hint that our fate might be changing. April is one of the hottest months in Thailand. It was ninety-five degrees with thick, oppressive, sticky humidity. The thatched roof on the patio overlooking the sea provided shade, but no relief from the heat. Our conversation wound down as we contemplated our fates. Looking over at Jane, I reached to take her hand, but she pulled it away to drink her coffee. Her face had changed.

"What's up?" I asked.

"Nothing."

"It feels like something."

"It's just hot."

It *was* hot. We swam to cool off but immediately started to sweat again as we walked back up the beach to our motorcycle.

The hotel we were staying in was a small set of wooden bungalows, set among the trees on a small isthmus of land jutting out into the ocean, with the murmur of waves hitting the beach directly below us. Shaded by trees, connected by dirt paths, it was a romantic hideaway. Or could have been. I had stayed there with friends two months earlier, fantasizing about what it would be like to be there with Jane.

The ceiling fan in our open wooden bungalow did little to help with the oppressive heat. We lay awake at night drenched in sweat, listening to the electric fan, and the sudden cuckoo-like calls of a gecko, sounding like, "Uh-oh...uh-oh...uh-oh."

Jane remained distant. She rolled away from my touch. I remembered lying next to her on our first and only night the previous fall, full of hope and fear. She had returned, against all odds, but now I could feel her slipping away. I tried to talk to her about it, but she couldn't engage. I guessed that her feelings had caught up with her. The betrayal by her fiancé, the confusion as to what to do, and the decision to move to Nepal had all been chasing her, and they finally caught up with her at the beach.

The next day we sat on the sand. Jane was topless, her smooth bare back and breasts making her achingly desirable, yet painfully out of reach. In the heat of the sun, I realized that Chokyi Nyima Rinpoche had told me that she would come back. He hadn't said that she would stay. I never even thought to ask that question.

We stayed a few more days and then flew back to Kathmandu. Jane couldn't talk about her feelings. She ate very little. She lost weight. I had to work at the clinic, leaving her alone a lot of the time. After a month, she told me that she was going to move into a friend's house. I helped her move her few things. She was really depressed.

"What do you want to do?" I asked.

"I don't know."

"Do you want to go back to Canada?"

"I don't know." She wasn't angry. She just wasn't there.

In the end, she booked a flight home. I drove her to the airport. Four months earlier I had driven to the airport to pick her up, feeling that a life of happiness and togetherness was within my grasp. Now all that was a shadow.

The monsoon had arrived. Large drops of warm rain pelted us as I kissed her goodbye near a crude tin-roof shack at a parking area about a quarter mile from the terminal. Another random security threat meant that I couldn't accompany her to the terminal. Jane would have to board a bus for the last quarter mile. We stood together in the rain.

"I really like you," she said. "You've been really kind to me."

"I love you."

"I know. I don't want to make you feel bad. I just don't know what I'm doing in my life right now."

I wanted to think that with some time and distance our relationship could recover, and we might get back together. But this time I knew deep down that it wouldn't happen. Jane got on the bus. It started raining harder. I stood in the rain watching the bus disappear up the short road to the terminal.

I turned and walked back to my car.

Things Will Slowly Get Better

FOURTEEN

"Things will slowly get better," Chokyi Nyima Rinpoche said. "It will take a little time."

"I don't know how to let go," I responded, and then added, "Maybe it's not a good idea to just let go of these feelings. Maybe I need to work them through somehow, to find out why they are so strong." He didn't reply. We were alone in his sitting room.

If there was a lesson to be learned, I still didn't know what it was. Don't fall in love? Don't fall in love and get dumped? Avoid love triangles? *That* would be worth trying.

Rinpoche sat back patiently on his small couch, letting me think it through. How could I not feel content living with a woman like Jane? How could I *possibly* feel content without her? As the Bangles sang, "What good is being strong when all I ever really want is you." For most of my adult life I had been either intensely in love or mourning the absence of love. I believed that it would be impossible to be truly happy without being in a relationship. Then it hit me. In order to be happy in the absence of a relationship, I would somehow have to learn to be content—with myself. Even all the great things that had been happening for me since I moved to Nepal hadn't overcome my sense of loneliness. I was more distracted and gratified by my activities, but that somehow didn't translate into being content within myself. Having experienced the high of being with Jane, I was back to feeling even worse than before. Being content would mean learning how to be happy within myself, whether I was with a woman or not. I looked over at Chokyi Nyima Rinpoche. He took a sip from his teacup.

"Yes, doctor?"

"I've heard what you've said about needing to learn to meditate in order to be able to calm my mind. Can you teach me how to meditate?"

He looked at me and nodded his head slightly. There was no smile of recognition, no sense that he felt that I'd finally come around. He greeted my request to learn to meditate with infinite patience—he undoubtedly knew that it would come to this long before I did, but he had just waited until the need to meditate had arisen in my own mind.

I had been to a number of his lectures by this time, and there was a common theme: we suffer because of our attachments, and our inability to let things just be. In order to learn to let things go, we need to train our minds. Our habit of clinging to thoughts and emotion is very difficult to break. Whatever thought or emotion that arises in our mind vies for our attention, and we are used to deciding how we feel based on the emotions that arise. We spend our lives waiting to find out how we are going to feel next. None of us are fully in control of our own mind—a strange thought. Whose mind is it, anyway?

Rinpoche sat up straight and proceeded to give me instructions. I should sit cross-legged on a cushion, my back straight, but not holding tension. My hands could rest gently on my thighs. He told me how to direct my attention during a meditation session. He said to try to practice for a short time every day.

I started the next morning.

I meditated for about fifteen minutes, directing my attention to my breath moving in and out, and trying to let thoughts go as soon as I realized that my attention had wandered. I welcomed the chance to try to stop obsessing about Jane. As I sat, I tried to visualize my breath going in and out, just watching, keeping my attention on the breath. As long as I was able to focus on my breath—which was just a convenient, neutral thought—it kept my mind from chasing after all the other thoughts that arose. However, the focus on my breath rarely lasted more than a few breaths. My mind would involuntarily start chasing after a thought—mainly longing for Jane, but could include anything else: the discomfort in my legs, a patient I was worried about, what might taste good for breakfast. When that happened, Chokyi Nyima Rinpoche said to just gently notice that my mind was distracted and direct my attention back to my breath.

In the brief moments when I could take my attention off the thoughts of Jane, I felt an instant sense of relief. My mind relaxed. The tightness in my chest eased. Then, just as quickly, thoughts of her would charge back as if breaching my wall of concentration. If I chased after them, they just ran around in circles, but if instead I tried to ignore them, the unwanted thoughts eventually slipped away by themselves. Even a very short-lived success in doing this gave me hope.

I meditated every morning for a week. I was disconcerted to find, however, that instead of growing more peaceful, I was getting more volatile in really obvious ways. If I was frustrated by a phone call, I threw the phone down and swore loudly. I would kick a chair in frustration. I threw a patient's chart down hard on a table in the doctor's area in a pique of anger, causing nurses and colleagues to quickly slip away. This was new behavior for me. What was going on? I had been meditating faithfully for a week, and now I felt that I was worse than ever. I went to see Chokyi Nyima Rinpoche.

I got right to the point. "This meditation thing is not working. I'm losing my temper really easily and acting worse than ever."

"Actually," said Rinpoche, "This shows that the meditation is working." *Really?* I thought. *If I keep this up, I may end up killing someone.* He paused. "Your mind is like muddy water, and meditation is like a filter. After you put muddy water through a filter, there is clear water on one side, but the remaining water is even more thick and muddy. The anger that you are experiencing has always been in there, but now you are more aware of it. Just keep practicing your meditation."

When he told me that, I realized that I wasn't completely surprised. Massage therapists over the years, trying to knead tension out of my over-stressed body, had often prodded something acutely painful and asked, "Do you ever feel angry?" And surprisingly, I usually answered, "No. Not really." And they responded with a knowing, "Hmmm." But I really thought I didn't get angry. Except when I was visiting my mother.

Like many adolescent Jewish boys, when I read *Portnoy's Complaint*, by Philip Roth, I recognized my mother in Mrs. Portnoy. My mother, who also read the book, swore that she was nothing like that: overly worried, hovering, needy, filled with a fierce love that had more to do with how she felt than how I felt. I had to fight my way out of that smothering cocoon to pursue the life of adventure that I yearned for, starting with the mountain climbing course at thirteen.

There were four of us children: my older sister, myself, and two younger brothers. My father was emotionally distant, always pushing us to do more, always thinking that what we had achieved was not enough. As we grew up, we all had different issues. My sister, Harriet, was worried that she would never get married. Three years older than me, she missed the breaking wave of hippie free love and drugs and carried a fifties mentality for some time. My younger brother, Mark, was the most creative of us all—a brilliant natural writer, cartoonist, musician, artist, and political radical. He couldn't find his place in the world or have the confidence to put his art or writing out on public display. My youngest brother, Larry, gravitated toward a career in photography, at which he was extremely talented, but he also was unable to bring that career to a well-recognized fruition.

It was Mark who drew my mother's love, attention, and worry. He lived alone in rural Oregon, growing his own food. He refused to take a job, and my parents were forced to support him, torn as to whether they were enabling him or helping him.

I was the successful one, albeit I had struggled as well. I managed to become a doctor, but I was unwilling to settle down and join my father in practice, or even stay on the same side of the globe. When I later started doing research and publishing papers, I would tell my mother that I published a new paper, and she would say, "Mark would have been really good at research."

Did that make me angry? I had to learn to hold it in. The tensions of unbalanced family love were rampant in me, and now, having sat down for the first time in my life to see what my mind was up to, these hidden angers were slipping out.

This early experience with meditation also confirmed for me why meditation techniques are passed on orally in the Tibetan tradition. If I tried meditation on my own, out of a book, and began to have these types of experiences, I might have quickly abandoned it as ineffective or even harmful. With the encouragement of Chokyi Nyima Rinpoche I persisted, and gradually the sudden bursts of anger happened less often. I began to experience a brief gap between the moment that I started to experience anger, and my expression of it. That gap sometimes allowed me to head it off before it flew out. It was a start.

In addition to the effect on anger, I noticed that the longing I felt for Jane felt different this time. I didn't have the same sense of self-pity and despair that went along with my previous painful break-ups. Knowing that Chokyi Nyima Rinpoche was there, along with my decision to take up meditation seriously, gave me hope that the future might be different.

Despite these baby steps of success, though, I still felt restless. I needed a distraction and yearned for an adventure. I wanted to go to Tibet, a place that had been closed to outsiders for more than a thousand years. After the Chinese took over in the 1950s, the country became even more tightly sealed off. However, in the early 1980s, China had finally started allowing tourists into Tibet, first in organized groups, and then—just a few months before—as individual tourists.

I told Chokyi Nyima Rinpoche about my desire to see Tibet. My meditation was getting a little more stable, and I wanted to ask him for some advice on how I should practice while I was there.

"Before you leave for Tibet, I want you to answer a question for me," he said.

"Okay."

"Can you have more than one thought at a time?"

Are you kidding me? My thoughts were like popcorn in a popcorn maker. Thoughts were constantly pushing each other out of the way, competing for attention. Of course, I had more than one thought at a time—it was the way everyone's mind worked.

"I have a lot of thoughts at once," I told him.

"When you are at home, watch your thoughts while you are meditating and tell me what you learn," he said.

I sat on my cushion and watched my thoughts. I could pick out one thought, then I would get the hint of another thought coming, and my attention would shift, like a quick flick of my eyes, and then I would focus back on the first thought. I'd pick up a stronger thought coming along, and my focus would go there. When that happened, the present thought would evaporate. I kept exploring my mind in this way, and soon I was convinced that what had seemed like many thoughts at once were really thoughts coming in very rapid succession. Even when thoughts appeared to be simultaneous, I could see my attention leaping from one thought to the next. I couldn't really look at two thoughts at the exact same instant.

I went back to see Chokyi Nyima Rinpoche a week later. "I think I can only have one thought at a time."

"Good," he said. He gave an analogy of how Buddhists view the act of thinking. "Picture a house in a tree with a window on four sides. You can only look at it from below. You see a monkey in one window, then a monkey in another window, then the first window again. It is difficult to know how many monkeys there are in the house. But if you watch closely, you will see that there is only one monkey visible at a time. One monkey, moving around rapidly, can seem like several monkeys."

"I think I proved that to myself," I said.

"Very good." He sat back. "Who is watching your thoughts?"

"Me."

"Who is me? Who is the watcher?"

I was confused. If it wasn't me, who could it be?

"Look at your mind more closely," he said.

I sat in my usual spot in front of the window in my home office, noticing that the bougainvillea that wrapped around the window was in bloom, the flowers a deep vermillion. I watched my thoughts. I looked to see who was observing the thoughts. I had to look quickly, as my thoughts were still jumping all over the place, as usual, but I noticed that when I tried to get a glimpse of who was observing the thoughts, the observer disappeared. I tried to look to see who was looking at the thought, but it was a trail that didn't lead anywhere. I couldn't pin down any sense of a solid observer. I tried this over and over for the next several days. I knew someone was watching, but when I tried to figure out what qualities the watcher had, I became less certain. Trying to define the qualities of the watcher just seemed like more thoughts—and who was watching *those* thoughts? It was disconcerting. The observer of "me" didn't seem to have any inherent qualities.

I went back to see Chokyi Nyima Rinpoche.

"I tried looking for the watcher, as you said."

"And...?"

"I couldn't find any watcher," I said tentatively. "Every time I looked, there was no one there."

"Excellent," said Rinpoche, smiling.

"But then who is the watcher?" I asked, still uncertain as to what I had learned.

"The mind is empty awareness. The mind is not the same as 'self.' What you think of as your 'self' are just concepts that you hold in mind. When you look to find the observer of your thoughts, it is empty. Mind is empty—no shape, no size, no color. Yet it is aware."

Had I seen that? Maybe a tiny, uncertain glimpse? But if my mind was empty, who was *I*? Who would I be if I'm not actually the person that I think I am? And where would that take me? How do you pursue spiritual practice if you are trying to prove that you don't really exist?

FIFTEEN

Tulku Urgyen Rinpoche, Chokyi Nyima Rinpoche's father and main teacher, started having chest pain and shortness of breath one night at eleven o'clock. He lived in a tiny room on the top floor of a small nunnery on a mountain called Shivapuri, high above the Kathmandu Valley. There was no electricity, no phone, and no radio. Unable to call for help, they also didn't have the option to send someone for help until the morning. The surrounding woods were called the King's Forest, protected by a high wall, with a gate that was locked from sunset to sunrise.

At dawn, a monk who served as one of the lama's attendants descended 2,000 feet to the gate just as it was unlocked, ran down the road, and finally got a taxi to Boudhanath, where he was able to tell Chokyi Nyima Rinpoche what was going on. Chokyi Nyima Rinpoche called me at 5:30 a.m., awakening me from sleep.

I drove to my clinic and started packing the battery-powered EKG machine, an assortment of medications, and intravenous fluid. Chokyi Nyima Rinpoche and two other monks pulled into the clinic driveway a few minutes later in a four-wheel-drive Jeep. We drove on empty roads, out past the Ring Road, through the bamboo forest, past rice fields and villages until we reached the gate at the base of the mountain. From there the path climbed through steep forest on a dirt road that alternated between loose sand and embedded sharp rocks, barely wide enough for the wheels of the Jeep. At times we inched past steep drop-offs with our outer wheels only inches from a fatal plunge. The road finally leveled off and doubled in width, and we parked. A steep red-dirt trail headed straight up the mountain to the nunnery, which took us another half hour.

Tulku Urgyen Rinpoche was waiting in his second-floor chambers, looking reasonably okay for someone who had been up all night in severe pain and shortness of breath. I asked him how he was feeling, and he said, through a translator, "It's better now. It got pretty bad for a while last night, and I thought I might die, but I didn't." Tulku Urgyen's voice had a casualness that startled me, like he was telling me what he had for dinner the night before.

He was sixty-five years old with close-cropped gray hair. His face was warm, open, and pleasant, his eyes enlarged by thick glasses he had acquired after having cataract surgery. He had full lips that reminded me, incongruously, of Mick Jagger. He wore a thin yellow shirt with an upturned collar underneath maroon robes. Traces of dried sweat on his forehead and scalp belied the amount of pain he must have endured during the night.

I asked him to take off his shirt and lie down on one of the low benches along the far wall. I kneeled next to him on the floor. His skin was cool and smooth and hairless. It took me a few minutes to untangle the leads from the portable EKG machine, attach them to his arms and legs, and then move the chest lead—held in place by a suction cup—to six different positions on his chest. Heat sensitive paper rolled out of the machine, and even the first few inches showed that he was having a massive heart attack, a complete blockage of the main artery that supplies the left ventricle—the left anterior descending artery—an often-fatal kind of heart attack known darkly as "the widow-maker." The EKG tracing was distorted in a way that made each heartbeat look like the top of a tombstone. It was the sign of dying heart muscle. By now, more than nine hours after his heart attack began, Tulku Urgyen Rinpoche's heart muscle was severely damaged. The nerves running through the heart would be disrupted, like rusted-out wires, subject to a sudden short circuit that could stop the heart without warning—a cardiac arrest.

I didn't know much about Tulku Urgyen Rinpoche beyond the fact that he was Chokyi Nyima Rinpoche's father. I didn't yet know that he was known throughout the world of Tibetan Buddhism as one of the greatest practitioners of the twentieth century. He had been one of the Dalai Lama's meditation teachers. Born in far eastern Tibet, he fled the Chinese invasion in 1958, lived in Bhutan, and now in Nepal, where he had settled a decade earlier.

I knew what care he needed, but I had no idea how to implement it. Ordinarily, a patient with a heart attack in those days would be put on strict bed rest, his heart monitored twenty-four hours a day for the least sign of instability. He wouldn't even be allowed out of bed to go to the bathroom. The heart would continue to be monitored for up to a week, with nurses and doctors always seconds away. The problem was that there were no cardiac monitored beds in Kathmandu to take him to. Which didn't really matter, because we had no safe way to transport him down the mountain to Kathmandu without the risk of killing him from the exertion.

Although it went against all of my medical training, I began to think that the best thing to do might be to do nothing at all—to leave him at Nagi Gompa. If he would receive no better care in Kathmandu, and the act of trying to transport him down there might precipitate a cardiac arrest, just leaving him here might actually be the safest course. I sat on a bench, trying to think it through. The monks and nuns were watching me, waiting to see what I was going to say. I wondered how Tulku Urgyen Rinpoche would feel if I told him that I was going back down to Kathmandu and just leaving him there.

When I told him that I thought he should stay where he was, he smiled in relief. He told me that he would rather not go down to Kathmandu if he didn't have to. I realized that Tulku Urgyen Rinpoche didn't seem to have any fear of dying, which was hard for me to comprehend. Among the hundreds of people having acute heart attacks that I had attended, I had never met a single person who was not genuinely afraid. I could see it in their eyes, a desperate, pleading look asking me to relieve the pain, to make sure they would be okay. With a cardiac arrest, the heart suddenly slips into a chaotic rhythm that can't pump blood, and the person gasps and stops breathing, often with their eyes still open. Sometimes we could resuscitate them and sometimes not.

Personally, I had a highly developed fear of dying, which I often tested when I went rock climbing, kayaking, or even just driving up that sketchy road to Nagi Gompa. I had learned to put aside the fear of dying while rock climbing. Although rock climbing is fairly safe, occasionally a piece of protection falls out behind you, or you find yourself off route in a way that could lead to a fatal fall. At that point, one has to stay calm and focus on the moves at hand, shutting out the fear of falling. It is an exercise in mind control; it doesn't address the actual fact of dying. It addresses the immediate issue—trying not to fall by giving into the fear. It is quite different than not being at all worried about the advent of death. The thought that it was possible to face death calmly had never occurred to me. It made me think, *Who is this guy? How can he not be afraid of dying?* I learned that he had spent over twenty years of his life in solitary retreat, practicing meditation in remote caves in eastern Tibet. Whatever the qualities were that he exhibited, he seemed to have earned them through training. But what was that training like?

I came to check on him each day for the next several days. After each trip, I realized that I was more afraid of driving up and down the treacherous road than *he* was of sitting on a remote mountainside after having a heart attack. It made *me* feel calm just being near him. It sowed a seed. Was there some way I could train in order to cultivate those qualities? Honestly, it seemed like a long shot.

Fortunately, his heartbeat remained stable, and his heart muscle was still strong enough to prevent heart failure. After my third or fourth visit, when he was feeling better, I sat with him in his very simple bedroom on the top floor of the temple. The room was eight feet square with two small windows that looked out over the forested mountains and green fields of the Kathmandu Valley. Thin yellow cotton curtains hung at the side of the windows. He sat on a low bed, a carved wooden table in front of him.

"What do you do up here all day?" I asked him.

"I practice nonmeditation," he replied.

I thought he was making a joke. How did that differ from how I spent most of my time, which was not meditating? I just assumed he was being humble about his practice. I didn't know that he had just revealed something important about the nature of Buddhist practice, something that only the greatest practitioners can accomplish.

SIXTEEN

I have to admit that I wasn't good at sitting through lectures on Buddhist philosophy and practice. Sitting on a cushion on the floor did not come naturally to me, and I would get fidgety and have to change positions frequently. The slow pace of teachings, first in Tibetan, and then repeated by the translator, gave my mind a lot of time to wander. Although I understood the importance of the teachings, the process of receiving them wasn't easy for me.

One day I drove my motorcycle up to Nagi Gompa to receive my first teachings from Tulku Urgyen Rinpoche. He had recovered from his heart attack, but I hadn't yet attended any of his teachings.

The fact that I drove up by motorcycle is not an incidental detail. The road was still treacherous, and almost impossible for my car because of its low clearance. Even with a bike of this quality, however, the road to Nagi Gompa still terrified me. The road had been improved slightly from when I had first gone up to treat Tulku Urgyen Rinpoche. Nonetheless, steep hairpin turns through loose sand were succeeded by even steeper stretches that featured large, sharp-edged rocks embedded in the dirt, too close together to ride between. The only way through was to commit to a medium speed through the rocky sections and try to stay balanced as the bike bounced from stone to stone. If I went too slowly, the bike would get stuck against a rock and I'd be thrown down; if I went too fast, I could careen off a rock and fly off the road, down a drop of hundreds of feet.

My fear of the road is relevant because after the first day of teachings (out of two), I had made up my mind not to come back the next day. However, as I walked out of the prayer hall during an afternoon break, Chokyi Nyima Rinpoche saw me and walked all the way across the lawn to where I was. He had never before made a point of walking over to me like that.

"You should come tomorrow," he said, before I could say anything. "It will be a good teaching."

How did he know I was thinking of not coming? What could I say?

The next day, still intact from two trips up and one trip down the road, I was back restlessly on the cushion as Tulku Urgyen took his place at the front of the prayer hall. He sat on a simple wooden throne that placed him about three feet off the ground. There were roughly forty students nestled into the small teaching hall. He spoke about having the proper motivation for spiritual practice. We needed to contemplate impermanence.

"None of us know how long we are going to live," he said. "We shouldn't postpone Dharma practice." The motorcycle ride down to Kathmandu immediately came to mind—it was possible I might meet the end of my life right after this teaching.

Tulku Urgyen went on to explain that the suffering of all sentient beings stemmed from the fact that we didn't understand the relationship between our perception of reality and reality itself, what Tibetan Buddhists call "dualistic thinking." We form opinions about everything we interact with: we like or dislike something or feel indifferent. As a result of these constant thoughts—like turning into desire, dislike turning into anger, indifference fading into dullness—we accumulate karma, the consequences of all our thoughts and actions. The only time we are not accumulating karma is when our mind rests in a state called "empty awareness," which he described as the quality of our mind when we don't form any concepts at all yet remain aware. This was the state of mind that Chokyi Nyima Rinpoche had described to me earlier. I had no idea what that state of mind could possibly be like.

"The natural state of empty awareness cannot be described in words," he said. "If you have never tasted sugar, how can someone describe the taste of sugar to you? What does the word 'sweet' mean to someone who has never tasted anything sweet? But if you give a person some sugar to taste, they will then know the meaning of sweet."

My body was rebelling. I leaned to my left, then shifted my legs around and leaned on my right arm. Tulku Urgyen talked about a specific way to view one's own thoughts. We constantly get absorbed into the content of our thoughts, labeling them as good or bad, not recognizing that the thoughts themselves are empty, like bubbles. When we take our attention off a thought, it simply disappears.

The sun started to set below the western mountains that rimmed the valley. It was getting dark in the prayer hall, as Nagi Gompa still had no electricity. Tulku Urgyen Rinpoche told us to sit up straight. I sat up and crossed my legs, my back straight. He chanted briefly in Tibetan, then paused. He raised his hand and made a simple gesture. And just like that, I experienced a brief instant in which my mind was empty of thoughts, yet fully aware. My body tingled with a gentle, electric bliss. The feeling gradually diminished, in the way that the sound of a struck bell slowly fades away. The actual gesture is a well-kept secret. He was a master of inducing a recognition of our natural state, and he was the only lama I ever met who did it in this way.

It doesn't sound like much, but I was stunned to my core. I had just experienced what my mind is like when it is aware, but no longer formulating any concepts or thoughts. It wasn't that he had made my mind like that; it was always like that. He just allowed me to see it for the first time. This fundamental nature of mind can only be pointed out by an experienced teacher. Having figuratively tasted the sugar, I would always recognize it when I encountered it in the future. The extraordinary moment of insight that I had just experienced left me with a glow of inner contentment.

"Ten thousand years of darkness in a cave," Tulku Urgyen went on to say, "can be illuminated instantly by lighting a single match. The darkness doesn't slowly and reluctantly give way to the light. It's instantly gone the moment that the match lights."

That's how it felt. But just like a match, the light had burned out within a few seconds. I wondered where I was going to find another match.

SEVENTEEN

I was finally headed to Tibet, to quench my desire to see that mysterious land and maybe have some spiritual experiences. I managed to fly all the way to Chengdu, China en route to Lhasa, only to be stopped there and denied a permit to enter Tibet due to a planned Chinese celebration of the "liberation" of Tibet. The Chinese army had invaded and nearly destroyed Tibet in the 1950s, killing hundreds of thousands of people, and sending at least an equal number into exile. This was not a day that was celebrated by Tibetans. Disappointed, I continued on my annual visit to the U.S. to connect with parents and friends and buy supplies for the clinic. At my parents' house in Portland, Oregon, I struggled to gain some equilibrium about Jane. I wrote a letter to Chokyi Nyima Rinpoche asking him about how I could use my current situation to gain a better understanding of Buddhist philosophy. He wrote back:

> As far as the situation with Jane, and all other such circumstances, it is the very nature of samsara to be full of hope and doubt, fear, and appreciation, without limit. These feelings fluctuate throughout all samsaric existence due to ego attachment, and they are not inherently bad, but should be seen for what they truly are. With this fact

in mind, please don't be too sad, as the situation will get softer in proportion to your lessening attachment.

Samsara is the Buddhist term for our ordinary life. When we remain wrapped up in our ordinary (samsaric) life, we experience hope and fear without limit. Rinpoche went on to write:

> Really, everything is mind, and in cultivating a mind of contentment, then everyone around you will be happy and at peace with you, and you will be more equal about any adverse situations due to the inner contentment. Conversely, if you always search outside of yourself for happiness, it will remain elusive, and whatever you have will seem bitter, and people around you will be unhappy. So now you know where to look for happiness.

If you always search outside of yourself for happiness, it will remain elusive. Where else could it be? I had been so convinced that happiness could only derive from a relationship with someone else that I truly couldn't imagine any other way. I had fallen in love with what seemed to be the perfect woman; she was the embodiment of a dream: a compelling beauty with an easy manner, a sense of humor, and an adventurous nature. Looking back, I wondered if she had, in fact, been a kind of dream—a real person, but serving a karmic purpose. She had appeared just after I connected with Chokyi Nyima Rinpoche, creating a circumstance I couldn't avoid, forcing me to decide which method—sudden romance or spiritual effort—was more likely to result in long-term happiness. Her appearance in my life had finally forced me to confront the fact that I always felt that happiness lay outside myself. *So now you know where to look for happiness.* But how do I do that?

As I flew back to Kathmandu at the end of the summer, I reflected on what I thought I was learning. Was it just a strange coincidence that I met Chokyi Nyima Rinpoche right before I encountered the most desirable woman I had ever met? The romances that I had enjoyed gave me a kind of blissful, transcendent feeling that I couldn't replicate any other way. I was far from the only person who felt that way. I had faith in something that a rock music critic, writing about Leonard Cohen, once called "romance as a path to enlightenment." The suffering that resulted just seemed to be the price one had to pay for being able to have those exquisite highs.

But as I listened to more Buddhist teachings, I began to realize that this was the very nature of suffering. We have many hopes about what we want and need, but they are not always fulfilled. The aching loneliness of a newly empty bed taught me that no matter how badly you want something, you can't always make it happen. If we are honest, we can admit that there is always an undercurrent of uneasiness, a sense that whatever we have can be lost at any time, and whatever it is we long for may not come to pass. And even if we attain that desire, it isn't going to last.

I realized that my understanding of suffering, in an otherwise fairly fortunate life, derived almost exclusively from my love affairs. They felt so wonderful that I couldn't help clinging to them. When they ended, I suffered a painful and overwhelming despair. However, this time when it happened with Jane, I was lucky enough to have a spiritual friend standing by whose name was not Schlitz Malt Liquor. Chokyi Nyima Rinpoche was able to convince me that my pain had not been created by the woman who left me. Her leaving me was the circumstance that caused the pain to appear, but the feelings of loss and hopelessness were being generated by my own mind. Nothing was causing me to suffer other than my own attachment to something that I had lost. The heartache and constant longing, I had learned, would eventually fade away, even if it took years. What I was now learning was a way to make that time frame shorter. *The situation will get softer in ratio to your lessening attachment.*

A slight jolt of the plane reminded me that I was still flying across the ocean. My knees pressed against the back cushion in front of me and I shifted in my narrow seat. Each new loss made me think back to other lonely times. Each year of medical school, I had driven alone to Chicago from Portland in the fall, and back to Portland the following spring. As I'd head west from Chicago in early June, I'd feel a bursting sense of summer freedom. I would pick scenic routes, camping out along the way in little-used National Forest campgrounds. Some nights I would sit by a campfire, a forested mountain at my back, and an incredibly full orange moon rising on a distant horizon, and I would wish desperately for someone special to share it with.

When it would be time to go back to Chicago at the end of the summer, I'd feel like a parolee reporting back to prison. I would delay the journey as long as possible, and end up having to drive two thousand miles in four days.

Before the start of my last year of medical school, my route took me from California through Arizona, up through Colorado, and across the plains to Illinois. I was driving across Iowa as the sky lowered and darkened and the radio warned of tornadoes having been sighted in the exact direction I was headed. Flat gray clouds with a strange greenish hue extended to the horizon. Growing up in Portland, everything I knew about tornadoes was from *The Wizard of Oz*. I was scared. I kept looking at the bottom of the clouds to see if any twisting tails had developed. What would I do if I saw one? Can you outrun a tornado in a car?

I didn't end up seeing a tornado, but the full fury of the rainstorm soon broke over me. Huge black clouds reared up into the sky, illuminated by an inferno of lightning flashes and thunder, the most dramatic rainstorm I had ever experienced. The deluge of thick raindrops overpowered my wiper blades, and I was forced to crawl down the interstate at a few miles per hour. As I squinted through my windshield, I became aware of a faint glow in the sky. As I drew closer, I saw that the glow was coming from four massive red letters on a yellow background, a hundred feet high in the sky, spelling out the word, "HELL." I had just crossed the Illinois state line and was already mourning my return to a lonely existence in the mountainless wasteland of Chicago. What the fuck was happening? As I crept slowly by the sign, I saw that it was actually a "SHELL" gas station sign, with the "S" burned out. I felt like it was mocking me.

This was the kind of self-pity that always nagged at my being. It was a combination of loneliness and a lack of self-confidence, even though from the outside I had plenty of reasons to feel confident. I spent too many hours, like I was now, feeling sad and wishing for something to get better.

The plane landed in Tokyo to refuel. We had to deplane and go into the terminal for a couple of hours, so I ended up watching sumo wrestling on high-definition Japanese televisions. Then I got back on the plane for another five hours to Bangkok. I waited through the long immigration lines, even though it was near midnight, Bangkok time. Walking across to the familiar Amari Airport Hotel was comforting. In the morning, I would board the Thai Airways flight to Kathmandu, revel in the view of the Himalayas, and be home again.

As soon as I was back, and starting to get over jetlag, I went to see Chokyi

Nyima Rinpoche. He asked me how my home leave was, and I told him that it had felt pretty lonely. Despite all that I had accomplished up to that point, I still felt very unfulfilled. I asked him if I was destined to just live alone my whole life.

"Before someone else can love you, you need to learn to love yourself," he said gently.

"What's there to love?" I blurted out and was instantly struck by the fact that I truly did feel that way.

"You need to accept yourself. You are much better than you think." He leaned over and touched my hands. He looked in my eyes with deep love. That genuine, unconditional love touched my core, and unbidden tears formed in my eyes. The power of his compassion reached through to me. It's hard to describe if you've never been in the presence of someone like that. I vowed to myself to start trying to take a more positive attitude. What happened in my life was not always—or even often—within my control. But how I reacted, how I felt—those were things I could work on. I could more actively pursue a practice that led to peace of mind. The alternative would certainly be to just continue to suffer.

I took some deep breaths and wiped the tears from my cheeks.

"Do you think I'll ever get married?" I asked him, the question popping out of my mouth before I had a chance to think about it.

"Yes, and I will perform the marriage ceremony in my monastery." Then he laughed.

When I arrived back in Nepal it was mid-August, still monsoon season. The weather was hot, with frequent, violent thunderstorms raging through

Himalayan-sized black clouds, larger than I had ever seen, even larger than the storm in Iowa. Lightning danced continuously in the sky among and behind the massive clouds. I was gingerly trying to get on with my life, feeling like I could finally handle being in Nepal without Jane, especially since I knew that she was 12,000 miles away.

Then Lisa called. "Good to hear your voice, darling," she said. "I wanted to let you know that I've heard from Jane, and she's coming to Kathmandu in September with her new boyfriend. I just thought you would want to know."

"It's good of you to let me know," I said. I *so* didn't want to know that. The news revealed as fiction the fragile belief that I was over Jane. I didn't know that Jane had a new boyfriend until that moment. Having to see them together would be unbearable.

A month later, Lisa called to warn me that Jane was in town, staying at the Hotel Vajra with her boyfriend. Suddenly, I found that I couldn't bear to go downtown. I avoided my favorite restaurants and bookstores. I just traveled between the clinic and my home. I felt like I would stop breathing if I saw them together. So much for Buddhist detachment.

After Jane had been in town for a week, she called me. She asked if she could come see me and when I agreed, she took a taxi to my house that same afternoon. "I wanted to call you," she said. "I wanted to see you before we left. We've been pretty busy."

I didn't know what to say. "I'm glad you did," I finally replied. I felt better that she had wanted to see me, rather than ignore that I was there. My chest was tight, but as we stood side by side in my kitchen, leaning against the stone counter, I still felt myself drawn toward her.

"Who's your boyfriend?" I asked.

"He's a photographer. I met him on a fashion shoot on the New Brunswick coast."

"Is he a nice guy?" I wasn't sure what answer I was looking for.

"We get along pretty well," she said. Then she turned toward me and looked into my eyes. "You know, you really changed my life."

"I did?"

"Yes. You were the first man I've gone out with who was really nice to me."

I stood there looking back into her eyes. "That's good, I guess." Despite all the time I had spent worrying about how *I* was feeling, it seemed that something had happened to Jane as well, and she needed to share it.

"Yes, it was." She put her arms around me and hugged me. We held it a long time, and I tried to memorize the feel of her body against mine. My dog stared up at us, wagging her tail expectantly. Then Jane walked out the door, gone—this time I was sure—for good.

EIGHTEEN

I had wanted to go to Tibet even before I started thinking about going to Nepal, but Tibet had been completely closed to foreigners during my lifetime. I first read about the country in Heinrich Harrer's book, *Seven Years in Tibet*, while I was in medical school. Harrer was an Austrian mountaineer who escaped from a British prisoner-of-war camp in India with fellow Austrian Peter Aufshnaiter and walked for almost two years across the Himalayas to reach Lhasa, a place that was untouched by World War II. He became a friend and consultant to the Dalai Lama until he was forced to flee ahead of the invading Chinese army. His book provided the first description I'd ever read of the life of the Dalai Lama.

Now that Tibet was opening up to tourists, I wanted to explore the roots of my Tibetan Buddhist teachers. During my first attempt in 1985, I'd been turned back, like so many of the early explorers who had tried to reach Lhasa. Since then, the Chinese had opened the border with Nepal to individual travelers, and I would be able to travel to Lhasa overland from Kathmandu, without having to fly to China.

Travelers have been drawn to the mysteries of Tibet for centuries. Geographically isolated by huge mountain ranges and great tracts of desert, the leaders of Tibet had consciously decided to keep it that way, to the extent that a Tibetan could be executed for trying to help a foreigner reach

Lhasa. A lot of what motivated the explorers was simply attempting to see what outsiders had never seen, but for some, there was also the sense that Tibet harbored spiritual knowledge unknown to the West. For example, the popular book and movie, *Lost Horizon,* introduced the concept of a Tibet that harbored "Shangri-La," a hidden spiritual valley where peaceful people lived to a great old age. James Hilton, the author, had no idea what philosophy might suffuse such a valley, so he portrayed it as a kind of tolerant Christianity introduced by a lost Jesuit priest, where nothing is done to extremes.

Even as I planned to go to Tibet in 1987, the country had received relatively few outside visitors. When tourism was allowed, starting in 1981, tourist infrastructure was so poor that I ended up treating dozens of foreign travelers who'd made it back to Kathmandu with pneumonia and other maladies acquired by hitching rides in the open backs of trucks. The tourists would sometimes land on the doorstep of my clinic late at night, dusty, bedraggled, underweight, and ill, with a chief complaint of, "I've just arrived from Tibet," as if that were enough explanation for their current state.

The lure of Tibet was so great for some that I saw numerous elderly travelers risking the journey, people in their 80s or even 90s who had apparently waited their whole lives for this opportunity and were determined not to miss it. Several of them died during their trip.

Tibet's isolation, both geographically and politically, fueled the mystery of what kind of secret knowledge and rituals they might be protecting. Perhaps recognizing that no one could go and verify whatever wild stories were made up, an industry grew, beginning in the 1920s, based on supposed spiritual guidance from Tibet. Yoga, from India, had begun to be imported to the West at that time, so some of the teachings from Tibet were supposedly derived from Indian yogis who had either physically lived in Tibet or were said to have magically transported themselves there to obtain secret teachings. One of the most successful frauds claimed to be a Tibetan named Tuesday Lobsang Rampa, whose first book was entitled *The Third Eye*. Frustrated by the fanciful accounts, Heinrich Harrer hired a private detective to expose the writer as a British plumber named Cyril Hoskins.

It was only after the Tibetans were forced into exile in the late 1950s that genuine teachers and books made their way to Western students.

The aura of magic and mystery pervades to this day. But is there real magic, and if so, would it always remain a mystery? As I delved into Tibetan Buddhist practice, it wasn't immediately evident that there was anything magical or inexplicable going on under the surface. However, as I gained benefit and experience from the teachings that I *could* understand, I was more willing to have faith in teachings that I had not yet been able to experience for myself. For example, I noticed that the start of all the major spiritual ceremonies I attended included making offerings to local spirits, asking them not to interfere and inviting them to share in the blessings. Who or what are these local spirits, and where do they fit into the scheme of things? I had no idea at the time, yet the wisest men that I have ever met, my Buddhist teachers, were certain that they were present. Who am I, with my limited view, to declare myself the final arbiter of what is possible or not?

I heard and read about great practitioners "achieving rainbow body." This concept, as wild as it seems, is still based on the Tibetan Buddhist concept of facts. It's a *fact* that everything is impermanent. It's a *fact* that solid matter is made up of tiny particles with great spaces between them, that eventually become just energy at the subatomic level. At that point, there is no longer anything left that can be called tangible. That's why Buddhists refer to what we see and experience as "empty appearance." It then becomes possible that those practitioners who can become so stable in their understanding of this "empty" nature of the body can dissolve into rainbow-colored light and disappear, leaving just the non-living parts of their bodies—the hair and nails—behind.

Tulku Urgyen Rinpoche told me that he saw this himself in Tibet when he was a young man. A well-known meditator, he said, had gone into a cave to meditate. Later, they saw a glow of light emerging from the cave, and when they went to see what happened, they found only the man's hair, fingernails, and toenails. In our modern age, one man's testimony would not constitute proof. However, Tulku Urgyen Rinpoche was the wisest, most sincere person I had ever met. Why did he tell me this? Was he lying? That would be out of character. Was he deluded, believing that he saw something that he didn't really see? That also seems unlikely. I was left believing what he told me.

What are we to make of these stories, so contrary to the Western requirement that facts be confirmed by our own eyes or detected by machines? Even as we cling to this material view of what constitutes science, the scientific world itself is replete with mysteries that can't be easily explained, such as the effect that particles can have on each other at a great distance with no means of communication, labeled by the world's greatest physicists as "spooky interaction at a distance." If we simply define any phenomena that are not materially measurable as being not possible, we will, by definition, never be able to expand our understanding of the world.

The way the stories from Tibet are told, they are always careful to say that the magic is not the point. It's just that these phenomena are the extension of an understanding of the empty nature of appearance. Chokyi Nyima Rinpoche told a story about one of Tulku Urgyen Rinpoche's teachers, who was out for a walk with Tulku Urgyen and other friends. They reached a cave that had been used by meditators for generations. The teacher placed his hand on the rock outside the cave and left a distinct handprint in the cliff, embedded into the rock as if it had been left in wet cement on Hollywood Boulevard. As they walked away, the teacher said, "I didn't mean to do that. Don't tell anyone." But of course, they later told everyone.

Exposure to these stories was a softening process, like the tanning of leather, that gradually wore away my resistance. By the time I witnessed events that are genuinely hard to believe, I was more open to accepting them as real, even if I still couldn't understand the mechanism. This was my background and my mindset as I prepared to go to Tibet.

However, before I get there, it's important to note that although all my knowledge of Buddhism came from Tibetan teachers, Buddhism did not originate in Tibet. The Buddha was born in Nepal 2,500 years ago, the only son of a king who ruled a small kingdom in the Terai, near what is now Chitwan National Park. The father pampered Siddhartha and tried to encourage him to follow in his footsteps. However, the prince, as he grew older, began to see old people, sick people, and dying people and was shocked by the inevitability of the suffering involved. He felt that life had no point if everyone was just doomed to suffer like this. Unlike almost everyone else in the world, he became obsessed with trying to determine if there was any possibility of going completely beyond suffering. He snuck away from his palace at age twenty-nine, leaving a wife and an infant son. After six years of wandering in forests and studying with all the available spiritual teachers, he still had not found what he was looking for. Finally, he sat down under a tree in Bodhgaya, India (where I first looked for Buddhist teachings) and vowed not to get up until he had his answer.

He meditated until he realized that people suffer because they don't see things as they are. The true nature of the mind is an awareness beyond the transient thoughts and emotions that dominate our lives. When fully realized, this awareness is beyond suffering, and is referred to as the enlightened state. He felt that this recognition was something so subtle and yet so profound that he wondered if he would be able to teach it to others. When Siddhartha stood up from his meditation, he eventually became known as the Buddha, which means "purified and perfected." He had purified all traces of selfish and negative emotions and perfected the intrinsic inner qualities of wisdom and compassion. He taught for the next forty-five years, and those he taught were able to use his teachings to come to the same realizations, and then pass them on to the next generation of students. This chain of instruction, from teacher to student, has been unbroken since the time of the Buddha, including Tulku Urgyen Rinpoche, Chokyi Nyima Rinpoche, and the other teachers that I met in Nepal. It is a living tradition. The authenticity of Tibetan Buddhism is the fact that it has been directly passed down in this manner and not left to the interpretations and whims of those who came after. The teachings given more than one thousand years ago in Tibet (available in translated books) are identical to the ones I received from my mentors' mouths.

Buddhism initially thrived in India for nearly fifteen hundred years. The philosophy gradually spread to other parts of Asia, but the form of Buddhism that we now know as Tibetan Buddhism was initially maintained in northern India. A massive university called Nalanda, with ten thousand monks, in the state of Bihar, was famous throughout Asia at the time.

In the seventh century, a Tibetan king, Songtsen Gampo, became aware of Buddhist philosophy and became convinced that his people could benefit from the knowledge. He invited a teacher from Nalanda, but it was initially impossible to translate the teachings from Sanskrit to Tibetan, as there was no written form of the Tibetan language. The king commissioned the creation of an alphabet, and since the language was created for the main purpose of conveying Buddhist Dharma, the Tibetan vocabulary created specific words for Dharmic concepts. These words allow for a precise transmission of Buddhist knowledge in Tibetan but as a result have been a challenge for modern translators trying to find equivalent words in English and European languages. These include Tibetan words for specific states of mind, and even the word *Dharma* itself, which resonates with so many meanings that it has defied an exact translation (which is why we still refer to the teachings as *Dharma*, rather than with an English translation).

Despite these efforts, the Tibetan people did not suddenly embrace the new philosophy, and some fought hard to oppose it. The king and his close advisors risked their lives as they persisted in bringing Buddhism to Tibet. It was touch and go as to whether Buddhism would succeed in Tibet until a subsequent king invited a teacher from India. Padmasambhava, also known as Guru Rinpoche, came from Uddiyana, the northwestern corner of India that is now Pakistan and Afghanistan.

Before the Buddha died, he predicted that he would return in another form to benefit beings. Guru Rinpoche is said to be this person, and he overcame many obstacles in Tibet, subduing both spirits and local resistance to Buddhist teachings. He fully established Buddhism in Tibet by encouraging the building of temples, establishing study and practice, and providing many of the texts that are still in use today. The philosophy, once established, flourished in this remote region for more than a thousand years of uninterrupted transmission that resulted in tens of thousands of practitioners achieving complete enlightenment. The spiritual leaders of

Tibet were so aware that the country was set up to produce so many great practitioners, that it was the main reason that they didn't want any foreigners coming in and upsetting the balance. Interestingly, there is no word for "Buddhism" in the Tibetan language. Followers of the Buddhist teachings are called "Insiders" in Tibetan.

The form of Buddhism that was practiced in Tibet was called Vajrayana Buddhism, a very direct form that focuses on the mind and its relationship to one's perceptions of the world. It is the form of Buddhism that most purely transmits the insight that the Buddha had under the Bodhi tree. However, the Buddha recognized that human beings have a variety of personalities and intellectual ability, so he taught not just this one insight, but a series of teachings that could be available to any interested person.

Vajrayana Buddhism, preserved in India, arrived in Tibet at a fortunate moment in time, as the practice of Buddhism in northern India was about to be completely wiped out by Muslim invaders. If the teachings had not been transmitted to Tibet, the Vajrayana form of Buddhism would have died out. The focus of Vajrayana practice stayed within Tibet, with virtually no exposure to the outside world until the Chinese takeover of Tibet in the 1950s. Ninety percent of the ten thousand monasteries that existed in Tibet were destroyed in the initial invasion and the subsequent Cultural Revolution in the 1960s. The teachers who managed to get out of Tibet at the time, such as the Karmapa, Tulku Urgyen Rinpoche, Chokyi Nyima Rinpoche, the Dalai Lama, and many others, were able to set up monasteries in India and Nepal, which allowed the tradition of Vajrayana Buddhism to be maintained. Due to the influx of Westerners attracted to the Himalayas beginning in the 1960s, the tradition of Vajrayana Buddhism began to spread to the Western world.

Chokyi Nyima Rinpoche, Tulku Urgyen Rinpoche, and a handful of other great lamas had the rare ability to induce certain students in their presence to recognize the nature of their mind when it is aware yet not forming any thoughts. This moment of awareness is so subtle, yet so profound, that these teachings can only be given by a master and then usually under quite restricted circumstances. For example, during all the times that I was present for these teachings, they were never allowed to be filmed or recorded. These teachings are referred to as "the pointing out instructions," as the teacher is, in essence, pointing to the nature of mind that already exists in each of us, but we don't usually recognize; it is the nature of mind that the Buddha recognized while sitting under a tree in Bodhgaya. Tulku Urgyen Rinpoche was unusual in his desire to transmit them more widely, maybe because of his confidence in transmitting them correctly. He was, as Sogyal Rinpoche described him, "one of the greatest masters of meditation in the twentieth century." I had stumbled onto one of the few teachers in the world who gave these instructions to Westerners, but at the time I had no idea how rare that was. Tulku Urgyen Rinpoche's confidence in his practice had been achieved through the teachings he received from the greatest teachers in eastern Tibet and refined during more than twenty years of meditation practice in remote caves and other isolated settings.

Four years after moving to Kathmandu, I was finally going to Tibet to try to experience for myself what it might be like to be a practitioner in this wilderness of high, wild mountain terrain and vast empty sky. The great practitioners who had achieved enlightenment in Tibet had left blessings that permeated the countryside. Now I wanted to wander this countryside and see if I could feel some of those blessings. Through my teachers in Nepal, I had cracked some of the mystery; would I now have the chance to experience some of the magic?

Tibet

NINETEEN

The woman behind the bars was Chinese. The angry crowd in front of her shouted at her and even spit on her. She worked in a ticket booth at a bus station in Lhasa and had just told a Tibetan woman in line that she needed to ask for her ticket in Chinese, or she wouldn't sell it to her. People in the crowd were shouting, "This is Tibet! This is our country! We can speak our language!"

I'd only been in Lhasa for a few days, but it was clear that Tibet was an occupied and deeply unhappy country. It was April 1987, five months before the cover would blow off the resentment, and there would be burning police cars, gunshots, and an end to any pretense that Tibetans were getting used to Chinese rule.

I couldn't find anyone to go with me to Tibet, so I invited Tashi, the twenty-four-year-old Tibetan monk who translated for me in my clinic at the monastery. To avoid the scrutiny that a monk traveling with a Western tourist would certainly engender, Tashi got permission from Chokyi Nyima Rinpoche to shed his monk's robes and go incognito in civilian clothes. He looked like a Japanese tourist, so much so that Tibetan touts would approach him and try to sell him trinkets, only to jump back as if slapped when he replied to them in their own dialect of Tibetan. Shedding his robes was more of a protection for myself than for him. I would be subjected to a lot more scrutiny if I were traveling with a Tibetan monk.

The night before, at the Lhasa Holiday Inn, we watched a movie in our room about the invasion of a country by a hostile army, while a nun wrestles with whether she can keep her vows. She joins forces with a family that is trying to resist the occupation, but eventually, they are forced to escape together over the mountains to a safe land. "I did that," Tashi said, who had escaped Tibet in the middle of the night at age fifteen with his own family. The movie wasn't about Tibet, however. It was *The Sound of Music*.

We rented bikes and rode towards Sera Monastery, a sprawling complex on a low hill just outside of town. As we rode on old cobblestone streets, we stopped for tea in the Muslim section of town. The Muslim section? This is why you have to go places yourself—you find out things that you never read about. The shop served tea that we might have gotten in Kyrgyzstan, served in thin white porcelain cups, with soft tea leaves floating in a gold-tinted clear liquid, sweetened by a marble-sized crystalline lump of sugar in the bottom.

Sera Monastery was one of two large monasteries on the outskirts of Lhasa that had remained physically intact through the Cultural Revolution. The monastery was a huge cluster of red-and-white buildings, set against bare dirt hills dotted with large, rounded boulders. Far up the hill were tiny retreat houses for long-term practitioners. Once housing thousands of monks, Sera now had a mere custodial crew. We wandered through the halls and temple rooms, speaking to the few monks that we met. The monks were wary—before they replied to Tashi in Tibetan, their eyes would dart around the room, trying to spot any Chinese spies.

The monastery, which was now run like a museum, closed for two hours over lunchtime. While we were waiting in a courtyard outside a large prayer hall, a sudden squall came up, driving a flurry of snow in front of it. We sought shelter under the portico of the temple. Several other Tibetans stood there with us, forced into closer proximity by the weather. I was the only foreigner.

One of the Tibetans, a man in his fifties with a dignified, weathered face, casually counting mantras on a *malla*, leaned over to Tashi. Tashi spoke with him for a few minutes, then translated for me.

"He wanted to know if you believed in the law of cause and effect. I told him that you were a Buddhist, and that you had a teacher in Kathmandu. He was totally amazed. He had always believed that foreigners were incapable of understanding the Dharma, but now that he has met you, he will believe that it is true."

Tibetans grow up believing that Westerners are incapable of comprehending Buddhist teachings. Alexandra David-Neel, the French explorer who became the first foreign woman to talk to a Dalai Lama, described their first meeting: "His conviction that the white race is mentally inferior [in regard to spiritual matters] remained unshaken." Later, she convinced him that she was sincerely interested in Buddhist Dharma, and he softened his view.

The Tibetan man we had just met had been a monk when the Chinese came, but he had been forced to give up his robes and get married. Now his children were raised, and he was free to pursue more Dharma practice; he was making a pilgrimage of the sacred sites in Lhasa.

My travels had taken me to many countries in Asia. Most of the questions I received from strangers were about where I lived, or how much my watch cost. This was the first time someone had initiated a conversation by asking about my worldview. I looked at the man, softly muttering prayers, and

I suddenly realized how fortunate I was. Here was a man who wanted to devote his life to spiritual practice. But an invading army cut that short, and now there were virtually no teachers left in Tibet to guide him further. Here I was, a Westerner, who, by moving to Kathmandu for an entirely different reason, had stumbled upon the teachers who had been forced to flee Tibet. My relationship with the teachers had started off as a nice diversion, and then as friendship. However, I was beginning to see that perhaps I should be taking it more seriously.

Later that afternoon, in a long narrow prayer hall, we met an elderly man with a completely unlined, serene face, dressed in the maroon robes of a monk. He sat on a cushion on the floor in the back of the room, behind a small wooden table that held his books, *dorje*, bell, and drum. He held a *malla* in his left hand, quietly slipping beads along the string one at a time with his thumb. He looked up and smiled, and Tashi started talking to him in Tibetan. After a few minutes, Tashi translated for me.

"He was imprisoned and tortured by the Chinese for twenty years. He was released three years ago."

The monk sat patiently as Tashi translated. He didn't seem to mind the interruption. I asked him how he felt about having been in prison.

"I was in prison due to my own karma," he replied in a gentle, matter-of-fact voice. "Now it is finished. There is no use in creating more negative karma by holding onto bad feelings about it."

His tone of voice carried the impression that twenty years of imprisonment and torture was just an interruption in his life, like having lost a job and having to move when he didn't want to. Prior to my trip to Tibet, I read and heard teachings about compassion, karma, and so on, but they seemed mainly like theories about how things could be, one choice among many options. As a Jew, I had been inculcated from an early age with stories about the holocaust, the horrors of which were revealed to the world only four years before I was born. The rabbis, my parents, and their friends made it clear that we must *never ever* forget, *never* forgive. "Only by holding those thoughts in our mind," they said, "can we do honor to those who died, and prevent it from happening again." Now, for the first time, I was witnessing a completely different approach: twenty years of horror and deprivation in a concentration camp, through cold, starvation, beatings, and forced labor, was dismissed as an unpleasant interlude that one needed to simply accept and move on. When we finished talking, the monk turned back to his table and resumed his chanting, his face as serene as before.

We went outside and crossed an open square paved with large, flat stones and entered another prayer hall. A ten-foot Buddha statue sat at the far end. A monk in his twenties was the only other person in there, dusting and adjusting things in the room.

The Buddha statue had an unusual posture. The depicted Buddha was tilted to his left, his left hand cupped near his ear, as if trying to listen to something in that direction. I'd never seen any statue or drawing of a Buddha in that pose. We asked the monk about it. He brought us over to the windows and pointed towards the courtyard outside. Several dozen monks practiced debate in the courtyard. Half the monks sat on cushions, and the other half stood in front of the seated monks, one-on-one. A standing monk leaned back, began his statement, and took a big stride. His right arm, holding a *malla*, slid forward and slapped the upturned palm on his left hand, looking like a baseball pitcher delivering a pitch, which in a sense, he was. This was a ritual debate, something I had read about but never seen. The standing monk put forth a statement, and the role of the seated monk was to refute it with logic. The contest of words continued until one had outfoxed the other. This was a unique and dynamic method of ensuring that the monks truly understood the teachings. If they couldn't win an argument with their logic, it meant that they hadn't fully grasped the concepts. Being educated as a monk meant diving deep into Buddhist philosophy. In the monastery, just getting a certain mark on a test was not enough to prove mastery.

The monk in the chamber told us that the Buddha statue had been cast in a normal posture, but one day it had become so interested in the debate outside that it leaned over and cupped his hand to his ear, and then remained frozen in that pose. This was new. I hadn't heard of or seen any statues in Nepal that were said to have moved on their own, but this monk delivered the information with a matter-of-fact manner. Tashi translated the words as if this was something that just happened in Tibet. I had traveled to Tibet to learn about the magic and mystery. And now here it was...sort of. Was it true? I didn't know, but I figured that I was probably not equipped to decide what was possible or impossible in Tibet.

I was unable to take a photograph of the statue, because I hadn't paid the ten-dollar photography fee charged by the Chinese. To add to the mystery, since then I have been unable to find anyone else who has seen this particular statue. I've asked several people who have been to Sera Monastery, or were headed there, to specifically look for this statue and get a photo, but so far no one has. I wonder if it has been removed by the Chinese.

As we toured the monasteries in Tibet, I found that statues coming to life was a common theme, something that, as far as I know, doesn't occur in statues made in exile. As we walked through the Potala Palace, the home of the Dalai Lama when he lived in Tibet, the monk attendants casually told us about specific statues that had spoken to them. In fact, I was finding the boundaries between inanimate and animate, solid and pliable, were blurred all over Tibet. The inside of certain caves, where great lamas meditated, had deities on the walls that were said to have spontaneously emanated from the rock. To my eye, they were not that distinct, but they were unusual protrusions nonetheless that resembled statues, and had no chisel marks or any other indications that they had been man-made. In many places, there were distinct hand, foot, and even head prints in solid rock, as if the rock had gone soft for a few minutes for a great master to leave his imprint. The hand and footprints were hard to explain away—how can you make these impressions in solid rock?

From a Buddhist perspective, these occurrences were not miraculous. Chokyi Nyima Rinpoche once defined a spiritual practitioner as "someone who is striving to see things as they actually are, not as they seem." The view that matter is not as solid as it initially seems is a key perspective of the philosophy. Saying that hard objects are not solid sounds deluded to outside ears at first, but if we think about modern physics, matter is made up of atoms and electrons and subparticles that have vast spaces between them at a sub-atomic level. Seeing solid things as empty, from this point of view, is just seeing them as they actually are—mostly empty. So why do things seem so solid? It's our mind that forms the concepts that make matter seem irreducibly solid; therefore, it's our mind that is also capable of perceiving things as not being solid. I was touring a land where some practitioners took this view to heart so clearly that they could manipulate solid matter by simply perceiving its intrinsically empty nature.

Of course, this takes some getting used to. But I was willing to suspend my skepticism to a degree because it was why I had traveled there—to see what spiritual life was like in Tibet. Chokyi Nyima Rinpoche believed in these things. Perhaps rather than trying to filter all experiences through what I already believed, I could expand what my mind was willing to believe.

The landscape itself had a surreal quality; the mountains looked as if they had been brushed with paint—black, white, rusty red, warm brown, pink, and purple. They were set against a sky so large and clear that it seemed as if it had been inflated over Tibet.

Despite the austere beauty surrounding me, I couldn't help thinking about how much the spiritual landscape had been decimated. The ruins of monasteries still dotted the hillsides wherever we drove. The teachers had been imprisoned, killed, or driven into exile, the texts and statues destroyed, pieces of which were still strewn around the wrecked walls of the monasteries. What had been a Buddhist oasis in the world for a thousand uninterrupted years had become a spiritual desert where the Tibetans' thirst for teachings could rarely be slaked. Just as refugees must flee a drought, Tibetans who yearned to pursue their spiritual lives had to go into exile.

In contrast, there were no obstacles to my obtaining teachings in Kathmandu, but I had taken it for granted, just one of many new experiences I was having in Nepal. A new feeling took root in me in Tibet, a recognition of the fact that it's not guaranteed that one will find a teacher in this life, and if one does, it may not last. I vowed that I would never again be so casual about my teachers in Kathmandu.

It was the birth of devotion in me. Devotion to a living teacher seems to come more easily for Tibetans, and Chokyi Nyima Rinpoche has often commented on that. Westerners often want to keep a slight distance or continue to believe that developing their own beliefs is more important than completely trusting someone else. For some, it may be a fear of falling under the influence of a cult-like figure.

What devotion can help with is the free flow of the lama's blessings. The lama is teaching with compassion and love, and to the extent that we can return those feelings, the teachings can also flow more freely. The lama's teachings are like the sun. The sun's light and warmth flows out in all directions. To be able to receive that light and warmth requires us to step out from the shade. Pure devotion is like stepping out from the shade. What's critical to safeguard this process, as described in many texts going back more than a thousand years, is to check and make sure that your teacher is worthy of that devotion before opening up completely.

Chokyi Nyima Rinpoche and Tulku Urgyen Rinpoche had consistently shown me their kind and wise intent, along with an authentic interest in guiding me towards understanding, and how to handle the most difficult obstacles that I may end up facing. To me, that was worthy of devotion. For this process to be both safe and genuine, one needs to have complete trust and confidence in the teacher. And for the teacher to open up to the student, he or she needs to have complete trust in the student as well. Trust and confidence are two-way streets and necessary precursors of devotion.

In Tibet, the physical manifestation of devotion is to perform prostrations to the statues in the temples, and to one's teachers. Doing a prostration is inherently humbling. You are consciously putting yourself lower than someone that you honor, touching the highest part of your body—your head—to the ground, where everyone else walks. One of the reasons that we might resist doing prostrations is pride—why should I place myself lower than this other being, or even a statue? Aren't I at least equal to them?

Each time we entered one of the prayer halls, Tashi placed his hands together in a prayer gesture, touched his hands to the top of his head, his throat, and his heart—signifying body, speech, and mind respectively—then went down on his hands and knees and bent forward to touch his forehead to the floor. He stood and did this a total of three times. I joined him in doing this, but I had never prostrated to statues or anyone else up until this time and I initially felt self-conscious. I carried with me a memory of a Jewish teaching that I thought said, "Don't bow down before idols," which was strong enough in my consciousness that it made me struggle to justify what I was doing on my knees in front of statues of the Buddha. What did it mean to do prostrations to a statue? Who was I pleasing, or offending?

As I continued to perform prostrations—despite my doubts—I thought of the kindness of my teachers, and their teachings. They taught only to help relieve the suffering of all sentient beings. Their insights came directly from the words of the Buddha. Doing prostrations is physically acting out the idea that we need to give up our pride and admit that we need help to overcome the inherent suffering in our lives. At the same time, we make the aspiration that we can eventually help all others overcome *their* suffering. Doing prostrations was a small step, but understanding why I was doing them was the start of my taking my Dharma practice to another level.

A major goal of the trip to Tibet was to visit the physical and spiritual center of Lhasa, the Jokhang Temple. Within the deepest reaches of the temple sits the country's most sacred Buddha statue, the Jowo, which was brought to Tibet as a gift from Nepal. In front of the temple, dozens of people performed prostrations on the hard stone surface. Bulbous white chimneys perched atop brick pillars billowed smoke offerings made sweet with juniper and other aromatic substances. A long sinuous line of pilgrims in grimy dark wool clothes, their long black hair tied in braids with red cloth, disappeared slowly into the darkness of the building itself. An eerie, deep sound emanated from the building, the composite tones of hundreds of individually chanted mantras.

Tashi and I joined the line. As we entered the temple, the bright high-altitude sunlight gave way to the dim flickering light of hundreds of butter lamps. They were set on tables in front of dozens of altars, and I could feel the heat on my face. Butter lamps are brass bowls of melted butter with a cotton wick in the middle; butter was readily available to the nomadic people of Tibet, while wax was a rarity. The pilgrims made small offerings as they passed each statue and sacred painting, consisting of a crumbled bill, a few coins, or even—surprisingly—sewing needles. In Tibet, sewing needles were precious items; often an entire village shared a single needle. The line of people smelled of sweat, butter, incense, and smoke, the odor of people who live in tents and small stone houses and cook with yak dung. I was now immersed in the chanting pilgrims, the low sound waxing and waning as we moved through. I was the only foreigner in the temple, and I felt like I could just disappear in the depths of the temple and never be seen again. But that flash of paranoia alternated with a surprisingly warm feeling of being included in the devotional line of Tibetans. We shuffled deeper and deeper into the temple. Finally, we entered a small open area in front of the Jowo itself.

The statue was three feet tall, seated cross-legged, and highly ornamented with gold and semiprecious stones. Tashi and I touched our foreheads to the base of the statue on four sides, offering our respect, and then left the line to sit on the floor with a handful of other practitioners. I started to meditate. After a brief time, I had a profound experience. My mind, emptied of thoughts, remained aware of itself, which generated a feeling of bliss. It was an incredibly strong experience, made more so by its unexpectedness.

I had been briefly shown this experience by Tulku Urgyen Rinpoche, and I had tried to practice like this at home, but I caught only vanishingly brief glimpses. This time, rather than flickering out like a quickly burnt match, it was like a small candle had been lit as I sat there.

I looked up and caught Tashi's eye, and he could see in my face that something was happening. He nodded and smiled in recognition. As I got up and rejoined the pilgrims winding their way out of the temple, I still tingled with the afterglow. The sacred environment—maybe even the statue itself—had helped induce an experience that I couldn't yet create for myself. Chokyi Nyima Rinpoche had told me that the term "blessing," in the context of Tibetan Buddhism, meant something that can help introduce you to the nature of your own mind. The sacred statue, imbued with the faith of thousands and thousands of pilgrims, created the energy—the blessing—to help my mind recognize its true nature: empty yet aware.

Without having received teachings, I would not have known how to look for this experience, and even if I had a spontaneous experience, I would not have recognized it. From these tiny glimpses, the path to enlightenment eventually unfolds; a single burning stick can light a thousand butter lamps.

Tashi and I set out from Lhasa in a rented Land Cruiser with a Tibetan driver, along with one of Tashi's uncles and a Tibetan friend. We were headed for Chokyi Nyima Rinpoche's original monastery that had been destroyed during the takeover of Tibet. None of Chokyi Nyima Rinpoche's students had yet succeeded in visiting his former monastery. As it turned out, we didn't succeed either.

After four hours of driving, we found that we were at the wrong monastery. Monasteries in Tibet were often connected by having the same lineage teachings, but the monastery we had just reached was not Chokyi Nyima Rinpoche's monastery, which was more than a week's walk from there. The monastery's main temple had been destroyed, but most of the monks lived in small retreat houses scattered up a long, bare hillside. Tashi found out that a monk that I had treated in Kathmandu several months earlier was in one of these houses.

We walked up the hill, pausing for breath in the thin air—we were now at 14,000 feet. We met the monk, and I remembered him quite well. He was close to eighty years old, with clear eyes and a soft, white, goat-like beard hanging off his chin. He had congestive heart failure, and when I first met him, he could barely walk, his lower legs thickly swollen with fluid, and his lungs filled with more fluid, making it hard for him to breathe. I put him on the appropriate medications, and he bought a two-year supply to take back to Tibet. He showed me his medicines and his non-swollen legs. He was happy and comfortable, spending all his days in meditation and spiritual practice.

Tashi and the monk had a lot of news to catch up on, so I walked outside and looked at the view over the broad valley, with a river running down the middle. I found a ladder and climbed up onto the roof and sat in meditation for a while. Then we said goodbye and walked back down the hill.

We had planned to spend the night, but I found myself feeling increasingly uncomfortable. The feeling was hard to describe—a kind of inner roiling of energy, as if I had drunk way too much coffee. I felt shaky, and I realized that if we spent the night, I would not be able to sleep at all. Tashi noticed me shifting from foot to foot.

"Are you okay? Do you have to pee?"

I said that I didn't have to pee, and when I described how I felt, Tashi understood immediately—he was feeling the same energy. We decided that it might be better to try to get away from the monastery and sleep somewhere else. I was grateful that he understood what I was feeling. It was 4:30 p.m. and it wasn't clear where we could go.

As we prepared to leave, a monk asked us if we wanted to meet Pachung Rinpoche, who was the head of the monastery. In his nineties, Pachung Rinpoche stayed full-time in retreat, receiving almost no visitors. It would be a rare privilege to meet him.

As we contoured around a hillside to his isolated little cottage, the monks told Tashi that Pachung Rinpoche had decided it was time for his life to end, and he had stopped eating a year ago. It seemed like wherever I went in Tibet, there was something that pushed the limits of credulity. I wondered if he would look skeletal. As I took off my shoes and stepped inside, I noticed that the air in the house had an incredibly fragrant aroma, exquisitely subtle and appealing, as if someone had collected the dew off of spring flowers, extracted the essence, and then released it gently into the air. Tashi perked up.

"Do you smell that?" he asked.

"Yes. Is it some kind of incense?"

"No. This is the smell that just comes in the house of a great meditator."

I had never heard of this before, and I wasn't sure what to make of that statement. But then it wasn't a matter of believing it or not—I was smelling it, and the aroma was so different and more amazing than anything I had previously experienced that I had to take it seriously. I searched for a source, but couldn't find anything burning, or any oil sitting out, or any flowers in a bowl. There was nothing that could explain the odor that seemed to be everywhere at once, and not coming from a single source. We stood outside a small door to an inner room. I was about to meet someone who most likely hadn't bathed in years, hadn't eaten in a year, and apparently exuded the most pleasant smell I had ever experienced.

We stepped through a hanging canvas curtain covering the door. A very old man was seated on a small bed platform in front of a window with a panoramic view of the valley. Wisps of long gray hair strayed across a mainly bare scalp. His weight seemed fine, and I had a hard time accepting that he hadn't eaten in a year. Yet in my experience, I felt that the monks had no reason to make up such a story. His eyes were filled with a great intensity, and as they met mine, I felt a jolt as he appeared to recognize me. He didn't say anything, but I had the strongest feeling that he was thinking, "*I know you. I didn't think I would see you in this lifetime.*" Even as that thought arose in my mind, I wondered if I was just inventing a grandiose conceit. I had no reason to think that I had a prior connection with him. It would have to be from a previous lifetime. It made me feel even more discombobulated than I was already feeling, a sensation that was subsequently made even more awkward when he offered us some food that had been blessed: balls of barley flour and butter, covered with a white yogurt sauce. He deposited it in our bare hands, and we ate the balls and tried to lick the dripping yogurt off our fingers. I had already been feeling an inner agitation just being at that monastery, and now my insides were doing flips. I was too wound up to even think of asking him a question about the Dharma. I later found out that Pachung Rinpoche was one of the greatest meditators in that region. As I was discovering, sometimes the power of blessing—this energy that I was feeling—is more than a novice can handle. We thanked him and backed out of the room.

When I got back to Kathmandu, I asked Chokyi Nyima Rinpoche why I might have felt so uneasy at this monastery. He explained to me that this monastery was where local people brought their dead relatives for ritualistic sky burial, a ceremony in which the naked body is hacked into pieces and fed to waiting vultures. I had read about this but have never seen it. In a country with little firewood, and frozen ground for most of the year, it was a practical way to dispose of dead bodies. The act of cutting up a body in the open served to reinforce the idea that the mind was the person, and the body was just the temporary vessel. Since the body is discarded when the mind moves on, there is no sense of desecration. The powerful energy of all the dead spirits could still be felt in the place. A more advanced practitioner can take advantage of this energy to supercharge one's meditation, but as a beginner, I just felt it as a kind of agitated discomfort.

So, it was with a sense of physical relief that we drove away from the monastery. The twitchy feeling subsided as we headed back down the valley. The only thing was, we didn't know where we could spend the night, and it was starting to get dark. Tashi's uncle knew of a nunnery that housed a famous hot spring and was only an hour's drive away. As we emerged from the valley, we turned onto a road that started to climb through a narrow canyon laced with frozen waterfalls, climbing into the mountains. It was getting dark, and we weren't sure where we might end up.

TWENTY

We ended up bathing in the hot spring at 10:00 p.m. A full moon shone behind white clouds from which large snowflakes floated gently down and dissolved into the hot water. Small bubbles, like carbonation, trickled up between our toes from the bottom of the rock-lined pool. When we came back to Lhasa the next day, a woman named Jill invited Tashi and me to a picnic at the Norbu Lingka, the Dalai Lama's summer residence, in the heart of Lhasa. It was from this compound in 1959 that the Dalai Lama—fearing capture by the Chinese who had already occupied the city—disguised himself and escaped late at night. Kampa warriors from east Tibet rendezvoused with horses, and they fled across Tibet, staying just ahead of the Chinese army during a desperate two-week race to the Indian border.

Jill was the assistant manager of the seven-hundred-room Lhasa Holiday Inn, a thirty-two-year-old Welsh woman who I had helped out on the first day I arrived in Lhasa. I assisted her in evacuating an eighty-two-year-old Swedish woman who looked like she had suffered a stroke but proved to have a previously undiagnosed brain tumor that had suddenly swelled at altitude. I later published a paper about her case.

It was May Day, the first of May, and a big communist holiday. The Tibetans could care less about that, but it was a day off, and picnics are the main social events in Tibet. For this occasion, ten thousand Tibetans brought brightly-colored Tibetan carpets to sit on, and then pulled out elaborate feasts of pre-cooked foods—momos and noodles and fried breads—stacked in metal tins. Huge, embroidered canvas sheets were hung from ropes strung between trees to block the wind. Jill had been invited to the picnic by some of the Tibetan staff at the Lhasa Hotel. Her boyfriend was off on a trek somewhere.

Jill, Tashi, and I walked through the bedroom and sitting areas of the Dalai Lama's former home. We could see his personal items—antique clocks, bronze statues, and an elaborate throne fashioned from gold offered by devoted Tibetans. I felt sad that we could walk through this space and the Dalai Lama could not.

May blossoms and sweet smells adorned the large compound. At the start of the day, I hadn't given much thought to joining Jill on the picnic, but sitting with her, sharing lunch, talking about the situation in Tibet, I felt something happening. Gradually, relaxing on a Tibetan carpet in the sun, I became aware of a familiar sense of attraction and possibility that I wasn't expecting to feel. I was suddenly conscious of being near her, how her bright white blouse fit, how her blue eyes formed a pretty contrast to her dark hair, the slight thrill I got when our eyes met. We were the only Westerners among ten thousand Tibetans, and now we were focused only on each other.

I enjoyed the edge of excitement, despite the obvious limitations. On the other hand, I had just finished three weeks of travel in which I felt surprisingly relaxed, comfortable, and consistently spiritual. I hadn't missed having a girlfriend at all. I was scheduled to leave Lhasa the next day and start driving back to Kathmandu.

Back at the hotel, Jill invited me to her suite, where we ordered dinner from room service and sat on her couch talking. At some point after eating, we started kissing, and suddenly we were making out like teenagers, pressing ourselves together, gasping for breath, stopping short of having sex. The fact that we were in the apartment that she shared with her boyfriend, and that I had been on a spiritual journey, was incentive enough for me to hold back, even as I felt Jill struggling with her own mixed feelings. In the end, we kissed goodbye, and I went back to the room I shared with Tashi around six in the morning, awash in hormones, growing attachment, and bewilderment that this could have happened on my last day in Tibet.

I left Lhasa that day, as scheduled, increasingly intrigued with the idea of being with Jill. She was pretty, articulate, worldly, and competent enough to run a seven-hundred-room hotel in the middle of Tibet. I had gone to Tibet to search for experiences that might lead me towards more peace of mind when I was alone. Now, the fragile calm I had achieved had been co-opted by an attractive woman.

"If you always search outside of yourself for happiness," Chokyi Nyima Rinpoche had told me, "it will remain elusive." *But I wasn't looking,* I thought.

Tashi wasn't going to accompany me back to Kathmandu. He had decided to stay in Tibet for a few more weeks and attempt to find Chokyi Nyima Rinpoche's destroyed monastery. To share the cost of renting a Land Rover and a driver, I put up a notice on a traveler's bulletin board in the hotel to find someone to go with me. A German doctor named Jurgen saw the notice and knocked on my hotel room door, setting up an extraordinary reunion. We had met once before, during a festival at Thyangboche Monastery seven years earlier, when I had been working at Pheriche. We stood side by side staring at Mt. Everest and shared a wish that we could someday see it from the other side, from Tibet. That was impossible to do in those days, so it was just vague wishful thinking at the time. We had not been in contact after that, and now we suddenly found ourselves together in Lhasa, planning a drive together to see the north side of Mt. Everest.

We drove to Shigatse and spent the night. The next day we drove up the Pang La, an 18,000-foot pass that is the last barrier to Everest Base Camp. I had seen a photo of George Mallory catching his first clear view of Everest from that exact spot in 1921. The view was staggering—the full range of the Himalayas, from Kanchenjunga on the far left, to beyond Dhaulagiri on the right, a span of almost three hundred miles. Everest was dominant in the middle, and we could imagine where we had been standing on the other side at Thyangboche. The sky was a cloudless blue, with little wind, and we stayed for an hour.

We drove back down the pass and got to the border with enough daylight left that we could conceivably get back to Kathmandu that night. A sudden huge downpour canceled that thought as it triggered a massive landslide just down the road, trapping us overnight at the tiny border station. The next day we managed to get a taxi that was waiting on the other side of the slide.

I was anxious to see Chokyi Nyima Rinpoche. After reconnecting with my house staff, I took a bath, and then took my delighted dog for a walk. As I strolled along the dirt roads next to the rice paddies near my home, I realized that Tibet had been as advertised: breathtakingly vast and full of mystery, with an energy that had somehow suffused me with greater devotion towards Buddhism.

The next morning, I drove to the monastery and found Chokyi Nyima Rinpoche standing outside on his porch, overlooking the Boudha Stupa. I immediately began three prostrations. It was the first time I had ever prostrated to him.

"No, no, no need. Please, doctor, one is enough," he said.

"No, I need to do these," I said, continuing with my last two prostrations.

"I've been prostrating to statues for three weeks. The least I can do is prostrate to my real teacher." When I finished, he reached out his arms to me, and I stepped forward into his embrace. It was the most important lesson I learned in Tibet: the key to the blessings and legacy of the Buddha is the teacher. Meeting a genuine teacher is a very precious thing. I knew that I would do whatever I could to stay in Nepal, for as long as possible, to be near my teachers.

Kathmandu

TWENTY-ONE

Wanting to stay in Kathmandu meant that I had to make the clinic a success. My visa and livelihood were tied to making the clinic viable. The clinic had been subsidized for two years by the Canadian aid project after which it was named, but they no longer wanted to put money into the clinic as they were subsidizing the medical care of a large part of the expatriate community. David Peterson, the original director who had hired me, left eighteen months after I arrived, and I became the director. When I took the position, the CIWEC project told me that not only did I have to make the clinic self-supporting, but I needed to pay them back $50,000 of their $100,000 start-up money. At the time, the clinic had never made a profit.

With my life taking off in every positive way, I needed to make it work. I won't go into all the details, but the logistical difficulties of running the clinic were massive. All of our medical supplies needed to be imported from the U.S., which meant that when I went home in the summer for a visit, I had to buy, pack, and ship supplies for a year of running the clinic: gloves, syringes, bandages, intravenous catheters, stool cups, vaccines, and virtually all of our medications. I needed to buy the reagents for our lab tests, and sometimes buy new machines for the lab. In a time before laptop computers, I had to rent a computer and printer to type out the detailed invoices that were necessary to clear customs when the supplies arrived in Kathmandu. Since the clinic didn't have any money, I would pay for all of these supplies myself, gradually paying myself back by the end of that year, only to loan it back again when I got home.

When the twenty or so cardboard boxes of supplies arrived in Nepal, they were thrown onto a heap of other shipments, with no rhyme or reason. When we went to get the shipment, we stared into a warehouse filled with pyramidal heaps of more than a thousand cardboard boxes. Of course, there was a Nepali solution to the problem. Workers hung around the warehouse looking to be hired to find one's boxes. Only after the boxes were found could the process of clearing them begin. I started spray painting my boxes fluorescent orange in Portland before shipping them, to help facilitate finding them at the other end.

Somehow, we made it work.

I mentioned that living in Kathmandu had been like going back to college. Although my cohort of friends were all there for different reasons, there was a remarkable sense of shared purpose that bound us together: we all loved living in Nepal. Despite all the chaos and uncertainty, there was the daily cheerfulness of most of the Nepali people, the aching beauty of the suddenly clear Himalayan peaks, the emerald green fields of rice that surrounded the city.

But it was to a large extent our friendships that made it so compelling to stay there. With no parents or siblings around, whatever happened, wedding or funeral, we celebrated or mourned with each other. It's rare to have a community like that.

Most of us were single at that time, in the mid-1980s, but there was a gradual pairing-up occurring. My friend Elliott, the dentist and drummer in our band, met his wife while he and I were on a grand motorcycle tour of Nepal. We stopped to spend the night in Pokhara, about 200 kilometers (120 miles) from Kathmandu. Elliott stood in the middle of a quiet street, looking around, and said, "I want to meet a woman." Moments later, two quite attractive American women walked up to us, one of them asking, "Are you Doctor Shlim?" I had seen her in my clinic a few days earlier. They asked us if we knew a good place to stay, and we steered them to our hotel—Hotel Nirvana—and ended up sharing dinner with them at a rooftop restaurant in town.

We went our separate ways the next morning, Elliott and I riding the most amazing twisting paved roads with almost no traffic because it was the biggest holiday of the year, and everyone was at home. The women went on a trek but looked up Elliott in Kathmandu a week later, and Frances, an elegant blond woman from Atlanta, decided to stay on in Kathmandu and eventually married Elliott. Her friend headed back to the States.

Besides the frequent dinner parties that bound us together, and the times that our band, Fear of Heights, put on a dance concert, we went on outdoor adventures together. The mountains were too far away and too high to visit on weekends. But there were convenient rivers that could be rafted and kayaked, with a night on the beach in between.

And so it was, that on the first weekend in May in 1988, we chartered a bus for an overnight kayaking and rafting trip on the Trisuli River for about twenty close friends. This band of friends could be recruited on short notice, and everyone arrived and traveled together without complaint. It was a great group of friends, all travel-hardened, thoughtful, adventurous, and appreciating each other. A trip like this was made nearly effortless by hiring a trekking agency to supply all the logistics: tents, sleeping bags, food, drinks, and a staff to put up our tent city and cook for us. Like everything else in Nepal at that time, this type of service was remarkably affordable.

On this particular trip, we drove past the usual put-in so that we could explore a cave that had been discovered just the week before. Don and Elliott had heard about the new cave on their way back from a kayak trip the previous weekend. Don was the kayaking guru of our group, one of the world's best paddlers; he had trained in public health and moved to Nepal to work in family planning. He was also dating Gilda, the nurse practitioner in our clinic.

The cavern became an instant tourist attraction for Nepalis. The entrance to the cave had been hidden for generations behind two large boulders halfway up a sparsely forested hillside. May is the hottest month of the year in Nepal, and it was close to a hundred degrees as we made the forty-five-minute hike up the steep hill. The nondescript entrance had gone unnoticed for centuries, but today there were hundreds of Nepalis traversing the bottom of the massive cavern while carrying every manner of light: candles, temperamental kerosene lanterns, fluorescent lanterns, dim handheld flashlights, and the occasional headlamps. We stood at one side of the cavern as this ant-like line of humans worked their way across the cave floor. We explored a side chamber that gradually narrowed and descended into the depths. The outside temperature had been nearly 100°F, but the air in the cave was cool.

The cave floor was covered in a thin layer of slippery bat guano and mud, and we were coated in sweat and dark brown muck by the time we returned to the bus. It was nearly dark, but we knew that our camp would be set up, and dinner was already cooking. The problem would be getting clean. James knew of a waterfall up a short trail from the road where we could rinse off the grime. All twenty of us walked up the trail, illuminated by a nearly full moon. The waterfall was about fifteen feet high, and fifty feet wide, falling onto water-polished flat rocks so that we could just walk into the cool refreshing water, with enough room for all of us to shower at the same time. We stripped off our muddy clothes and stood under the cascades of water that glinted off our naked bodies in the moonlight. Intimate and primeval, it was the first time that we had all been naked together, as it was very rare to be anywhere in Nepal where there was enough privacy to be without clothes in public.

The next day we ran the river, a succession of class II and class III rapids, for four hours in rafts and kayaks. The pre-monsoon heat was intense, in the high nineties Fahrenheit, so at one point we spilled out of the rafts and swam through a set of small rapids that threaded through a narrow canyon. As the current slowed, we spontaneously formed a floating circle of eight people, heads in, arms linked, and our feet pointed out. For some reason, Gilda started incanting a low "ommmm" sound, and we all picked up on it. As our voices joined, it created an otherworldly resonance, something I've never heard before or since. Waves of harmonics filled the area in the canyon with vibrating overtones that created a shimmering wall of reverberation that made us feel like we were hearing an organ in a cathedral. Don and Elliott, sitting in kayaks at the outlet to the canyon, were stunned by the sound. We would remember this odd and beautiful moment a week later, when all of our lives suddenly changed.

Later that night, we sat around a driftwood bonfire, our feet in the sand.

"I'm getting the coolest truck this week," Elliott said. "A Land Rover, with a long wheelbase. I'm going to put in a bed, a refrigerator, and a stove. It'll be my weekend getaway playmobile."

"Where's it coming from?" I asked. I knew there were no such trucks in Nepal.

"I first saw it in Kenya when Frances and I went there last year. The British couple that owned it were already planning to drive it to Kathmandu and sell it before going to Thailand. I've been in touch with them. They arrive this week."

"Where are you going to go first?" I asked him.

"I saw a new road up a side valley near Bhote Kosi, up near the Tibet border. There's a river running down the valley that we think has never been run."

As I went to sleep that night, I thought about the international lifestyle that we all lived. An American living in Nepal could travel to Kenya, meet a couple from England, admire their truck, and then end up buying the truck when it was driven to Nepal.

The following weekend, on a Saturday night, I went over to Brot and Didi's house for dinner. Brot was a former Peace Corps volunteer in Nepal who had stayed on to do remarkable aid work. He had brought the first electricity to the Everest region in the form of a mini-hydroelectric project. Didi had hitchhiked to Nepal in the early 1970s and stayed. She and Brot were now a couple, and they were gracious and fun hosts. By 9:30 p.m. I was sated with food and wine and lying on the floor of their living room, trying to summon the energy to drive home. I could relax because I wasn't on call for the clinic. The phone rang, and I was surprised when Didi handed me the phone.

"It's for you," she said. I wondered who had tracked me down. It was Don. He and Elliott and Gilda had gone up the Bhote Kosi River that morning with Elliott's new truck.

"I've got the worst news in the world," he said. In the few seconds, before he carried on, my mind struggled to grasp what that could be. All I could think of was that Elliott's dog had been killed. Not very imaginative.

"Gilda's dead."

"That's not possible." Those were the words that came out of my mouth, but even as I said them, I thought that it was. My body froze. I struggled to add, "What happened?"

"The truck went off the road while she was driving it down for us. Must have been three hundred feet. We found her by the side of the river. The truck is in the middle of the river."

"Oh my God! Where are you right now?"

"I'm at my apartment in Dilibazaar. I caught a ride back to Kathmandu on the back of a motorcycle. Elliott's still out there at the police station, and Gilda's body is still by the road. We need to go get her."

I had been organizing rescues, searches, and body retrievals for several years now, and my mind slipped into professional mode. "I'll try to get an embassy truck and driver. I'll call you back in a few minutes." We needed a truck to be able to carry Gilda's body back, and I figured it would be safer to have a driver who wasn't totally in shock that Gilda had died.

I called Chokyi Nyima Rinpoche. He was very close to Gilda, and he would want to know.

"Oh my! Oh my!" he said. "This is so bad." He agreed that it was a good idea to get her body back to Kathmandu that night if we could. I phoned the American consular officer, who was a good friend. He said he would organize the truck and driver and supply a body bag. A few minutes later he called me back.

"I'm really sorry," he said. "We can't do it. I didn't realize that the embassy has a policy against taking any of their cars out of the valley at night."

"Really? That seems overly cautious," I said.

"I know," he said. "I wish I could help. I can still get you the body bag."

My next-door neighbor was a wildlife biologist named Eric who had a pickup truck with two rows of seats in the cab. I called him. He immediately offered to drive out with us. Word was spreading quickly of the accident, and Brian, Elliott's partner in the dental practice, called and wanted to come along to help.

As we drove east out of town in the pickup truck, Don went over what had happened. The road had been scary, more like a scar in the hillside made by a single pass with a bulldozer than a proper road. The Land Rover had done fine, though, and they managed to find a place to turn the truck around. Gilda wanted to drive it back down, while the boys kayaked the river, but they made it clear that she didn't have to. "If it gets too scary," Don told her, "just park it and we'll walk back up the road and drive it down, no problem. She was fine with that."

We were quiet as we tried to think about what it might have been like for Gilda trying to finesse the truck down the narrow road. We still didn't know why the truck had gone off the road. Finally, I asked Don, "How was the run?"

He paused, shaking his head. "It was great," he said, with a rueful smile. "It's a really nice stretch of river. We had a good time, and we weren't really worried about Gilda. We got to the confluence, took our boats out, and looked around for the truck. When we didn't see it, we just assumed she had parked it and was waiting for us."

We were driving along a narrow asphalt road. There was no moon, so we could only see what the headlights illuminated as we flashed by—a stack of hay, a cow lying down at the edge of the road. There were no other cars on the road. The houses in the villages were dark.

"We started walking back up the road in our swimsuits. Some Nepalis saw us and waved for us to follow them. We followed them up the road a short way, but they turned off and headed down towards the river. We rounded a ridge, and then we saw the truck, nose first in the middle of the river. And we saw Gilda lying on her back on the bank, and we had this initial huge surge of relief that she was okay." He paused. "But when we got to her, she was dead."

"What did she look like?" I asked.

"She looked fine. She didn't look like she was hurt. I don't know how she got to the side of the river. The truck was at least seventy-five feet out into the river. Maybe the Nepalis swam out and got her."

After two hours of driving, we arrived at the police station. Elliott was lying on a cot in a back room in his swimsuit, unable to sleep. The walls were bare plaster, peeling off in large chunks from past moisture damage. Above Elliott's head on the wall was one of the largest spiders I had ever seen, at least five inches in diameter.

"Good to see you guys," he said, glancing back at the spider. "I didn't know if you'd make it back here tonight." We brought Elliott some clothes, and as he changed, I talked to one of the policemen.

"We can't let you take the body," he said. "We must first have an autopsy report." I knew that no one could perform an autopsy out here in the countryside. I'd been through this before in trying to claim a body.

"I'm a doctor," I told him. "I can make sure that you get an autopsy report from Kathmandu." He looked down at the paper in front of him and pursed his lips. A long pause. Finally, he sighed and said officially, "We *must* receive a copy of the autopsy report." He made me sign a paper promising to send him the report. He was now satisfied that he had done his duty.

The three policemen all stayed at the station when we got back in the truck and drove along the main river. We reached a bridge and crossed to the sketchy dirt road.

"The villagers carried her up from the riverbank to the road, so that we will be able to pick her up," Don told us. About a half-mile up the road, our headlights lit up the scene of a small group of Nepali villagers sitting calmly on a blue tarp in the middle of the road in complete darkness, with Gilda's body right next to them. The villagers had offered to guard the body, all night, if necessary, to keep animals away. The generosity of that offer—to sit outside all night next to the body of a complete stranger and a foreigner—was breathtaking, yet also typical of the Nepali nature.

I put my headlamp on and examined Gilda's face. She looked peaceful and composed, still pretty. She looked like she should be alive. I felt along the back of her scalp with my bare hands, her dark curls still damp from the river. My fingers encountered a large laceration, and a bony prominence that shouldn't have been there. She had fractured her skull. Her torso was completely okay, but her right thigh had a bulging deformity that showed that the femur was broken. We stretched out the body bag next to her, and we all joined together, Nepalis and foreigners, to lift her gently into it. I zipped it up. We carried her to the truck and had to lay her diagonally across the short bed in the back. Don sat in the back with her the whole way back to Kathmandu.

It was 3:00 a.m. We drove back along the dark road past the sleeping villagers. As we reached the outskirts of the city, the sun rose and illuminated the terraced fields. Elliott and Don kept replaying the day, and the different decisions they, or Gilda, could have made. We had talked to a villager who witnessed the fall of the truck from across the valley. He had seen Gilda stop the truck at a point where the road made a sharp curve back towards the mountain. She got out and looked at the outer wheels and the road for a while, then got back in and started to drive down. The back right wheel missed the edge of the road as she came to the apex of the curve and started to turn right. The truck teetered briefly, and then plummeted down the steep brushy hillside to the river. He hadn't seen Gilda fall out of the truck, but she must have been thrown out to have ended up on the bank with the truck in the middle of the river, or else someone had swum out to get her. We later concluded that the Land Rover had a longer wheelbase than a normal Jeep, and the back wheels didn't automatically follow in the tracks of the front wheels, something the driver had to compensate for on tight curves.

We reached Kathmandu around 5:30 a.m. and drove to Phora Durbar, where the American medical unit was located. They had the only body freezer in the country, and I had been there several times with the bodies of other foreigners who had died. It sat outside under an open roof, like a long, narrow filing cabinet with two drawers. We drove up, lifted the body bag onto the sliding metal stretcher, pushed it back into the freezer, and closed the door with a solid metallic click.

I felt exhausted but satisfied that we had gotten Gilda's body to a safe place. We'd had all night to experience and talk about the range of emotions that we were going through: mainly shock and sadness, but we were also conscious of how close we felt to each other under these extreme circumstances. We'd even been able to crack jokes and laugh a bit. It's not a normal thing to lose a friend in the countryside, and then have to go get the body yourself. It was just the nature of living in Nepal, where government infrastructure was nearly non-existent, and we had learned to take care of ourselves.

Getting Gilda's body back was one thing. Processing her loss was something else. I was trying to fathom how I could have lost a friend and colleague so unexpectedly. Don and Elliott were experiencing the death in a whole other way. They felt responsible—that their decision to go kayaking and have Gilda drive the truck down the bad road had led directly to her death. They could understand—intellectually—that Gilda had chosen to drive the truck down and could have stopped at any time, but that's not how it felt to them.

I took them out to talk to Chokyi Nyima Rinpoche. Neither Don nor Elliott were actively interested in Buddhism, but like most people who knew Chokyi Nyima Rinpoche, they had faith in his kindness and wisdom. Plus, he had been very close to Gilda.

"Gilda was my good friend," Rinpoche said to us. "I'm very sad that she has died." He turned to Don and Elliott. "I know that you feel bad that she died, and you feel—how to say it—guilty?"

They both nodded. Chokyi Nyima leaned toward them and asked, "Did you set out that day to kill Gilda?"

Surprised, they both replied, "No."

"Do you feel that you were careless in the way that you allowed Gilda to drive the truck down the mountain?"

They both shook their heads no. "We really thought about it," said Don.

"Would you have allowed Gilda to drive the truck down the mountain if you had known that she was going to die?"

"No way," said Elliott.

"Of course, it is natural to feel sad that Gilda has died, but you should not feel guilty—you didn't do this trip to harm Gilda."

His reassuring words helped, but the men were still reeling from the loss. The next day, I went back to see Chokyi Nyima Rinpoche by myself, and he had a different explanation for what had happened to Gilda. He told me that he had seen her earlier in the week and noticed that her life force was diminishing. What?! This was completely out of the blue—he had never said a single word about life force before and had never hinted that one could see something like this. He described it as seeing an aura around her that was changing. When he had seen her, he said, he realized that her life was going to end soon and that nothing could be done to stop it. He hadn't said anything to Gilda because it was unavoidable; telling her would only have created unbearable anxiety. I tried to pin this down.

"Does that mean that if Don and Elliott had not let her drive the truck down the mountain, she would have died soon from some other cause?" I asked.

"That's true," he said. "If the life force is diminishing, this is due to karma, and no one can change the outcome."

"So, if this is true, Don and Elliott shouldn't feel so bad that this accident happened the way it did, because her natural life span was coming to an end anyway."

"That's right."

This was uncharted territory. What was he able to see? I later thought of it like this: let's say that each person has a propane tank with fuel when they are born that burns with a steady flame. We can't see how much fuel is in the tank to start with, or how much is left at any given time. But when the fuel runs out, they will die. What Chokyi Nyima Rinpoche might have been able to see, figuratively speaking, is that the flame was beginning to flicker and diminish, meaning that the fuel had almost been used up.

Being able to see another person's life force, as an otherwise invisible aura, would be an unimaginable responsibility. Who would want to know that? On the other hand, if it were true, it made accepting Gilda's death a lot easier—the accident wasn't due to anyone's negligence. It was somehow inevitable, and therefore must be accepted. Could he just be making this up to make us feel better? That hardly seemed likely, given everything I knew about him. It was more likely that he was pulling back a corner of the cover to give us a glimpse of a greater world of Buddhist capacity, far beyond just taming our own minds to ease suffering.

Later that week, while still trying to decide if I could accept what Chokyi Nyima Rinpoche said, I ran into another high lama who was also a close friend of Gilda's. The Sharmapa Rinpoche came to my office to see me for a medical problem. In the course of that visit, he casually mentioned that he had seen Gilda the week before she died and saw her life force diminishing. I had no idea whether he had talked to Chokyi Nyima Rinpoche about this, but I didn't think so because they didn't live near each other. It was as if the cosmos had sensed that I was about to doubt what Chokyi Nyima Rinpoche said about Gilda's aura. *Not so fast. I saw it too*, he was saying. Curiously, the observation that someone's life force was diminishing has never come up again in all my time with Tibetan lamas.

This is obviously an astonishing power to think about. I don't pretend to understand it or know how the lamas utilize this gift. All I can do is report on what these two lamas said. If only Chokyi Nyima Rinpoche had said this, it would have been one thing, but when the other, more distant lama said the same thing, I felt that there must be something to it. I don't know how this capability is used. I think there are extremely few healthy people who could handle being told that they are going to die in the near future, for no apparent reason, not knowing how it will happen.

Three days after Gilda died, Tulku Urgyen Rinpoche arranged to perform a *puja* for her. As I drove up to Nagi Gompa, I thought about what she might be experiencing. I had started to believe in the fact of rebirth, that our mind separates from our body at death and spends time in an intermediate state before seeking another body. It is described as a terrifying time if one has not achieved some mental stability through meditation practice; the dead person has experiences as if in a dream, able to travel wherever their mind takes them. I had heard that the mind of the dead person may visit their close friends and family, trying to figure out why no one can see them anymore, until they finally realize that they are dead. The night before, I felt uneasy looking out my window into the dark, fearful that Gilda's face might suddenly float into view, or I might step out into my hallway and see her standing there. I wanted to help her, wish her well, but I wasn't at all sure I could handle seeing her.

Thirty people drove up to Nagi Gompa and we walked up the trail as the sun was setting. We sat cross-legged on the floor of Tulku Urgyen's fifteen-by-twenty-foot greeting chamber. He sat on a low bench with a wooden table in front of him and began chanting prayers, accompanied by a handbell and drum. The deep resonance of his voice was punctuated by the clear ringing tones of the bell and the sharp rapid clicks of the rotating drum. We had been told that he would summon Gilda's mind and give her instructions that would help guide her to a favorable rebirth. Having experienced the fear of encountering Gilda myself the night before, it now felt reassuring to be in the presence of someone who appeared to know what he was doing—someone who didn't fear the prospect of seeing Gilda, and indeed was inducing her to come.

I found myself staring at a photograph of Gilda. It was clipped to a thin stick that had been propped upright on a tray in front of Tulku Urgyen. The darkness was now complete, and the nuns lit candles that cast a soft yellow glow on the rapt faces of the participants. Seeing an image of Gilda brought a sudden pang. Tulku Urgyen paused in his chanting, looked up into the space in front of him, and emitted three loud guttural, unworldly sounds from deep in his throat with startling force—*Hiiicccccckkaa!... Hiiicccccckkaa!... Hiiicccccckkaa!*—unlike any sound I'd ever heard before. He turned to Gilda's photo, gave a blessing, and then signaled the attendant to light the picture on fire. It curled as it burned, revealing a last glimpse of Gilda's pretty face before the ashes dropped onto the ceremonial plate.

There was a stunned silence in the room. The two assistant monks moved around as if this was routine. In the Buddhist tradition, death is just a transition from one lifetime to another. Not that big a deal, and not avoidable in any case. For the person who has died, however, the transitional period between incarnations—called *bardo* in Tibetan—can be difficult, and that's why the thoughts and actions of the surviving friends and relatives are focused on helping the person who has died, not just in mourning their loss. I was surprised to discover the benefit of focusing my attention on helping the person who has died, rather than focusing on my own fear and loss. I couldn't just sit back and feel sorry for myself. Gilda still needed our help. She was in a difficult transition, and we couldn't just abandon her.

The comforting presence of Tulku Urgyen Rinpoche in the candlelit room in the nunnery high above Kathmandu allowed many of us to feel better about dealing with Gilda's loss. But for Gilda's family, it was a different story. I was standing in the office of the American consular officer when she placed the call to her parents, who were traveling in southern China. The worst news in the world, as Don had said. Their daughter has just been killed in an accident. They cut short their trip and flew home to Florida.

While they were en route, I returned to the body freezer at Phora Durbar and prepared Gilda's body to be shipped to Florida for her funeral. We obtained a metal-lined casket from the American embassy and put her frozen body inside. I had a very special sacred Buddhist text from Chokyi Nyima Rinpoche that he told me to place on her chest. I then soaked a hundred meters of muslin cloth in formaldehyde and packed it all around her still-frozen body so that it could remain preserved as she thawed during the flight. We sealed the lid by soldering it shut. I had already done this half a dozen times for other families. During my first trip to Nepal, I had feared that working in Nepal might mean that I would have to cremate a patient. I hadn't yet imagined that working in Nepal would mean having to embalm my close friend.

Life and Love

TWENTY-TWO

I had work to do—on myself. At the start, it seemed to me it was an impossible task. If I was able to take to heart what Chokyi Nyima Rinpoche kept telling me, I needed to learn how to become content within myself. *Now you know where to look for happiness* seemed initially like a false hope—if I look to myself for happiness, there's not that much to see. Good sense of humor, athletic, kind, a doctor, a musician, but it never seemed like enough. What I always needed was to meet a beautiful woman who responded to my attention, in an instant and complete way. This could be seen as an unattainable fantasy, as many people go through their whole lives without experiencing this kind of instant, complete connection. However, it kept happening to me, fulfilling the fantasy, and once again allowing me to experience hope for the future. And then it would fall apart. Jane—the first Jane—was the last time I had been through this, and her aftermath resulted in the first time I tried to see if I could change things. I was working diligently, if reluctantly, to imagine myself content on my own.

Having met Chokyi Nyima Rinpoche, I was forced to question for the first time the fact that romance may not be a very effective religion. None of the relationships that began in this way ever lasted, and as a result, I spent far more time pining for love than enjoying it. It seemed that the only thing romance was effective at was making me want more romance. When each dramatic connection ended, I suffered a torment of longing and grief, not knowing when or if I would feel those feelings again.

I didn't have an effective way to try to mitigate the pain, given my limited strategies: get stoned and listen to music, drink alcohol, or go rock climbing. After one particularly sad break up I tried yoga. Not wanting to get sucked into some kind of Eastern religious cult (yoga in the 1970s was not the universally accepted, fashion-driving activity that it is today), I signed up for my first yoga class at a university. Yoga taught me that I could get my mind off loneliness and despair for brief moments of concentration and relaxation, which was a big revelation to me. However, after pursuing yoga instruction for a number of years (and even going to yoga camp, where I started yet another sudden, intense, but ultimately brief relationship with a Swedish yoga instructor), I couldn't figure out what the endpoint was. Once I became flexible and could do all the poses easily, how did that help me with my life? It didn't help me get over my sense of loss any faster. Yoga, for me, was a Band-Aid. Band-Aids protect wounds while they are healing; they don't make them heal faster.

Yoga led me to wonder, however, if there might be another kind of spiritual path that could help, but I had no idea what that would be. It was a vague notion anyway, as I was not ready to give up my religion of romance. How could any spiritual path compare to the intoxicating sight of the female form, the touch, smell, and taste of romance? At best, I was looking for a path that would serve as a safety net rather than an end in itself, something that would allow me to fall in love as usual, but not spend as much time regaining my equilibrium when it ended.

Yoga had possibly been an opening toward something more, but just what that could be, I didn't know. It had stayed like that for years, through my strange frustration outside the Thyangboche Monastery, until I finally met Chokyi Nyima Rinpoche. Even then, I needed to go through it one last time, one final toss of the dice to see which one it was going to be: instant and lasting romantic bliss, or some difficult internal work to see if I could learn something about contentment on my own.

Chokyi Nyima Rinpoche had set me on this path. Four years later I had arrived at a point that I had genuinely, really, thoroughly believed would never be possible. I was starting to be able to envision a future without a romantic partner. I began to think, if I didn't find a woman, what would I do? I had a vision of that as well. When I eventually left Nepal—no idea when—I would move to Spain. In my mind's eye, I felt more comfortable thinking about still living outside the U.S.; the expatriate lifestyle suited me. Why Spain? No idea at all. I had never been there, and I didn't speak Spanish. But I could see it: rugged forested low hills, a view out towards a distant blue Mediterranean Sea, a small village that I could walk to and from which I would buy food and the *International Herald Tribune*. I would live simply, and practice Dharma in semi-retreat. It was a concept, but nowhere near a plan.

Besides, Chokyi Nyima Rinpoche had told me that I was going to get married. He just hadn't said when.

The phone rang in my living room. Many life-changing events begin with the ringing of a phone. A female voice. "Hi. This is Jane Gallie. Do you remember me?" I did remember her. The other Jane. A bit surprising that I did, as we hadn't had any contact since I left her at her hotel four years earlier.

"You had a boyfriend the last time we met," I replied, surprised that those were the first words out of my mouth.

"We broke up. What happened with the girl you were hoping would come back?"

"It didn't work out. Do you want to go out to dinner? Where are you staying? I'll pick you up." Why was I so eager?

The Yak and Yeti Hotel was a few blocks down from the Royal Palace. She was in town to help lead a trek in the Annapurna region. As I stepped into the hotel lobby, I was hoping I'd remember what she looked like. I headed toward the garden behind the hotel, where the group was having a small reception. Jane was wearing a sleeveless denim dress over a blouse. Her blond hair was cut shorter than last time, but I had no trouble recognizing her.

During dinner at my house, we caught up on what had happened in our lives over the past four years. Her boyfriend had abruptly decided that he couldn't marry her, and therefore they shouldn't be together anymore. Jane had been devastated.

"I couldn't sleep. I couldn't stand to be alone. Luckily, I moved into a house with two guys, and they looked after me." She had never experienced this degree of heartbreak before, and I sensed that she was still shaky from the experience. The appearance of this sudden vulnerability drew me closer to her; when we had first met, she couldn't fully relate to the heartbreak that had been such a part of my life.

I was pouring the last of the bottle of wine I had opened for dinner when I looked at my watch. It was nearly eleven and I offered to drive her back to the hotel. She hesitated, flashing a slight, playful glance that caught me off guard. She didn't say anything. The evening up to then, although warm and pleasant, had not been overtly romantic. Our eyes met while I tried to figure out if an invitation had just been extended.

"Do you want to stay here tonight?" I finally asked.

"Do you want me to?"

I realized that I did.

As if we were already married, we brushed our teeth, got undressed, and got into bed. Everything about being with Jane was strangely natural—the way we could talk about anything, and not feel anxious about what we were doing together.

Jane went back to her group the next morning but spent the following night with me again. She left for her trek the following day. She was scheduled to be out for twenty-one days, and then back for only two nights before leaving the country. However, on what should have been the sixteenth day of her trek, she unexpectedly phoned me from the Yak and Yeti. She had helicoptered out with a seventy-four-year-old man from her group who had developed pneumonia, and she needed me to come see him.

I saw him in his room, where I confirmed that he had pneumonia and started him on antibiotics. Then Jane and I walked down the hall to her room and made love. We got up and went out to dinner, and she moved into my house for the next week. These extra, unexpected days gave us a chance to feel what it was like to be together. She fit in easily with my friends. Being in her company was warm and fun and comfortable. By the time she left, I didn't know what to think. It wasn't the rush to enlightenment through romance that I was more familiar with. It was something I'd never experienced before.

The following July, I visited Jane at her summer job working for Exum Mountain Guides in Jackson Hole, Wyoming. We stayed in her small cabin at the base of the Tetons, went rock climbing, and took a long hike. I had never experienced this combination of attraction and amazing ease.

The previous spring, I had invited her to meet me in Hawaii for a week, but just before we were to go, I got cold feet and asked her not to come. I was still struggling with a fantasy that I might meet someone in Hawaii that would kindle my romance-as-religion tradition: if it's not instant, it can't be real. Bailing on the Hawaii trip would have wrecked most relationships, and the fact that she still wanted to see me in Jackson said a lot about her.

Jane came back to Nepal that fall, having led a trip to Tibet that finished in Kathmandu. She moved into my house while we tried to figure out how serious we were. Lisa, the friend who introduced me to the first Jane, dragged me outside from a party and said with unusual earnestness, "You need to marry this one."

Jane seemed to be leaning towards marriage as well, but she felt I had to pass a final test. She said we needed to go on a trek together to make sure we were compatible in an adventurous setting. Despite my having spent almost a year living near the base of Mt. Everest and spending most of my twenties camping and mountain climbing, she wanted to see for herself if I was comfortable in the mountains. Adventurous-seeming people occasionally reveal that they don't handle stress well in difficult surroundings. If I were going to start whining when I were hungry or cold, she wanted to know about it prior to making a lifetime commitment.

TWENTY-THREE

Friends told us about a rarely-visited valley north of Kathmandu, near the Langtang region. The valley, at 13,000 feet, was in Nepal, but was used by Tibetans as a summer pasture for their yaks. These dual claims of ownership made for some political sensitivity and the valley was officially off limits to trekkers. The only trekkers who had ever been there were the few close friends who told us about it. We went with four other people: Brot, his friend Thekla, Don, and the new woman in his life, Vanessa, whom he had just met a couple of weeks earlier when he was in New York. Vanessa had flown halfway around the world to go on their second date, which would be two weeks long.

By the third night, we reached the far end of a forest at the confluence of two rivers, one of which flowed out of the narrow canyon we would enter the next day. Jane and I were cozy in our tent. I was reading a Dharma book, and I mentioned to Jane how lucky I felt to have met the Tibetan lamas and learned about Buddhist philosophy.

"Don't get me wrong," she said. "I like Chokyi Nyima. The problem I have is that if the Buddhists are right about karma and reincarnation and needing to learn about meditation in order to ultimately escape suffering, then everyone else is screwed. How can one group be completely right, and everyone else in the world be completely wrong?"

"I've thought about that," I said. And I had. I was beginning to think that it was unlikely that what happened to people in life—and afterward—could be just due to what they believed or where they were born. I expressed this to Jane. "The way I've started to look at it is like this: do you think that the same thing happens to everyone? If consciousness continues past the death of the body for one person, it must be true for all people. If it doesn't continue for one person, then it doesn't continue for anyone. Does that make sense?"

"It doesn't have to be that way. It could depend on what you believe."

"That doesn't make as much sense to me. Beliefs change so much during life. It could change at the last second of life, or you could get scared and not know what to believe. Then what would happen to you?"

"But it still isn't right to think that one set of beliefs is completely true, and everyone else is wrong." It was important for Jane not to negate the views of others. Even if the views were completely opposite and incompatible. I thought, *Consciousness continues after death, or it doesn't. Both things can't be true.*

I blew out the candle we had been using for reading. Chokyi Nyima Rinpoche had taught me that every time we go to sleep, it's like a small death. Our consciousness of our surroundings disappears, but an inner consciousness emerges again, having experiences in dreams. He said that this is similar to what happens when we die—we are unconscious for a time, and then our mind emerges with a dreamlike body and begins to have experiences in an in-between realm. In fact, every religion believes that our consciousness continues past death, and they also believe that there are consequences to our actions. In that way, Buddhism is not so much an outlier.

The Buddhist view is not dependent on a creator, however. They believe that the mind is never created or destroyed—it has existed since what they call "beginningless time." Through a law of cause and effect—karma—the mind incarnates in lifetime after lifetime until one encounters a teacher who can point out the nature of mind and help set the person on a path that can transcend this endless cyclic existence. For whatever reason, I had come to believe that the Buddhist view was right. Why was that viewpoint so attractive to me but not to others? Maybe that was karma as well.

The morning dawned sunny and cold, and our fingers froze as we packed up our things and then thawed out painfully. Crossing the river on a high, shaky, cable-and-wood-plank bridge, we followed a trail on the right side of the canyon. Fresh snow and ice spotted the trail, which was little more than a narrow ledge that had been cut into the cliffs. Icicles hanging on the steep rock cliffs above us began to drop like spears as the sun hit the upper walls of the canyon. A falling icicle shattered on a rock just above Don's head, and a flying chunk of ice gave him a tangerine-sized bruise on his forehead.

Vanessa was having a hard time on the trails. The narrow icy path was intimidating enough, but she had also developed a fever the night before. At times, the path disappeared altogether, and we had to scramble around bulges in the cliff, lowering our weight onto icy exposed steps, with a two-hundred-foot drop below us. Vanessa, however, managed to display the courage that can be called upon while trying to impress a new lover.

After several hours, we exited the far side of the canyon to find ourselves in a large meadow below Ganesh Himal, a 24,350-foot peak. The 11,000-foot south face dominated the head of the valley. To our left was a graceful spire that looked like a slender Matterhorn. In another mountain range, this smaller peak would have been the main attraction; here it was just an unnamed spike on a ridge.

As we stood in the meadow, we spotted a small, fast-moving bird of prey high in the sky. We got out our binoculars and tried to figure out what it was. As best we could tell, it was either a female merlin or a male Eurasian kestrel. We spent some time trying to determine if it had a black band on its tail—the distinguishing feature between the two birds—but it was too far above us.

"The merlin is described as 'scarce,'" Don quoted from *Birds of Nepal*, the definitive guide. "Scarce means people like us never see them. I think it has to be the Eurasian kestrel."

"Somebody has to see birds that are 'scarce,'" I said. "Just because it's scarce doesn't mean this bird can't be a merlin." It was a philosophical point as much as an ornithological one.

After two nights at our high camp, we turned around and negotiated the scary canyon one more time. Jane had hiked and skied in the Canadian Rockies since she could walk and had no trouble with the tricky terrain. As we returned to a lower altitude, the temperature warmed up, and we strolled along in t-shirts. I appeared to have passed the test, and we were hugging and holding hands often.

I thought about Don's remark about the merlin. It may have been rare to see that bird in the Himalayas, but it was possible. Tibetan Buddhist philosophy is believed by a tiny percentage of humans on the planet, but that doesn't mean that just because it's rare, it can't be right.

TWENTY-FOUR

What we ended up calling "The Honeymoon Trek" was a success, both for Don and Vanessa, and Jane and me. We were edging towards a decision to get married, without really talking about it. Then I was confronted with an unexpected problem that, while not so serious in itself, served to bring our relationship to a head, thanks to the magic of stress and alcohol.

I had been the medical director of the Himalayan Rescue Association for six years, ever since I moved to Nepal when I took over from Peter Hackett. I found out that there was a Nepali doctor who wanted me to step aside so that he could become the director. He had gone to the HRA committee—all of whom were Nepali—and asked them to make that change.

As the medical director, I had overall responsibility for staffing and operating the two aid posts in Pheriche and Manang. This meant recruiting, screening, and training four volunteer doctors per season, twice a year. In addition, I had overseen the opening of an HRA office in Kathmandu, to give trekkers advice before they started on their trek. The medical director job was unpaid—I just wanted to help make trekking as safe as possible, and make sure that people who got in trouble could get rescued. I had streamlined helicopter rescue, and I was also trying to complete the building of a new HRA aid post in Manang, for which I had raised all the funds.

That evening I met my close friends, Gil Roberts and his wife Erica Stone, at the private bar that Stan Armington had equipped in a corner of the Malla Hotel. Stan had lived in Kathmandu for almost thirty years, running a trekking agency, writing the Lonely Planet trekking guide for Nepal, and running the Northwest Airlines concession. He lived alone and enjoyed close friendships with a handful of people who passed through Nepal regularly. Although Stan had created the popular Rum Doodle Bar in Thamel, he had given that up. We were now drinking in Stan's private club—not open to the public but only to his close friends. Gil and Erica had become close friends over the years, and I usually stopped in Berkeley to stay with them for a few days at the start of my annual home leaves. Gil was a giant among mountain doctors—large, bearded, and fearless, with great judgment.

Gil handed me a large drinking glass full of Scotch, and I gratefully drank it.

"I hate this kind of shit," I said.

Gil reached over casually and refilled my glass. "It's always like this in Nepal, isn't it?" he asked.

"Maybe so," I replied. "It's true that Nepalis often try to push Westerners aside once something is going well."

"It happened to Stan—he got forced out of the trekking company that he built up for twenty years."

"I know the time will come when I'll be okay to step down."

"But now's not the time," said Erica, putting her hand on my arm.

Erica was more than twenty years younger than Gil, but just as tough— she was the top female Tae Kwan Do practitioner in America. She was blond, with intelligent blue eyes, and her lithe body moved like a cat. On top of that, she was Canadian. A few years earlier, I remembered standing on top of a parking structure in downtown San Francisco with my arm around her. I told her that I would like to find my own blond Canadian woman who would be as easy to get along with as she was. Jane was now sitting on the other side of me. I was beginning to think that maybe Jane was the blond Canadian woman that I had been looking for.

The bar gradually filled up with a collection of friends, some of whom were well-known Everest climbers and Himalayan adventurers, such as Pete Athans, Hugh Swift, and Gary McCue, the author of a detailed trekking guide to Tibet. It was dark, around nine o'clock, when I walked unsteadily out of the bar into the parking lot of the Malla Hotel. I was holding hands with Jane. I turned and looked at her. The parking lot light backlit her hair, and her face looked content.

"Will you marry me?" I blurted out, without thinking.

She looked at me for a moment and smiled. "Oh, probably," she said. There was a pause. "You need to ask me again when you're not drunk." That made sense, I guess. We put our arms around each other and waited for the others.

We all squeezed into cars and drove to the New Kabab Corner. The owners looked at us, an unruly group that had grown to twenty or more, and shuffled us upstairs to an unfinished banquet hall, where we arranged a four-by-eight-foot sheet of plywood as our table. Stan went downstairs and ordered an elaborate meal for all of us, and in the meantime, we kept drinking. Two of Erica's girlfriends from Berkeley were there—both beautiful and both lesbians—and I remember one of them following me into the bathroom to help me pee, which seemed more natural at the time than it does in the retelling. The party became a haze of laughter and good feelings. Tandoori chicken arrived, along with fresh baked naan, *dal makhana*, and more beer. It was my last truly debauched night in Kathmandu. I was no longer worried about the HRA position, or really anything, including who I was in the bathroom with.

The next morning, I woke up next to Jane with less of a hangover than I deserved. I kept my head still, and listened to the bird sounds and someone ringing the temple bell on the corner up the street. I rolled over and embraced Jane. I remembered that I had asked her to marry me.

"Are we going to get married?"

"You need to ask me again."

I looked into her eyes. "Will you marry me?"

"Yes."

"Good."

Jane would be in town for another week, but then she had to join her parents at Lake Louise for Christmas and work one more term as a teacher in Vancouver. Although we had just decided to get married, we would be apart for the next four months. If everything went well, she would fly back in early May, and we would tie the knot. Somehow that felt okay. It was as if we were being carried along by a current of trust and warm feelings, something that I had not previously experienced in a relationship.

TWENTY-FIVE

However, everything didn't go well. Jane and I were fine, but Nepal was entering an uncertain time. The king had long ruled with absolute power in Nepal, but in the early spring of 1990, a democracy movement gained steam—inspired by the changes taking place in the Soviet Union and Eastern Europe. Their goal was to achieve a multi-party system within a constitutional monarchy, which would greatly diminish the power of the king. Demonstrations began as peaceful gatherings, but when the government's response was to suppress the demonstrations with baton charges, people grew angry, the crowds increased in size, and anti-government groups called for strikes and demonstrations every couple of days. The most common form of strike was a *bandh*, which was an announcement that any car, truck, or bus that drove on the street that day would be attacked. It was a way of shutting down the city to protest, and the *bandhs* were enforced by angry gangs of demonstrators, usually young men in jeans and t-shirts who would stone or burn any vehicle caught trying to evade the strike. Walking through town was safe enough, but without vehicles, sick people had a hard time getting to the clinic. I could get there on foot or by bicycle, but I ended up having to try to diagnose and treat many patients on the phone.

The most unsettling thing about a revolution is that you don't know how it's going to turn out. It's one thing to talk about it in the past tense, when the outcome is known, but living through it is filled with uncertainty, and it's difficult to keep one's mind from playing out all kinds of apocalyptic scenarios. Would the U.S. embassy evacuate me if it came down to it, or would I be on my own as a private citizen? If there was a complete collapse of order, would I have to flee on foot across the middle hills with a backpack, trying to make it to the Indian border? Would I be admitted to India without a visa? Would I be able to take my dog?

Services were already starting to fall apart. There were shortages of gasoline, butane, and rice, with people waiting in ever-longer lines to obtain necessities. The level of violence led to several deaths and escalating threats of retaliation.

The potential demise of the country was not the only threat to my being able to stay in Nepal. For the past two years, I'd been in an increasingly nerve-wracking struggle to obtain a new agreement to run the CIWEC Clinic. The CIWEC engineering aid project that sponsored the clinic had finished its work and departed Nepal, leaving the clinic without an operating agreement with the government. Without an agreement, we couldn't get work visas. Without work visas, we couldn't legally stay in the country, operate a business, or import supplies. The three foreign doctors and our nurse practitioner were in danger of being deported at any moment without warning. I kept up a steady round of meetings with government officials that managed to convince the immigration officials that we still had a possible future, so they left us alone for the time being. The stirrings of revolution, however, meant there was a real possibility that even if we could get an agreement, there may no longer be a government to sign it.

Meanwhile, the demonstrations grew larger and more violent. The police shot and killed five peaceful demonstrators, and a policeman was killed in retaliation. Curfews were imposed regularly, sometimes lasting twenty-four hours at a time. I ran up enormous phone bills talking to Jane in Canada— the cost was three dollars per minute, and I ended up spending thousands of dollars. Each time I spoke to her, I didn't know if it might be the last time before the phone lines were sabotaged or—more likely—cut off by the government to prevent the leaking of unfavorable news from Nepal.

One night I was huddled on the floor of my office, trying to work by the faint light of a candle, while gangs of slogan-shouting protestors marched through the neighborhood, enforcing a ban on anyone having a light on at home. This was just an additional way to disrupt normal life until they could get their way. Rocks crashed against the side of my house, just missing the windows until I blew out even that faint light.

Didi called to ask me if I had heard what happened that afternoon.

"There was a mass shooting at the Palace," she said. "A lot of people are dead."

Having stayed at home all day, I was unaware that a hundred thousand people had marched to the Royal Palace to demand peaceful change. Policemen had positioned themselves with machine guns in a semi-circle facing outwards in front of the palace gates. The crowd slowly pushed towards the palace, increasing tensions. As the front of the crowd pressed within fifty feet of the gates, the police opened fire without warning. People tried to run, but the shots continued, spurring total panic in the crowd. Bleeding bodies were strewn across Durbar Marg. Amidst the chaos, army trucks appeared from side roads and soldiers seized the bodies, never to be seen again, or even counted. The wounded found their way to poorly equipped local emergency rooms. A British tourist, amid the crowd, was shot in the neck and killed. Another tourist was shot below the knee and ended up losing his leg.

The revolution had come to a head. In the next few days, fate would decide whether Jane could fly to Nepal as scheduled so that we could begin our married life there, or whether Nepal would descend into the chaos I had feared. A twenty-four-hour shoot-on-sight curfew was imposed, which kept the lid on things for the moment.

The next morning I realized that the king was stuck—if he lifted the curfew without changing the government, the people would riot. The country was boiling with intense shock and anger over the shootings at the palace. People would pour into the streets and the army would not be able to contain them. If the King relented and allowed a constitutional monarchy, the crisis would end, but ten generations of absolute power would be forever abandoned.

At 11:00 p.m. the following night, the king announced on television that he would legalize a multi-party system. The news of the lifting curfew was broadcast over the radio at the same time, but sadly, was not communicated in time to the soldiers patrolling the streets; several more people were shot and killed as they came out of their houses to celebrate.

As I drove to work, Nepalis everywhere were smiling and celebrating a hard-won victory. The idea of transitioning to democracy was hopeful. I felt celebratory as well, for now I knew that I wouldn't have to flee Nepal, Jane could arrive on schedule in a week, and we could get married. We could then look forward to living together in Nepal—if I could solve the agreement problem.

As with so many things about my life in Nepal, more than one thing was happening at the same time. Due to the visa crackdown, a boyfriend of one of the Pheriche doctors had been arrested and marched back to Kathmandu. His girlfriend went with him, leaving just one doctor at Pheriche for the season. I wouldn't have blamed her if she got fed up and wanted to leave as well, so I was worried when she sent word that she needed to talk to me on the radio. The aid posts could only communicate with Kathmandu through the National Park Headquarters radio system. It was the day after the king relented, and the clinic was maxed out with patients. However, there was only one scheduled radio contact per day from each aid post, and that was less than an hour away, so I rode my motorcycle out of the clinic and headed towards the center of town, unprepared for the level of joyful chaos I would encounter. Tens of thousands of giddy, grinning people were laughing and shouting and pelting each other—and me—with red powder, which is often used in large celebrations. I was reduced to straddling my motorcycle and walking it down the middle of the street, smiling at the joyous throng.

The radio connection with Jan at Pheriche was patchy and filled with static. Jan still didn't know what had happened to her friend, the other doctor. I told her that they were not in jail, but they were not returning to Pheriche. To my relief, Jan said she had decided to stay on by herself and keep the aid post open—a decision that dramatically and irrevocably changed her life. But more on that later.

TWENTY-SIX

When it comes to religion, what many people long for, more than anything else, is proof that what they believe is true. So, what do you do if what you're seeing can't be true, and yet is? I had gradually gotten so close to the world of Tibetan Buddhism that I came to accept the possibility of inexplicable happenings.

One evening, I went to see Chokyi Nyima Rinpoche. I rarely saw him after dark, and I can't remember why I was out there that night. He was relaxed and alone in his chambers. He reached into a cloth bag next to him and took out two sheets of paper with writing on them. He said that these were two original "songs" that he had recently composed. Every once in a while, a great master will write down a spontaneous moment of insight gained through meditation. These poems, which are sometimes sung, describe a moment of genuine realization. When he handed me the first sheet of paper, I noticed a faint rainbow across its surface which gradually grew more vivid as I watched. I looked around for a source—a reflection off a crystal perhaps—but it was dark outside, and I couldn't see anything that was refracting the light. When I moved the paper, the rainbow moved with it, staying on the page rather than continuing to shine on the spot where the page had just been. Which is impossible, right?

I glanced up and saw that a rainbow had also appeared on the copy that

Chokyi Nyima Rinpoche still held. I pointed out the rainbows to him, and he just laughed.

"The rainbows must be an auspicious sign," I said, trying to get him to comment on what was happening.

He laughed even harder. "Actually, that's really true," he finally said. I took the two sheets of paper and put them in my pocket. The rainbows were no longer visible. I was still looking around trying to figure out how these rainbows had appeared out of nowhere. Before I could ask any more about it, he said, "Come with me, I want you to meet someone." He jumped up and swept out the door of his chambers, leaving me trailing behind.

It was dark, but Rinpoche moved without hesitation down the stairs and through the outside hallways. The monastery was adding another floor for monks' quarters, and we needed to avoid hitting scattered pieces of concrete and jutting pieces of rebar. We entered the room of an elderly monk. He was lying in bed, in the dark. His breathing was raspy, with a distinct rattle coming from his chest. When we walked in, he looked up, quite cheerful despite his profound weakness.

"How old is he?" I asked Chokyi Nyima Rinpoche.

"I think he's seventy-four years old. He has cancer—it's in the tube between his mouth and his stomach."

Esophageal cancer. Once advanced, it blocks any food or water from reaching the stomach. It can be a difficult and painful way to die. The monk, with long, straggly hair and a thin beard, had a huge grin on his face that revealed both of his remaining teeth. He had the incongruous eager look of a child who had just been tucked into bed, anticipating a big event the next day. I helped him sit up a bit so that he might be able to breathe more easily.

"How are you feeling?" I asked him, as Chokyi Nyima Rinpoche translated for me.

"I'm grateful that I have been a practitioner my whole life," he said, in a weak whisper. "Now I have nothing to regret."

I stepped back, and Chokyi Nyima Rinpoche went over to the monk, took his hands, and said something to him in Tibetan. The monk smiled and nodded. We went back outside.

"This is a great example for all of us," Chokyi Nyima Rinpoche said, "because it shows that Dharma really works. It can truly ease the biggest suffering of sickness and death."

We climbed a flight of stairs onto a flat roof that had no guardrail. We could see the Boudha Stupa, three blocks away, with its all-seeing Buddha eyes illuminated by a spotlight from below. We looked out over Boudhanath beneath bright stars and a half-moon overhead. It was beautifully quiet—for Kathmandu—with only the occasional motor noise and barking dog. Chokyi Nyima Rinpoche seemed to savor the moment. "Dharma practice is no joke," he said. "It can really help. I teach about these things, but I can't always tell who has really taken the teachings to heart. I knew this monk for a long time, but I didn't know he was such a great practitioner. He has no fear, no attachment, no regret." Chokyi Nyima Rinpoche stood for a moment, looking out over Boudhanath. "It's amazing," he added.

Indeed, here was a person in his last days or hours who was completely content, with no fear, no attachments. I thought about the hundreds of dying patients I had treated who were terrified, sad, and hopeless as they faced their death. How could I help them? If I was ever going to be able to help give them the confidence to let go of their attachments and face their death a little more easily, I would have to learn how to do that for myself. Otherwise, my encouragement or advice would carry no real weight; the words would sound hollow to someone who is facing imminent death. I realized that Chokyi Nyima Rinpoche wanted me to see this practitioner not just to inspire me to be able to face my own death someday, but to inspire me to learn how to help others deal with their own deaths as well.

The evening had started with what seemed like a miracle—rainbows spontaneously appearing on the surface of paper. However, Chokyi Nyima Rinpoche had laughed those off. The real miracle he wanted to show me was an accomplished practitioner facing the end of his life with a profound yet seemingly matter-of-fact acceptance.

TWENTY-SEVEN

It was a hot, bright day in early May when Jane flew back into Kathmandu. As I went to the airport to meet her, I thought back five years to when I picked up another Canadian woman named Jane, believing that she would become my wife. A lot had changed in half a decade.

Just before Jane had phoned me in Kathmandu about eighteen months earlier, I had begun to feel that I could either end up in a long-term relationship or not, and it would be okay either way. The fact that I could honestly feel that way was, to me, an astounding transition. Right after that, Jane called, and we started down this new path, which was culminating with her arriving to marry me.

And here she was, in a white dress decorated with scattered flowers, fresh off the plane and into my arms. It had been a long and eventful four months. We drove back to our house. I had hired a sign painter to add Jane's name to mine on the gate. This city of half a million people still had no street names and addresses. If you invited someone to your home, you sent a map. A name on the gate was a helpful clue for anyone who had not been to your house before.

I also hung a large, red cloth banner across the second floor of the house, the kind of banner that decorated Nepalese wedding parties. It was painted with silver letters that read: "Dear Jane: Welcome to the Rest of Your Life."

My house staff stood in a row in the driveway with huge grins on their faces. They all knew Jane from her fall sojourn.

Jane would stay in Nepal for a month before we flew back to the States for the summer. We needed to get married as soon as we could so that she would have time to obtain a green card to work legally in the U.S. Because she was Canadian, working in the U.S. each summer for Exum had been complicated. She had managed to do it legally, using different strategies, but she had recently run out of options.

We arranged to get married the following Wednesday, May 9th, which happened to be Buddha's birthday that year. Chokyi Nyima Rinpoche would conduct the ceremony in the afternoon. My life was unfolding as he had predicted—he would perform my marriage ceremony in his monastery.

On the day of the ceremony, we had little to prepare. A few friends had been notified, but we planned to have a bigger celebration in the fall, when our parents could attend. By the afternoon, we had already obtained the fruit, flowers, candles, and *katas* that we needed for the ceremony. With nothing else to do, we rode our bikes along the Ring Road and turned off at the road up to Kakani, a beautiful ride past the edge of the Queen's Forest, and—somehow fittingly—past the spot where I had once seen a leopard sitting by the side of the road.

The monastery was filled with the customary rows of monks, and about thirty of our friends. We were seated in a position of honor on the right side of the prayer hall, closest to the statues in front. There were three seven-foot-tall statues behind glass. They had been fashioned from clay by Tulku Urgyen Rinpoche personally: one was the Buddha, one was Guru Rinpoche, and one was the female Buddha named Tara. The walls of the prayer hall were elaborately painted with scenes from the life of the Buddha.

Our friends sat in rows on cushions placed behind low wooden tables. The monks chanted prayers, punctuated by horns and drums, and served us all tea from a large metal thermos. Finally, Chokyi Nyima Rinpoche called for us to come forward. We stood at the head of the prayer hall, backlit by the bright light of the open monastery doors. We performed three prostrations, which were the first Jane had ever done. Although she remained extremely supportive of my Dharma practice, she had not taken it up on her own. We walked up to the dark green marble mantel in front of the three large statues that adorned the front of the prayer hall. We offered the fruit and flowers and lit the candles. Chokyi Nyima Rinpoche, sitting on a raised throne to the right, gestured for us to come over. He put an arm around each of us and drew us in close to him.

"Since you are getting married," he said, "you should make up your minds to be nice to each other. That's the main thing." He draped a large *kata* across both our shoulders. That was all he said. That single sentence of advice, though, has proven to be extremely useful. What more do you need to do to keep a relationship thriving? Plus, the advice went along with something I had been telling my friends: if you are going to wait until you are forty to get married, you might as well marry someone you like.

Since our wedding had come together in just a few days, we hadn't planned any party. Jane and I went home, broke open a bottle of duty-free champagne, and called our parents to share the announcement. However, getting married does create a honeymoon mood, which we enjoyed throughout the evening.

The next morning, my office called to let me know that the police had come to the clinic looking for me. Consistent with the unpredictable intensity of life in Nepal, I found out that Mr. Singh, the Director of Immigration, was trying to deport me. After two years in the country without a visa, he somehow picked the day after my wedding to go after me. Luckily, he didn't know where I lived, which is why he sent the police to my office, but I assumed he would find me eventually.

I needed help at a high level. One of the clinic's most powerful supporters had been Les Douglas, the Australian ambassador. We provided all the medical care for the Australian Embassy, and his wife worked as a receptionist at our clinic. I called him, and he said, "Don't worry. I'll take care of this." He said he would contact the Foreign Minister.

While I waited, I wondered whether to pack, just in case. I changed clothes; I didn't want to get deported to India in my shorts. After two long hours, Les phoned to say that things would be okay, at least for now. One of the lessons that all foreigners in Nepal eventually learn is that nothing happens until it happens. It's the lesson that I started to learn as a traveler. You need to take things in stride, or you're not going to last in Nepal.

TWENTY-EIGHT

When a young person travels to the Himalayas, they likely have a parent somewhere who will worry about him or her while they are there. The remoteness, altitude, and disease risks, along with concerns about personal security, will all hover in their minds while their children are away.

Only about thirty percent of visitors to Nepal go trekking into the mountains. When I first came to Nepal, the risk of trekking was completely unknown. People were aware of occasional altitude sickness deaths, but once I had lived in Nepal and worked in the mountains, I became aware of the fact that more people seemed to die in accidents or from some other medical problem. I formally studied trekking deaths from 1984 to 1991 and published the results in two papers. I found that about 1 in 6500 trekkers died on their trek.

In the course of those studies, I documented a tiny subgroup of trekkers who simply went missing and never returned. This created a nightmare situation for their families, who ran endless scenarios in their heads, with no way to bring any of them to resolution. Each day that slipped by made it less likely the loved one would be found safe, but until they were found—either way—there remained the possibility of hope.

I was consulted on most of these cases. I didn't have any professional training in searching for missing people. I just tried to use common sense and knowledge of the trekking environment to try to piece together what might have happened, and then send people out to see if there were any clues. The first case that I was aware of involved an American Peace Corps volunteer, a twenty-seven-year-old woman, who went trekking from Jiri towards the Everest region. No one knew she was missing until she failed to turn up for an international flight more than three weeks later. We sent people to investigate, and because she was a foreign woman trekking alone who spoke fluent Nepali, the people in the teahouses where she stayed remembered her. She was last seen leaving a teahouse on the morning she headed into a long stretch of woods that go over Lamjura Pass. I had hiked over this pass when I walked into Pheriche for my second season, and I could picture the long stretches of forest trails, often immersed in fog.

Then, two weeks after that, a Canadian woman who was trekking alone also disappeared in the same stretch of woods. I learned that local people tried not to walk alone through these forests, as they were far enough from villages that people had occasionally been attacked and robbed. Violent crime against foreigners, however, was extremely rare in Nepal at that time. We made posters, circulated photos, and had people slowly hike the trails to look for remains, but there were no clues.

A few years later, I was asked to investigate another missing American. This man had last been seen heading over a ridge from the Kali Gandaki Gorge toward the entrance to the Annapurna Sanctuary. The trail traversed a forest of densely growing rhododendron trees, with eerily twisting trunks interwoven into a dark canopy. I had walked through that forest myself a few years earlier and found it easy to get confused.

Someone would have to go to the area and try to retrace the man's steps and find out where he had last been seen. I recruited an experienced

American mountain guide, Carl Harrison, who was the husband of one of the CIWEC nurses. Since the missing man was a tourist and didn't speak Nepali, there was little reason for the teahouse owners to remember him. He did have red hair, which helped. Carl was able to trace him within a day's walk into these woods.

The man's parents flew to Nepal about a month after he went missing. There had been rumors that a man matching the missing person's description had been seen staying at teahouses in the region, openly smoking marijuana and acting strange. The family decided that this could be their son—who had no known history of drug use—and that perhaps he had lost his mind and was wandering in the hills, or some Nepalis had locked him up somewhere. The family checked into the Yak and Yeti Hotel, which was next door to our clinic, and they asked to come and talk to me.

We sat in my office on the second floor of the clinic. The father, mother, and a sister all expressed a positive belief that he would be found safe. "We'll find him," they said. I sensed that they were bolstering their hope with an optimistic bravado. I was much less sure of a positive outcome. After a month, I couldn't imagine a scenario in which he was still alive and had not walked out or been seen by someone. The dope-smoking tourist had been found, and it wasn't their son.

It was time, I thought, to gently suggest the possibility that their son may not be found alive. Since it still wasn't impossible, I tried to find a way to phrase it so that I would not suddenly and completely shatter their dreams.

"We've been able to trace the general area where your son disappeared. It's a small area, and it is not at high altitude. It's possible to walk back to Pokhara within a day or two from there. If he were all right, he would have walked out by now. He wouldn't want you to worry about him."

"But what if he has become psychotic and is not thinking clearly?"

"A psychotic tourist would still have to eat and get shelter somewhere in order to survive, and the Nepalis in the area would certainly remember seeing such a person."

"Then what could have happened to him?" the father asked with a slight quaver in his voice.

"I'm not able to say for certain that he won't be found alive." I felt it was important to say this, although I didn't believe it to be true at the time. "All I can say is that, after all my experience of working in Nepal, I'm having trouble coming up with a scenario in which he will be found alive. It's possible that such a scenario exists, but my imagination is unable to come up with how it could happen." This sounded a little stilted to my ears, but it was the best I could come up with.

They sat there, suddenly subdued. "What could have happened to him?" the mother asked again.

"Most likely he fell from a trail. There are steep hillsides, and some of the trails can be unsafe at times and break loose underfoot, particularly if he lost the main trail and took some kind of side trail. The Nepalis go into the forest to cut wood, so someone may find him someday."

It was a sad moment. What could it be like to have your son disappear from the planet, from your life, from your hopes and dreams? But maybe not disappear, maybe be trapped somewhere, suffering, longing to come home. What if you stop looking too soon? I tried to leave some hope. There could be some reason to believe he would be found alive. But I truly didn't know what that reason could be. The family stayed on in Nepal for a week or so, went to Pokhara, and asked around. Then they flew home.

Sometime after that, a Nepali woodcutter found some skeletal remains and a Canadian passport down a steep ravine in the Lamjura Pass region. It was the passport of the Canadian woman, and the bones were presumed to belong to her. We suspected foul play, as there was no way to fall off the trail near where she was found. The remains of the Peace Corps volunteer were never found.

A failure of imagination—the inability to think how someone could still be alive after a prolonged period—could have serious consequences if a search was called off too soon. Someone could be stranded, but alive, unable to walk out, completely reliant on persistent search efforts to track them down. That was always in the back of my mind. But once the trail went cold, it was completely impractical to try to scour the steep, forested, trailless terrain. It would fall to the woodcutters to stumble upon any remains.

There is a trekking area just north of Kathmandu called Helambu. Because it does not go as high into the big mountains, it isn't visited as often. The trails are not well developed, but there is a trail that goes over a pass to Gosainkunda Lakes at 15,000 feet, and then loops back to Kathmandu. In December of 1991, an Australian medical student named James went trekking with a friend into this area. They had been in Nepal for a couple of months doing medical student clerkships and had done one short trek already. Before they returned to Australia, they wanted to squeeze in one more.

They arrived at a teahouse at the base of the pass where they met a lone German trekker headed in the same direction. James's friend developed knee pain and decided to turn back. James decided he would head over the pass with the German man the next day. However, the morning dawned cloudy and cold, and it looked like it could snow. The teahouse owner, however, guaranteed them that it wasn't going to snow that day, so they headed out.

They made it a few hours up the pass before the snow began. Gentle at first, it started coming down harder, and James, already nervous about getting stranded on the pass by deep snow, prudently turned around. The German trekker apparently still felt comfortable with his decision and carried on. They agreed to meet up in a restaurant in Kathmandu in three days' time. The German man crossed the pass and returned to Kathmandu as scheduled. He was surprised when James did not show up. Instead of shrugging it off, he contacted the Australian Embassy to report James missing.

Again, I was asked to help investigate. I called on my friend, Carl Harrison. Carl hiked the route up to the area. He met some other trekkers who thought they had met James, but it proved to be a false lead. The teahouse had closed when the two trekkers left that day, so there was no one there to have seen James's return or to offer him shelter. If James had returned to the teahouse seeking shelter from the storm, he would have encountered a locked, empty building. The trail that he had counted on following was blanketed with snow and no longer visible. The circumstances suggested that James could have become lost. The question was, where did he go?

Carl hiked the area for weeks. James's sister flew to Nepal and was tireless in pursuing leads and encouraging people to keep looking. But a month had gone by, and again I could not imagine a scenario in which the man could still be alive. The sister even consulted a Tibetan lama, whom I didn't know. The lama had performed a divination , called a *mo*, and told her clearly, "You will meet your brother again." The sister called to ask me for some help in finding her brother, but I told her I was in close touch with Carl, and I had no new ideas of where to look. After five weeks, I once again could not imagine a scenario in which he would be found alive.

The lama had indicated an area on the map where James was likely to be found. The area that the lama pointed to was virtually impassable. The snow that had fallen the day that James had started to cross the pass remained on the ground. The area in question had dense underbrush and the snow was waist-deep and soft. After a few forays into the area, Carl, who was an incredibly tough mountaineer, decided they couldn't explore it on foot. They hired a helicopter for one last flight over the area, even though it seemed like a long shot. If Carl couldn't walk into the area, how could James have done it?

The helicopter flew past a large mountain ridge. Carl thought he spotted something. When they flew back closer to the ridge, a man was waving from about halfway up the ridge. They flew closer to take a look, and it was a very weak, emaciated man, lying on his side in a sleeping bag. It had to be James. He had been missing for forty-two days.

The hillside was steep jungle. Above were vertical cliffs. The helicopter could not land anywhere near the man, so they landed in a clearing a few thousand feet below where he had been spotted. Carl led a crew of Nepalis up the incredibly difficult hillside, post-holing in deep snow, sliding backward, bashing through underbrush, grabbing branches to try to move uphill. By nightfall, they hadn't yet found him. The crew needed to find shelter for themselves, as it was the beginning of February and still quite cold. As they moved along the hillside, they spotted a large overhanging rock and decided to take shelter under it. As they stepped into the shelter, they spotted the man in a sleeping bag inside.

He was coherent but very weak, unable to stand. A Nepali rescuer, who had climbed the hill barefoot, said, "Are you James?" When the man answered, "Yes," he hugged him. The rescue crew offered him his first food in forty-two days. They all settled down to spend one more night.

Carl got the story from James that night. As Carl had determined, James had returned to find the teahouse shuttered, with no one to ask directions. He started down what he thought was the trail, but the new snow blanketed the area. Finding a river, he reasoned that he could follow it back to civilization. He bushwhacked alongside the river but had to detour around a cliff when the river went over a steep waterfall. After descending the steep terrain next to the waterfall, he found himself slogging through waist-deep snow. He was now in a steep valley, but he thought he could climb out over a high ridge. Fighting his way up the steep slope through snow-covered bushes, he made it to the base of a vertical 3,000-foot cliff, which was totally unclimbable. This journey had already taken him three days. He began the odyssey with two candy bars. Completely out of food and water, he was too weak to retrace his steps. He found shelter under an overhanging rock, and after a few more forays to try to find a way out, settled down to wait to be rescued. He packed snow into his empty backpack each day and melted it in the sun for water. Otherwise, he lay in his sleeping bag. He saw helicopters flying around, presumably looking for him, but none came close enough to spot him until yesterday.

The steep, jungly hillside made a helicopter landing impossible. Carl had a radio, and the next morning he organized a short-haul rescue. Anticipating this scenario, he had rigged the helicopter with a rope and a harness before he hiked up the hill. The helicopter flew up the next morning, and they accomplished the first-ever short-haul rescue from a helicopter in Nepal. The helicopter flew James from the end of the rope out from the cliff and over the jungle to a clearing, where he was lowered to the ground, placed inside the helicopter, and flown to the Patan Hospital in Kathmandu.

I received word that he had been found alive while I was attending an international mountain medicine conference in Chamonix, France, that was being held in conjunction with the 1992 Winter Olympic Games. None of the mountain medicine doctors at the conference—some of the most experienced mountain doctors in the world—had ever heard of such a survival story. I was happy for James and his family. I had been willing to believe the Tibetan lama who had been so sure that he would be found alive, but I still couldn't imagine how it could play out. My years of experience with missing persons and search and rescue had, in fact, blinded me to the possibility that someone could survive for so long, and later be found. We had never found anyone alive who had been missing for more than two weeks. If his sister had not stayed in Kathmandu for six weeks and promoted the continued rescue efforts, no one would have found him. He would have survived for just as long, but then died anyway, an unsung hero. It made me wonder how many people had survived for inordinate lengths of time, only to never be found. It gave me a lot to think about. It seemed that every time I thought I was sure of something, based on my own experience, I encountered a situation that forced me to change my view. What would I tell the parents of the next missing trekker to come along?

A year later, a Nepali woodcutter found the skeleton of a Western man lying in the woods below a steep, unstable section of trail near Gandrung. It proved to be the body of the red-haired American man.

TWENTY-NINE

Tibetan Buddhists believe that our mind, in the intermediate state between the death of our current body and the start of our next one, can sometimes choose who our parents will be. There are detailed teachings as to what we will encounter when we leave our body, how to avoid the loneliness and fear that can occur in this state, and how to direct our mind towards a favorable rebirth. If we are too frightened, we may take refuge in any available shelter, which could trap us in the womb of an animal, for example. They say that if we are destined to be reborn as a human being, we will see our parents making love, and enter the womb at that time. I knew about these teachings, but that didn't prepare me for what happened one night, shortly after Jane and I married.

Jane and I were still in a honeymoon mood. We were in the basement guest room of her parents' house in Calgary. We were not yet trying to get pregnant, as we planned to lead a trip to Tibet in the fall, and then start trying to have a baby. Just after we finished making love, I experienced an incredibly vivid vision—profoundly immediate and clear. I had never experienced any kind of vision before, not even in my youthful mescaline-dropping days. I felt surrounded by vast empty space, dark, but with a faint pervasive light that didn't seem to have a source. The basement room was dark, and it didn't seem to matter if my eyes were open or not. I sensed something emerging from this space, and I suddenly felt like I had attracted someone into my life. I felt a being arriving, accompanied by an overwhelmingly good feeling, like the reunion of an old friend, a loving companion from some unknown past. It was clear that this person would be reborn as our son.

Then the vision abruptly ended, and I lay there next to Jane, stunned. I found I couldn't utter a word. What could I say? ("Honey, I just had a vision that we attracted a being from some unknown realm and he's going to be born as our son. Felt great.") It would come out in time, especially if she proved to be pregnant in the ensuing few weeks.

Within two weeks, we had driven down to Jackson Hole from Calgary and settled into our cabin in Lupine Meadows in Grand Teton National Park for the summer. It was a twelve-by-seventeen-foot one-room shack with no running water, but it was at the edge of a spectacular meadow at the foot of the Tetons.

Jane was a week late for her period. I got up as usual and Jane went off to work at the Exum Mountain Guides office. On that particular morning she left me some urine to test for pregnancy. I was used to doing pregnancy tests at the CIWEC Clinic, so I drove into town and bought a couple of home pregnancy test kits and followed the directions. Sure enough, the vertical and horizontal lines both lit up to form a bright red plus sign. She was pregnant.

I drove over to the Exum office. Jane was busy talking to a client. She looked up and I nodded. She kept on talking to the client. When the client finally left, she said, "No way. I don't believe it. We need to do the test again." I told her that it was clearly positive. I had run it twice. She said, "Why don't you run *your* urine and see if the test is accurate?" I said I had already run two tests—there was no doubt. I had no problem accepting her pregnancy, as it was the natural follow-up to the powerful vision that I had experienced. The positive pregnancy test was just the manifestation of something I had already known at another level. Why I had been given this knowledge, I had no idea.

Finally, Jane accepted that she was pregnant and scheduled an appointment with a doctor. We had to cancel our plan to lead a trip to Tibet that fall, but since we were both over forty years old, we were glad that Jane had been able to get pregnant so easily.

One thing that felt nice about the prospect of being older parents was that we'd both had a lot of adventures in our lives. A child would not interfere with any unfulfilled dreams of travel. Plus, we would still be living in Kathmandu, which, after all, was an adventure for many people just to visit once. Making it easier to contemplate was the fact that we would have household help. A cook, a cleaner, a laundry person, a gardener, and most importantly, a nanny (called an *ayah* in Nepali), would all help ease us into parenting.

We returned to Kathmandu at the end of the summer, at the end of Jane's first trimester. The question we had to decide was where to have the baby. Kathmandu was not a safe environment in which to give birth. The delivery could be handled safely, but if the baby was compromised—meaning unable to breathe or experiencing other difficulties—there was no neonatal intensive care at all. There wasn't even an incubator to keep a premature child warm. We recommended to all our expectant mothers to give birth either in Bangkok or in their home country. We opted to give birth in Bangkok, where there was an excellent hospital with a birthing suite and a well-known doctor who had delivered dozens of babies from expatriates living in Nepal. After the delivery, there would only be a short three-hour flight back to Kathmandu, rather than a thirty-six-hour journey from North America.

We needed to go down to Bangkok a month before the expected time of delivery. It was particularly important to be there if the baby were to come early. Steve Blake, the consular officer with whom I had worked on many rescues of American tourists while he was stationed in Nepal, was now working in Bangkok. His wife and child were going to be away for a month, so he invited us to share his apartment there, complete with a swimming pool.

The month in Bangkok was one of the most relaxing times of our marriage. Neither of us were distracted by work, and Jane's condition limited our recreational or sightseeing options. We needed to stay within a few hours of the hospital just in case she went into labor early. We enjoyed great Thai food, swam a few laps in the pool, and wandered through air-conditioned shopping centers. Jane developed an irresistible once-a-day craving for McDonald's hamburgers during this period of time.

After four weeks, Jane went into labor on a Thursday morning at 6:00 a.m. We phoned the doctor, and he told us to head for the hospital once she was having strong contractions about ten minutes apart. We reached that stage around 6:00 p.m. We got into a cab and told the driver to go to Samitivej Hospital.

Only we didn't go anywhere. The traffic was in its usual early evening gridlock. Jane was having a strong contraction every ten minutes; the taxi was barely moving a block every ten minutes. We had several miles to go, and every time a contraction came, I thought about what it might be like to deliver our son in the backseat of a taxi. Motorcycles zipped by on the traffic dividers and the sidewalks, and it occurred to us that—in a pinch—we could wave down a motorcyclist and get a ride to the hospital.

The contractions didn't progress that much, however, in the two-and-a-half hours it took to get to the hospital. My brother, Larry, and his girlfriend happened to be in Bangkok on a long trip in Asia, so they joined us in the birthing suite. Tulku Urgyen Rinpoche had given us a special herbal pill that had been blessed. The blessing of a single lama is nice. However, these pills, which have no power or side effects on their own, are a vehicle for carrying the blessings of past masters, or the combined prayers of an entire monastery. Jane was to take it when the labor was well advanced. He said that it would completely protect both mother and child during the birth. I gave Jane the pill and this gave us both a lot of confidence. I trusted that my teacher was wise enough not to give us something that could be harmful, and I had faith that the pill and its blessings would safeguard Jane and the baby.

Jane labored through the night. Each contraction gave her intense pain in her low back, and I needed to stay at her side to constantly massage her back. There was not much progress. Finally, the nurse called the obstetrician to come in, and at 4:00 a.m. he realized that Jane's tailbone was jutting forward just enough to prevent the head from getting through. He clamped big metal forceps around our son's head, and with more force than is comfortable for a parent to watch, assisted him into the world.

Despite the long labor and the use of the forceps, our son cried only briefly and then looked serene. The Thai nurses were kind and efficient, and after letting him lay on Jane's breast for a while, they swept him off to the nursery to get him cleaned up and examined, and then brought him right back.

Unlike after most modern deliveries in the U.S., we stayed in the hospital. We had a private suite, our own refrigerator, and a couch for me to sleep on. We named our son Matthew after my friend, the French Tibetan Buddhist monk, Matthieu Ricard. Matthieu has a remarkable life story: while studying for a PhD in biochemistry in France, he saw rough video footage of some Tibetan lamas that had just emerged from Tibet into India in the early 1960s. Just by seeing their faces he was moved to travel to India to try to meet them. After establishing a connection and starting to learn Tibetan so that he could communicate with them, they told him to go back to France and complete his studies, which he did. Then he immediately moved to India again to be with them. He eventually took the vows of a monk and settled in Nepal. He became fluent in Tibetan, translated many Tibetan books, was an accomplished photographer, and served as the in-person translator for His Holiness the Dalai Lama when he gave teachings in France. On top of that, he was remarkably compassionate, and I had known him through the Dharma community for many years. His name fostered a nice connection in my mind.

Although I was a doctor, and Jane was a special education teacher, neither of us had spent much time caring for an infant up until then. But it was okay; anytime Matthew cried or fussed, the Thai nurses came and got him and made him better. After three days of this, the doctor gently suggested to us that since both mother and son were doing well, we could leave the hospital whenever we wanted.

Jane and I looked at each other. There was an awkward silence. "We'll let you know," was all we were able to say. Take this fragile infant away from these competent nurses and rely on our own skill and judgment? What were they thinking?

After two more days, during which we built up our courage, we moved into the Royal Hotel. Steve had left Bangkok to join his family in the U.S. The Royal Hotel was the very first hotel in Bangkok, and the place I had stayed when I came through Bangkok my first time in 1979. It was near the Grand Palace, and at night we could see the temples lit up with thousands of lights. In three more days, we had obtained a passport for Matthew and flew back to Kathmandu.

THIRTY

Her feet were perched on the edge of a trash can. Her toes were stripped of skin—bare bones stuck out, loose tissue hanging around them. I looked at her toes and then at her face. She turned to me...and smiled. She was eleven years old, her face burnished red from the high-altitude sun and wind of Tibet, her relatively short black hair pulled back. She had just survived a multi-day epic battle through the snow to get across a 19,000-foot pass to escape from Chinese rule in Tibet. Her parents weren't with her. They had taken the chance, like so many Tibetan parents, of sending her out to school in Dharamsala, India, where she could get a traditional Tibetan education. She would have to sacrifice all of her toes to frostbite to get there. But at least she was alive.

Another girl around her age was not so lucky.

A few weeks earlier, I had treated a different group of refugees that had been engulfed in a snowstorm that blew for five days, dumping heavy snow whipped by violent winds. The oldest members of the group were only in their early twenties—several were children sent alone without their parents. The children struggled to keep up through the drifting snow and bitter wind, their clothes, hair, and faces coated with ice, trying to plow through drifts as high as their chests.

A twenty-two-year-old man named Taga told me the story. "There was a young girl, maybe twelve years old," he said. "She got so cold. She couldn't walk. I put her on my back. She was so cold she was a blue color. I had to try to keep walking through the deep snow."

"How long did this last?" I asked.

"We had to spend the night. We had no tent, no warm jackets. We just sat together close, to try to keep warm."

"Did the storm keep going?"

"The next day was still strong snow coming and wind. I walked with the girl on my back. I was so tired. She turned bluer, and finally I realized that she had died. She was still on my back."

"What did you do?"

"We had to just leave her in the snow. I don't even know how to contact her parents." A wave of anguish passed over his face. "After she died, I finally looked at my feet. I could barely walk. My boots were frozen solid. Like wood. I couldn't feel anything in my legs. I only cared about saving the girl."

"Did you know the girl before?" I asked.

"No. She was just in the group. I think at this time also three other people died, but I didn't see them myself."

"Then what happened?"

"I couldn't walk anymore. My girlfriend had to carry me. The whole day, and next day. Finally, we came down from the snow."

When they got below the snow in Nepal, they encountered the Nepali police, who arrested them and stole their few remaining valuables. They were released to the Tibetan reception center.

I met the group the day after they arrived. Taga had a sweet face, with an open, innocent expression. Then I looked at his legs. It was as if they had been dipped in tar up to mid-shin, and then dried; the skin was utterly black and shriveled, with a sharp line that demarcated where the normal skin resumed, about eight inches above his ankles—just where his boots had been tied. He had been wearing leather work boots instead of the usual Chinese sneakers. He would have been better off in the sneakers. His boots had gotten soaked, and when they froze solid, they cut off the circulation to his feet. There was no hope of recovery. Both his legs would have to be amputated below the knees.

I looked him in the eyes as I told him that he would have to lose his feet. I said that we would take him to a good hospital for the amputation.

With an endearing naivety, he asked, "Will they put me to sleep before they cut off my legs?" I reassured him that they would.

I arrived at the hospital just as he emerged from surgery. Taga moaned and cried as he woke up from the anesthesia. He said that he wished he could have died. Then, he clarified, "I wish that I could have died if it would have prevented the suffering of all the others on my journey."

His brother, a monk from a monastery in south India, came to Kathmandu to help take care of him. However, Taga needed to stay in Nepal and let his stumps heal for at least two months before he could be fitted with prosthetic legs that would allow him to walk again. The refugee center, with its rutted rough paths and uneven houses, would not accommodate a wheelchair, and the pit toilets would be impossible for him to use without legs.

I had seen a Tibetan family going in and out of a room down the hall from Taga. The husband was recovering from gallbladder surgery. I made a point of speaking to the wife. She and her husband had been refugees themselves, but now had a good carpet manufacturing business and a nice home in Kathmandu. I brought her to meet Taga and his brother.

"Taga is going to have a problem going to the bathroom unless we find a place for him to stay with a Western toilet," I told her. Without hesitation, she offered to take both men into her house for as long as they needed.

The Tibetans who attempt to escape Chinese rule in Tibet have to take on extraordinary risk. The only way out is over the few passes in the Himalayas that form the lowest point between the peaks, which is still 19,000 to 20,000 feet high. The journey involves a lengthy trip by truck or bus to get near the border, and then about five to seven days of walking to get over the pass. The most challenging factor is that they can't be seen outfitting themselves for the journey or buying hiking shoes, warm clothing, tents, stoves, and sleeping bags. Often, they literally head out with just the clothes on their backs. Roaring rivers can create an impassable obstacle at times, so refugees have learned to go in the winter when the water freezes over, finding that the bitterly cold temperatures are still easier than fording fast-running, ice-cold streams. Even with all those hurdles, most of them make it over without injury, provided there wasn't a storm.

Their goal is to get to Dharamsala, India, to see His Holiness the Dalai Lama, and then get on with their lives. Parents sometimes are forced to make a cruel choice—send their children alone with strangers in an attempt to get them a Tibetan education in Dharamsala or allow them to grow up with a completely secular, Chinese-language education. If they die along the way, sometimes no one in the group knows how to contact the parents. It may be months before the parents find out whether their child made it to Dharamsala—or whether they were never seen again.

Tibet is an occupied country. Nearly thirty years after the Chinese cemented their hold on the region, those who remained, or had been born since then, faced constant reminders of the occupying army: lack of freedom, destruction of their culture and language, and suppression of their cherished spiritual practice. When this deprivation becomes too much to bear, people have the choice to either rebel or leave. Rebellion leads to torture and imprisonment, and attempting to leave the country is illegal, also punishable by torture and prison. If you commit to escape, you've got to keep going.

The refugee crisis grew out of an eruption of protest in the fall of 1987. A group of Tibetan youths staged a protest on a side street near the Jokhang Temple. The police removed the protestors and took them to jail. Four days later, a riot ensued. Protestors burned police cars and attacked government offices, and the police fired directly into the crowd, killing six protestors and injuring two Westerners who were watching the riots. The subsequent crackdown was severe, with hundreds of Tibetans imprisoned and brutally tortured. Many of those spared no longer saw any hope of living in a free Tibet and began to sneak away across the Himalayas into Nepal. Those who were incarcerated also fled soon after they were released, creating a steady stream of refugees crossing into Nepal.

Their plight flew under the radar of local and international news. I didn't know about them until I got a phone call one day from Tsering Lhamo, the Tibetan nurse who took care of practically all the newly-arrived Tibetan refugees in Kathmandu. There was a sudden influx of patients with severe frostbite, and she didn't know how to manage them. She asked if I would be willing to come see them at the Tibetan refugee reception center.

I picked her up in town and as we drove, I asked her about her past, which turned out to reflect that of so many Tibetan refugees' sad experiences. The Chinese killed her parents in Tibet. As a ten-year-old orphan, she escaped across the mountains with her aunt to a refugee camp in India. Food was scarce, conditions were abysmal, and her aunt soon died of tuberculosis, leaving Tsering Lhamo alone in the world. She was taken to Dharamsala, where the Dalai Lama had made his home, and she lived in an orphanage called the Tibetan Children's Village. She proved to be a diligent student and scored high enough to enter training at one of India's most respected nursing schools in Vellore. She was later sent to Kathmandu by the Tibetan authorities, who had set up a government-in-exile in Dharamsala to look after the medical needs of the increasing numbers of refugees.

A cluster of prayer flags strung in some tall trees along the Ring Road marked the turn-off onto a dirt road. It had huge ruts, and I picked my way along slowly, trying not to get high-centered. We stopped near a group of old buildings in deplorable condition. Their tin roofs were bent and rusting, plaster was peeling off the brick walls, and the windows were broken. Dozens of Tibetan refugees sat against crumbling stone fences in the winter sun. Newly-arrived Tibetans had a different look than the refugees that had lived in Nepal for some time. Their cheeks were a perpetual red, their eyes were clear, and they had a kind of calm gaze, as if they were used to patiently looking across vast distances, as if waiting for a caravan to arrive. A few dozen refugees were lined up in front of a small wooden table outside in a dirt field, waiting to be registered by a representative of the United Nations High Commissioner for Refugees.

Tsering Lhamo led me through a low door into the nearest building, where I saw fifteen or twenty young Tibetans with bandages on their feet and hands. They sat on a row of low beds pressed together to form one big platform. A few days before, most of these Tibetans had been in a jail in Kathmandu. Robbed by the police of their last few possessions, they were penniless, unable to speak or understand the Nepali language, with no idea what lay in store.

Then a tall, broad-shouldered woman in a traditional Tibetan dress marched into the jail and started reassuring them in their native language. Turning to the Nepali police, Tsering Lhamo scolded the officials into letting the refugees go: "Why are you holding these people in jail? They are refugees, they are not criminals. They need to go to the refugee camp. You must release them." And so they did. They didn't really know what to do with them in any case and were just as glad to have them off their hands.

The relationship between China and Nepal was delicate, and the Chinese did not like the Nepalese authorities tolerating the influx of Tibetan refugees. On the other hand, thousands of Tibetan refugees already lived in Nepal, and the Nepalis were very supportive of Buddhism. The Tibetans could not be officially labeled as refugees, since the Chinese insisted that they had no valid reason for fleeing China. Instead, they fell into a netherworld as "people of concern," and were given a modicum of protection by the UNHCR. The registration that they obtained would allow them to cross the border into India. They were not initially allowed to stay in Nepal, but they could return to Nepal after spending some time in India. The vast majority did not have a passport.

Most of the Tibetan refugees I was seeing were former monks and nuns in their late teens or early twenties. They had a wide range of frostbite injuries, from bulging sausage-shaped blisters that would slowly heal completely, to one young woman whose toes were already starting to shrink and turn black, and who would eventually lose the front halves of both her feet.

As I reviewed each case of frostbite, I also undertook the tedious and time-consuming work of washing each foot carefully with betadine and water, then drying them off. I placed pieces of cotton between the toes to keep the skin from breaking down while wrapped in the dressings. I draped cotton gauze over the wounds and then unfolded ten to fifteen four-by-four-inch gauze pads to make "fluffs" to pad the feet and keep the skin safe from accidental bumps. The fluffs were held in place with carefully applied roller gauze and secured with tape. Each dressing change took fifteen to twenty minutes. Traditional protocol called for frostbite dressings to be changed daily, which had proven to be a huge burden with so many cases and a limited supply of bandages. I had discovered, though, while taking care of mountain climbers and trekkers in the mountains with limited supplies of bandages, that once the area was properly cleaned and dressed, I could leave the dressings on for three days at a time. Tsering Lhamo had been changing them every day, and when she found out she could do it every three days, it freed her up immensely. She had often spent entire days changing all the dressings.

Once the frostbite damage has been done—once the tissue has been frozen and killed—the damage cannot be undone. Treatment is aimed at preventing infection and further trauma and waiting until either natural healing takes place, if that is destined to happen, or the dead tissue starts to separate from the remaining healthy tissue, at which time the dead tissue is amputated. Waiting to see what will happen takes about a month, which is the hard part for the patient, watching the tissues turn black and shrink and start to be pushed away from the remaining healthy tissue. Once the dead skin and bone are cut away, the remaining tissue can finally heal.

The Tibetans were extremely stoic by nature, but the ordeal was still very difficult. I could see the flickers of loss in their eyes, but they rarely said anything about it. Even the children had an amazing tolerance for looking at their damaged fingers or toes during the awful waiting period without complaint.

The next step was to find a hospital and surgeon who could perform the amputations. Tsering Lhamo had tried using local doctors, but their lack of experience with frostbite led to some unfortunate outcomes. I knew that Ashok Banskota, the best orthopedist in Nepal, could care for these injuries, and he had a private hospital. I had met him eight years earlier, when he first moved back to Nepal after completing orthopedic training in the United States. At that time, he was offering free surgery to crippled orphans, and I had introduced him to a Swiss-funded disabled children's aid project, which made him their medical director. He now had his own hospital, but he told me that he couldn't afford to donate the care at his hospital when so many of his patients were also poor and had difficulty paying. I needed to find a donor.

I contacted Erica Stone, who had become the executive director of the American Himalayan Foundation, a very effective philanthropic organization. The amount of money we would need was small, by their standards, and she readily agreed to cover all the surgeries for Tibetan refugees in the future, which was a great relief.

The frostbite cases came in waves. One storm could create ten to twenty frostbite cases. Between storms, the refugees had few medical problems—occasional dysentery, a rare case of TB, or persistent pain and limitation of motion after being tortured in prison.

Even the refugees who had not been in prison had endured Chinese police coming into their monasteries and nunneries every night to force them to sit and listen to propaganda that denounced the Dalai Lama as a traitor and a "splittest," and attempting to denigrate the role of religion and promote the value of communism. In the period after the riots, the repression of Tibetans had worsened significantly. Just keeping a picture of His Holiness the Dalai Lama could send a Tibetan to jail to be tortured.

Until that moment in time, I had never met any victims of torture, and the experience was both horrifying and inspiring. Horrifying because of the painful experiences but inspiring because of the incredibly matter-of-fact way that the Tibetans could talk about their torture without apparent self-pity or post-traumatic stress. The Chinese government publicly denied—and still does—that prisoners are tortured in Tibet, but I heard convincing first-person accounts as Tsering Lhamo translated for me.

"The pain was like my heart was exploding out of my chest," said a twenty-two-year-old nun. "It blacked out everything in my mind. Then they would do it again." She was describing the feeling of having an electric cattle prod shoved into her vagina and discharged.

Some were beaten with clubs. Most had been tied in painful positions for extended periods of time, days or even weeks. A common torture position was having one's hands handcuffed behind one's back and then suspended off the floor by the wrists. Several people I saw had permanent problems in their shoulders and arms following their torture.

The story that stuck with me the most—maybe because I ended up moving to the high-altitude wintry climate of Jackson Hole—was told by a young man in his twenties who had been tortured with cold. "It was the middle of winter—January. They took me out of my cell at night and took me up to the roof of the prison. They took off all my clothes and then dunked me completely in freezing water. Then they tied me to a pole on the roof and left me there the whole night," he said. "It got so cold. I felt like I was freezing to death. In the morning, I was barely alive. They took me back inside my cell, and I started to warm up. That night they did the same thing to me again."

"How long did that go on?" I asked.

"They did it for one month."

I was staggered, trying to imagine the suffering involved in nearly freezing to death every night, naked and wet in the bitter high-altitude cold. I could imagine the shock of the icy water, with no chance to warm up or dry off, tied naked on the roof of a building at 12,700 feet in altitude, the bitter cold on the skin, shivering, going beyond shivering, slipping into confusion, not knowing if you were going to die or how long the night was going to last.

I asked him, "Why did they do this to you? Did they want you to tell them something?"

"They just wanted to make us suffer. There was nothing we could do or say that would make them stop." Every time I step out onto my porch at night in the sub-zero winter air of Jackson Hole, I still think of the suffering of this Tibetan man, and I stay just a few extra seconds to feel the cold start to penetrate my skin, trying to imagine not being able to step back inside again until dawn.

Unsurprisingly, many of the prisoners decided to leave Tibet once they were released from prison. In addition, as I had discovered on my trip to Tibet, almost all of the great Buddhist teachers had left Tibet or been killed. The monasteries that were allowed to operate were mostly shells, without genuine transmission of the teachings. To get genuine teachings, the monks and nuns had to risk the trek over the Himalayas to reach one of the many monasteries in Nepal and India that had been founded by the Tibetans in exile.

The stories they told fueled my compassion. If they could endure torture and be willing to talk about it, I would be their willing witness. When I finally moved away from Nepal several years later, the patients I missed most were the Tibetan refugees.

THIRTY-ONE

I was brushing my teeth in the upstairs bathroom of our house in Kathmandu when our neighbor ran into our front hallway. He was an American who worked at an English language school.

"Please come! Hurry! Please! Please!"

Jane ran up the stairs to get me, as I couldn't initially hear him. As I reached the head of the stairs he yelled, "Come quickly! It's Nicholas! He's not breathing!"

Nicholas was his sixteen-month-old son. I ran back into the bathroom for a second to spit out my toothpaste, then ran down the stairs, slipped on my shoes, and followed him out the door. Because every house is walled off into a compound to keep out thieves and wandering cows, we had to run three blocks, even though his house was only about thirty yards away.

Slightly out of breath, I entered the living room to see the boy lying on the floor. One of my CIWEC nurses, Jill, who lived next door on the other side of his house—herself a mother of four young children—was kneeling next to the boy doing chest compressions and breathing into his mouth. I offered to take over. I put my lips over his small mouth and his face felt as cold and smooth as marble. After giving a couple of breaths, I paused and looked into Jill's eyes. I'll never forget how calm and kind she looked. Her eyes met mine, and she told me with her eyes that she also knew. It was hopeless. I put my ear to the small boy's chest. There was no heartbeat. I felt for a carotid pulse. I watched for signs of an attempted breath. There were no signs of life.

Just the afternoon before, he had been in our backyard with his nanny, and he had looked fine to me, despite having battled croup for the past three days. He was being seen by the American Embassy doctor, so I didn't know the details of his case, but croup usually gets better within one or two days, and he showed no signs of distress. His father had slept next to his crib, in case he woke up with any trouble breathing. "When I woke up," he said, "my initial reaction was relief that he had slept through the night. I stood up and reached to pick him up, and he didn't move. He wasn't breathing..." He started sobbing.

"He seemed better," said the mother, "when he went to sleep." The mother picked the child up off the floor and cradled him in her arms. She walked around for a little while, and then placed him carefully in his crib.

Word spread through the tight expatriate community. Friends began arriving, some bringing food. The parents were Buddhists, students of Chokyi Nyima Rinpoche and Tulku Urgyen Rinpoche. As the day went on, a succession of friends sat in the child's room and meditated, trying to create a calm environment. The child was left in his crib all that day. It was important to allow the child's body to lay undisturbed to allow the mind to get its bearings before moving on to the intermediate state. When the Sherpas had done this for the child up in the mountains, I didn't have any understanding of what they were doing.

The next morning, two lamas from Chokyi Nyima Rinpoche's monastery came to the house to perform rituals that would help guide the child's mind through the intermediate state to a favorable rebirth. The prayers of an accomplished practitioner can reach across the divide between living and dead and help reassure and instruct the person after death.

The monks chanted in a deep, confident, droning tone, punctuated by their bells and drums. At one point, the senior monk with long gray hair and a beard stopped and turned to the mother. "It's natural to grieve," he said gently. "Just don't grieve too much. What's happening here is natural. The cause of death is birth."

The words were startling in their elegance and directness. They would never be spoken at a Western funeral. He meant his words to be comforting, a reminder that once we are born, death is a constant possibility, with no guarantee of even growing up. The lama was invoking impermanence, that unique and deeply resonant Buddhist concept that is meant to remind us of the fragility of life while at the same time helping us accept that it is the very nature of life to be impermanent. We can grieve when we lose someone, but we shouldn't go completely to pieces. *What's happening here is natural.* He was describing what the Sherpa parents and friends had known in Pheriche when the little boy died of croup up there.

That afternoon the mother sat on a low porch, leaning back against a red wooden pillar in the courtyard of a small monastery at the base of the hill leading up to Swayambunath Stupa. She held her child, draped in a thin white blanket, against her chest. All our love cannot stand in the way of impermanence. The image of my American friend is frozen in my mind, holding her child for the last time, preparing to make the impossibly poignant motion of having to relinquish him forever. Any parent watching this scene would find it impossible not to think of their own children at that moment and hope that they would never have to go through this. Although we try to live as if the things surrounding us can stay the same, we know in our hearts that they are impermanent. It's why we experience so much hope and fear; it's why we check our children in their cribs at night to see if they are still breathing.

Thirty close friends accompanied the family to the cremation site. The thick pieces of hardwood, almost the size of railroad ties, had already been stacked on the concrete stand built for cremations. When it was time, the mother stood up and surrendered the child to the senior monk. She did so with remarkable grace and courage. My stomach clenched at the awful finality of the moment. The head monk carefully placed the child onto the pyre. The monks chanted as the fire was lit. There was no coffin, so the body was visible as the flames took hold and slowly engulfed the tiny body.

Eleven years had gone by, and I no longer needed to hide from the reality of cremation, in which the fire confirms what our minds struggle with—that the body is not the person; that the body is impermanent, and the mind continues on. Now I had my own son, almost the same age as Nicholas. It made it even harder to fathom the mother's poise. Even while processing all of those feelings, I could sense that I had become more capable of thinking about the mother, father, and child, and not just thinking about how hard it was for me to have to watch this.

I could see that I was changing, but there were still so many eventualities that I feared. How can you learn to live with your fears and uncertainties, while at the same time recognizing that all human beings are in the exact same situation? Isn't that the basis of compassion, recognizing that everyone suffers even though no one wants to? How could I learn not to worry about my son? I could barely stand it when Jane took Matthew to Canada to attend a wedding a few months earlier. Parenthood had taught me about unconditional love, but it had also brought a new kind of attachment that I had never felt before. I couldn't grasp what it would mean to hand my child over to that monk to be placed on a funeral pyre. All I could do was hope that I would never have to find out.

THIRTY-TWO

I was working at my desk at home when I suddenly felt I needed to go see Chokyi Nyima Rinpoche. One minute I was working on a research manuscript, and the next moment I was driving my motorcycle out to the monastery, without knowing why I was going. As I started up the last of the four flights of stairs to Chokyi Nyima Rinpoche's chambers, I heard the deep murmur of Tibetan chanting, which was unusual. Ceremonies were always performed in the main prayer hall downstairs. I came into the reception area and one of Chokyi Nyima Rinpoche's attendants came over to me, leaning his head in close as he spoke.

"Chokyi Nyima Rinpoche's mother has just died," he whispered, pointing to a room off the waiting room that I had rarely visited. He pulled aside a cloth curtain and motioned me in. The room was larger than I remembered. Twenty monks and nuns sat cross-legged on the floor, including Chokyi Nyima Rinpoche, Chokling Rinpoche, and Tulku Urgyen Rinpoche. They were chanting continuously. Chokyi Nyima nodded at me when I stepped through the door and pointed to where I could sit. I stayed for the rest of the puja, which lasted about an hour.

Chokyi Nyima Rinpoche's mother, Mayum, was sitting up in her bed in the far corner of the room, propped up by pillows against the wall, her arms resting on her thighs. Her long hair, streaked with gray, hung in two long braids down her chest. Her eyes were open, and she looked as if she were meditating. She was staring straight ahead, her face calm.

Her death was not unexpected. Mayum had been ill with pancreatic cancer for the past three months. I had made the diagnosis myself when she first became ill. The cancer was advanced, and she had not wanted to have any surgery. She continued living at the monastery, and a French doctor, living nearby to study Dharma, was available to give pain medication when necessary. The pain of dying from pancreatic cancer is often severe, but Mayum didn't like to take pain medication because she said it clouded her mind. I hadn't seen her in a few weeks, and I hadn't known she was this close to dying.

Two days later I went back to talk to Chokyi Nyima Rinpoche. We got a chance to talk alone. He told me that many people had come to see him because they were so upset about the death of Mayum. She had been a major source of inspiration for many female practitioners.

"It's funny," he said with a smile. "The people come to me for comfort because Mayum died, but they forget that she was actually *my* mother."

The mother figure is extremely important in Tibetan culture—children remain devoted to their mothers throughout their whole lives, and the word "mother" is synonymous with unconditional love and affection. The example used to encourage us to care for all sentient beings equally is to think that all beings have been our mothers at some point in a previous life. Since our mind has been in existence since beginningless time, the nearly infinite number of lives we have lived allows for the possibility that we have been in past relationships with all the other beings on Earth: the deer in the forest, the mouse in your house, the mosquito flying noisily around your face have all been our mothers in our past lives, as precious to us then as Chokyi

Nyima Rinpoche's mother had been to him in this lifetime.

I touched his arm and asked, "Are you okay?"

"I'm a little sad, naturally," he said. "But it's impermanence." We sat quietly for a moment.

"My mother was a really strong person," he said, breaking the silence. "When we had to flee Tibet, it was just her and myself and my brother, Chokling Rinpoche. I was eight years old, and Chokling was six. The Chinese were searching for us—they wanted to arrest or kill the *tulkus*, and we were trying to get to Sikkim. I had never slept outside in my life at that point, and we had to sleep out on the ground. My mother lay in between us and pointed to the stars and the moon, and said how beautiful it was, and how lucky that we got to sleep outside. She kept us from feeling afraid."

"You know," he went on. "I went in to see my mother last week. She had been left alone for a short time, and when I went into her room, she was crying. I felt bad, like maybe she felt abandoned. We almost never left her alone while she was sick." Chokyi Nyima Rinpoche was sitting on his couch, his legs folded under him, leaning forward. "So, I asked her, 'What's wrong, Mother?'"

She told him that her former teacher, who had died years before, appeared to her as a vision when she was alone and told her not to worry. The teacher told her that she had been an extremely diligent practitioner her whole life, and after she died, they would be together in a favorable realm. He told her not to have any fear at all.

"That's amazing," I said.

"On the one hand, it seems amazing," said Rinpoche, "on the other hand, this is the result of her many years of devoted practice."

"Yes."

"Her former teacher still wants to benefit all his students. He is still there for them. He came to reassure her, and due to her karma and the stability of her practice, she was able to meet him in person. That's what made her cry: the kind words of her teacher, and the promise they held. They were happy tears."

I would have reason to recall this conversation many years later.

Mayum was an extraordinary practitioner. Married to Tulku Urgyen Rinpoche for more than forty years, she had benefited from his teachings. She had never truly wasted a day in her life, always filling her time with practice, or working for the benefit of others. Tibetan Buddhist practitioners traditionally do the *ngondro*, the preliminary practices, until they have done one hundred thousand repetitions of each of the five parts. One part involves doing full prostrations one hundred thousand times. At that point in time, I hadn't even started my *ngondro* practice, while Mayum had completed the full set of one hundred thousand repetitions six times and had continued to do them until she was no longer strong enough to practice that way. As a result of her karmic connections and her diligence she had died peacefully, not experiencing pain, not clinging to this world, having confidence in what would happen after she died.

Just hearing about Mayum's vision of her teacher as she lay nearly dying didn't prove that it happened. I tucked the story away as another hard-to-fathom Tibetan Buddhist mystery. I couldn't imagine, at the time, that I would someday see for myself that this could be true.

THIRTY-THREE

The spring of 1996 was a watershed for ordinary people's interest in climbing Mt. Everest. It was the first expedition that broadcast events from the mountain in real time via the internet. When a big storm hit, computer users around the world were tuned into the life-and-death dramas on the mountain. Those stories were memorialized in a book by Jonathan Krakauer that became a huge international bestseller called *Into Thin Air*. The expedition had one of the most poignant moments ever recorded in the history of Everest climbing, and in the middle of that moment was that same Himalayan Rescue Association doctor named Jan.

By choosing to stay at Pheriche, Jan changed the course of her life. At the end of the season, she met one of New Zealand's greatest climbers, Rob Hall, as he was coming down from an Everest expedition. They fell in love, and after they got married, she climbed Mt. Everest with him. Six years after they met, Rob was back on Everest, while Jan had to stay home in New Zealand, seven months pregnant with their daughter.

I knew Rob before he met Jan. In 1988, I had given Rob and his climbing partner, Gary Ball, a Himalayan Rescue Association award for performing a remarkable two-day rescue of a Polish climber who was stranded on the West Ridge of Mt. Everest, injured and snow blind in a tent. Then, in 1993, I spent a long, emotional evening debriefing Rob and Jan in my living room, after Gary died of altitude illness on Dhaulagiri. The world of extreme high-altitude climbing is filled with constant peril.

In late spring 1996, I got a phone call at 8:00 a.m. from Everest Base Camp. It was Caroline McKenzie, who was the doctor for the Rob Hall Everest expedition which along with several other expeditions, was guiding clients to the summit.

"There was a huge storm yesterday, and as far as we can tell, there are twenty-one people unaccounted for above the South Col," she told me. "Rob Hall is stuck above the South Summit somewhere. We don't know where everyone else is."

"Are there people up on the mountain who can help?" I asked her.

"The Breashears IMAX expedition is letting people use all their oxygen. And Pete Athans and Todd Burleson are climbing up to the South Col today. I just don't know what I'm going to be dealing with here at base camp."

"We need to wait and see what happens. Maybe people will start showing up this morning." It was too soon to know what might happen. But spending the night out above the South Col, the last camp at 26,000 feet, was often unsurvivable.

In the meantime, I was on call for my clinic. I went in to see a young American woman who had been helicoptered out of the Annapurna region. Her hands were tied behind her back. The leader sent a brief note along with her. All it said was, "Don't untie her."

"How are you doing?" I asked her.

"I'm fine. I don't know why they sent me back to Kathmandu." She was twenty-three-years old, blond, pretty. The note said that she had been completely psychotic in the mountains, tearing down tents, paranoid. She seemed calm now, but I thought I should leave her hands tied for a little longer while I tried to figure out what to do with her.

"You can untie my hands," she said, smiling.

Caroline called back in the afternoon. Her voice was stressed, but she was under control. "Beck Weathers and Yasuko Namba have been found, and they are dead," she told me. "Scott Fischer is stuck high on the mountain and can't move. Rob Hall is still alive, but he seems unable to move down. He says his hands are frostbitten. Two Sherpas went up the ridge to try to reach him, but the wind was too severe, and they had to turn around." The fact that the Sherpas couldn't reach Rob was really bad news.

The American Embassy had already been on the phone with Beck Weathers' family. It fell to the consular officer to tell Beck's wife, Peach, that Beck was dead.

By 4:00 p.m., I had arranged for the young American woman in my office to go to a new private psychiatric hospital. I couldn't make sense out of what she was telling me about what happened in the mountains, and I couldn't trust her to be on her own, at least for a day or two.

Around 6:00 p.m. I got another call from Caroline. She was a levelheaded New Zealand doctor whom I had appointed to work as an HRA doctor a few years before. She had become an experienced high-altitude physician, but now her emotions were being tossed around by events on the mountain.

"Beck Weathers walked into camp," she said.

"He must not have been as dead as they thought," I replied.

"I guess not," she said. "But I don't think he's going to survive to be brought down to base camp," she continued. "I've told the rescuers not to try to bring him down. They need to use their resources to get the other people off the mountain."

That may sound practical, but that's a tough call to make, I thought. I didn't say anything to Caroline. *If Beck's alive at the South Col, and doesn't die right away, they're going to have to try to rescue him.* In the meantime, Beck's wife was going to get the phone call that everyone who thinks they have just lost a loved one secretly longs to receive. A call that says that it was a mistake, he's not dead after all. But this call was going to come with a catch—he's alive, but we're not sure we can get him down. Peach asked the American consular officer, who was new to his job, why they couldn't send a helicopter to get her husband off the mountain? The consular officer, unfamiliar with the altitude limits of helicopters, said he would ask the army what they could do. I knew that helicopters had not landed and picked anyone up above 18,000 feet in Nepal. Beck was currently at 26,000 feet.

Jan had been following the news hour by hour in New Zealand. When the two Sherpas had turned around before reaching Rob, she knew that he almost certainly could not survive a second night out near the summit of Everest. He was in touch with base camp by radio, and by holding the radio up to the satellite phone at base camp, he was able to be patched through to Jan. They were able to share one last heart-wrenching farewell, during which they chose a name for their unborn daughter. The other climbers, listening on the radio at camps scattered across the mountain, wept as they listened. I choked up when I heard about it the next day.

Beck Weathers survived the night alone in a tent at the South Col. When the others realized that he was still alive, and asking for water, they knew that they had to try to get him down off the mountain. He was walked down the fixed rope on the Lhotse face by some of the top mountaineers in the world: Pete Athans, David Breashears, Todd Burleson, and others. His frostbite was tended to in Camp II, at 21,000 feet.

On Monday morning I was busy seeing patients in my office. I took a phone call from the American Consular officer.

"We've sent a helicopter to get Beck Weathers from Camp Two," he told me.

"They can't land that high," I replied.

"Well, they told me they were going to go get him. When they do, we'll bring him to your clinic."

I was incredulous. If it was going to happen, it would set a world record for a high-altitude helicopter rescue. Two hours later, an embassy SUV arrived with Beck Weathers, and a Taiwanese climber named Makalu Gau. A Nepalese army pilot, Colonel Madhan KC, had landed twice above 21,000 feet and brought out the two injured climbers. He set a new world record for high-altitude helicopter rescue.

Nurses took the climbers to two separate examination rooms. The waiting room had suddenly filled up with people.

"Who are all those people?" I asked the receptionist.

"The press."

"Why?" We received injured climbers all the time, but they usually didn't attract much attention.

"I don't know."

I went upstairs and met Beck Weathers for the first time. He was walking on his own. He greeted me warmly, with a southern accent. His nose was black, and his right hand looked normal except for a bluish discoloration that ended abruptly at his wrist. The fingers on his left hand showed the same discoloration. There were no blisters, and he could move his fingers, but he couldn't feel them.

"I'd like to call my wife," he told me, "if that's okay." I dialed the phone and held the receiver for him. Peach had not wanted him to climb Everest. Then she heard that he was dead. And now she was talking to him. A lot of emotions wended their way through that first call.

After he said goodbye, I turned my attention to his hands. "There's a possibility that the injury is not as bad as it looks," I told him. "I've seen this kind of discoloration once before, and the outcome was surprisingly good." I knew, however, that he had been out overnight in high winds in subzero temperatures and that he had lost a glove on his right hand, so the potential for severe frostbite was extremely high. In the short term, we just needed to protect his hands from trauma and the possibility of infection, which would mean cleaning them with betadine and bandaging them. The bandages on his hands would render him somewhat helpless, so we needed to figure out where he could stay and who could help him.

"My brother's flying in this afternoon," Beck told me. "He's an ER doc." Beck was going to stay at the Yak and Yeti Hotel, just down the street from our clinic, and his brother would be there with him. I went down to look at Makalu Gau, whose frostbite injuries appeared much worse and involved both his feet and hands. When the two climbers were cared for, I helped them out through the waiting room, where the reporters descended on them. Ignoring the reporters, they both got into cars and drove off.

That night I was packing to go on a short trip to Mustang the next morning, with three close friends, including my close friend Erica Stone. We were going to helicopter directly to Lo Manthang, a medieval walled city on a barren plateau behind the Himalayas that had only recently been opened to foreigners. Around 10:00 p.m. I got a call from New York.

"I'm Dan Rather's assistant, and Dan Rather would like to speak to Beck Weathers."

Dan Rather was the news anchor on the CBS evening news, one of the most important news figures in the U.S. at that time. "He's not staying here.

He's at a hotel."

"I tried the hotel, but he's not answering his phone," he went on.

"Then I guess he doesn't want to talk to anyone."

"I was wondering if you could go down to the hotel and tell him that Dan Rather wants to interview him for the evening news."

"I'm his doctor, not his agent. I don't feel like it would be appropriate for me to do that. I think if he's not answering the phone, that's his answer."

He called back a few minutes later, trying to impress upon me how much Dan Rather *really* wanted to talk to Beck on the news that night. I told him there was nothing I could do, but I did tell him that Beck would be flying home within a couple of days. The phone rang again, a local photographer who was a friend of mine had been asked to get a photo of Beck. I told him that it wasn't up to me—he'd have to ask Beck. Beck still wasn't answering his phone.

"Are you just going to leave me hanging here, David?" he asked. "You've got to help me."

I thought about what to do. As a doctor, my responsibility is for the well-being of my patient. Helping the press get access to the patient not only wasn't my job, but it also didn't feel right. After what Beck Weathers had just been through, I didn't blame him for not wanting to be interviewed right away. He had told me that all he did was screw up and get rescued—the real story was the "dream team"—his words—of rescuers who had gotten him off the mountain. I wasn't going to drive down to the hotel and knock on his door even to help a friend.

The next day I was on a helicopter, sitting in Jomsom, the last airport before the final short hop to Lo Manthang. There were two helicopters, and the pilot of the other helicopter had decided it was too risky to try to fly through the forty- to fifty-mile-per-hour winds blowing down the gorge from Lo Manthang that afternoon. He was going to fly back to Pokhara to wait until morning. We watched as the smaller helicopter took off and flew down the valley. Prayer flags snapped in the wind, and dust flew around us on the runway. I assumed that we would do the same thing.

Our pilot leaned to the right and looked back down the aisle of the helicopter and smiled. I immediately recognized him as the pilot who had made the record-breaking landing at Camp II on Everest the day before to rescue Beck Weathers and Makalu Gau.

"Do you guys want to go to Lo Manthang today?" he asked.

THIRTY-FOUR

"One of my monks has died," said Chokyi Nyima Rinpoche when he called me one evening. "If you have time, can you come out and see him?" This was about as direct as Chokyi Nyima Rinpoche ever was with me. Since he rarely called me to come out to the monastery, especially in the evening, I knew I needed to go.

Namdrol, Chokyi Nyima Rinpoche's secretary, met me in front of the monastery. He led me to a second-floor room in the older wing. The deceased monk had been the chant master for all the ceremonies in the monastery, an important position. I didn't know why he had died—he wasn't very old, mid-fifties, and if he'd been ill, I hadn't been asked to see him.

We entered his small, square room. The first thing I noticed was that there was no odor at all in his room; the room smelled fresh and sweet. Since most of the monks did not have easy access to hot showers, this was unusual in itself, quite apart from the fact that there was a dead body lying on the bed, wrapped in dry white muslin cloth. No fluids had apparently leaked out of his body. Namdrol unwrapped the body so I could see it. The face of the dead monk looked relaxed and composed—not sunken in any way. The skin tone was good—when I pinched the skin, it quickly went back to its original position, instead of having the doughy texture ordinarily seen in dead people. His limbs were easy to move; there was no rigor mortis. The only sign that something wasn't right was that the very tips of his fingers had begun to atrophy, looking slightly yellow with tinges of black at the very tips, as if he had been frostbitten.

"How long has he been dead?" I asked.

Namdrol stopped to consider. "It's eight days now."

I wasn't ready for that. It didn't seem possible. It was springtime in Kathmandu, with daily temperatures reaching into the high 70s and low 80s. How could the body have not started to decompose in eight days? Bodies usually start to decay within hours.

I went upstairs to talk to Chokyi Nyima Rinpoche. "How can this be?" I asked him.

"He's resting in meditation."

"But he's not alive," I said.

"The mind doesn't die," replied Rinpoche.

"But why is the meditation going on so long? Why doesn't his mind just leave his body?"

"Actually, he was an extremely good practitioner. He was our *Umtse*, our chant master. He led the chanting at all our pujas. He was very good at visualization practice. His mind is now resting in meditation, as he visualizes himself as the deity."

I tried to take that in. From a Buddhist point of view, it wasn't a miracle; it was a reflection of having achieved a high degree of awareness in meditation. Although the fact that this monk had not shown any signs of decomposing for eight days seemed unbelievable to me, to a high lama it was a sign of remaining undistractedly in practice. It was a good sign that he was able to meditate with such stability after death. I would later learn that a practitioner with an even higher realization would not have remained in this stage of meditation for so long.

The next day I insisted that Prativa, my partner at CIWEC Clinic, go out and see the monk. Although raised as a Hindu, she tended to be a skeptic about spiritual matters. However, after viewing the body—now nine days dead—she could offer no scientific explanation for how the corpse could remain in that condition.

On the eleventh day, the monk's meditation must have ended, for his body suddenly leaked fluid, the tissue firmness collapsed, and he began to smell. Chokyi Nyima Rinpoche said it was now time to take him for cremation.

The body remaining in this state of suspended decomposition is called *tukdum* in Tibetan. It's not considered uncommon, but it's rarely been observed by outsiders. I may have been one of the first Western doctors to ever see this. Since then, there has been a growing interest in trying to document a genuine case, and film the body, but it's not easy to catch the right circumstances, and the Tibetan lamas are always reticent to promote events that seem to confirm supernatural circumstances. They don't want people to get distracted by what seems like magic until—like me—they are willing to try to understand and accept what they are seeing.

Although this was a remarkable event, I saw it as a continuation of the teachings that I had been receiving. If the mind is separate from the body but connected during life, then there can be different ways that it disconnects from the body. In fact, years later, Namdrol—Chokyi Nyima Rinpoche's administrative assistant, who had shown me the body—underwent *tukdum* himself after he died, remaining fresh for six days in very hot summer temperatures, observed by dozens and dozens of friends and monks, Westerners, Nepalis, and Tibetans.

Nonetheless, I wasn't that distracted by seeing or hearing about this. The one miracle that meant the most to me was the extraordinarily unshakeable and profound compassion and wisdom of my closest teachers. The truth of what I had discovered in Nepal was that human nature *is* perfectible. Or to express it in Buddhist terms, the obscurations surrounding our already perfect Buddha nature can be purified and removed. The point of Buddhist teaching is that every sentient being has this potential—the potential to overcome the endless cycle of suffering that we experience due to ignorance of our true nature. What brings this possibility to life is the chance to meet living examples. Tulku Urgyen Rinpoche and Chokyi Nyima Rinpoche were the proof that what they taught could be accomplished. In all my years in Nepal, it was their living example that was the true miracle. The rest was just icing on the cake.

THIRTY-FIVE

And then, all too soon, things changed.

"Jane called this morning," said Wendy. "Tulku Urgyen Rinpoche died last night."

I was in Sikkim to teach a first-aid course to trekking guides, and Wendy was the American woman who had organized the event. She looked anxiously and compassionately into my eyes to see how I would take this news. I felt a sudden chill. It was too soon, in my mind. I would never see him again.

Before I had left Nepal, I had gone up to check on Tulku Urgyen Rinpoche. His heart problems had gradually grown more severe in the past several months. He was on maximum medication, but still having intermittent chest pain, sometimes at rest. Eleven years had passed since his heart attack, and he was now seventy-six years old. He told his students that most of the lamas from his part of Eastern Tibet only lived to be sixty. The reason he had lived so much longer, he said, was due to the care of Western doctors treating his heart disease and insulin-dependent diabetes.

None of his medical concerns affected his unfailing kindness to everyone he met. He was so precious to everyone around him that they were perhaps over-protective. They didn't want him to walk, but he wanted to get up from time to time and walk on his porch outside his room and look at the exquisite view over Kathmandu Valley. One day while I was visiting him, I helped him up, over the protests of the nuns who watched over him, and we walked together around the porch. He held my hand the whole time and gave me a conspiratorial squeeze to let me know he appreciated my giving him this glimmer of freedom.

Wendy took my arm. "Are you alright?" she asked. I must have been just staring blankly, reminiscing. "I didn't want to tell you before your lecture this morning. I hope that was okay."

"I'll be okay," I said. I was trying to put up a brave front, but I felt numb. I thought about Tulku Urgyen Rinpoche—his kindness to me in explaining the teachings over and over again, his unbelievably direct meditation instructions, his advice on the clinic, my career, my life.

"This is what Tulku Urgyen has always tried to teach," I finally said. "Impermanence." Impermanence is easy to say, harder to live up to. These are the times when you find out whether you have been able to take impermanence to heart or not.

I had a three-hour workshop to teach. I thought about the scene taking place at Nagi Gompa. Chokyi Nyima Rinpoche and his brothers would all be there. I wanted to go back right away, but I felt that I was obligated to do the teaching that I had come to do.

I taught my workshop that afternoon. The group of aspiring guides that I was teaching had not done much trekking, and as a result, they seemed to be only half interested in what I was saying. They hadn't been out in the mountains enough with clients to know that emergencies can happen. Hopefully, it would prove useful to them as they gained more experience. In contrast, whenever I taught Sherpa trekking guides in Nepal, they were extremely focused and receptive. They had all seen many accidents and illnesses among trekkers, and always wanted to improve their knowledge and skills.

The next day, I rode in a Jeep back to the Nepal border. At the border crossing, the driver got out to take my passport to the immigration officials. An old man, toothless, unshaven, and reeking of alcohol and body odor, came to my window and asked me for money. I ignored him, but he yelled loudly, gesturing with his arms, stumbling. It felt awkward at first, but the more he carried on, the calmer I felt, a kind of blissful detachment that I couldn't explain. Even after the driver returned and we continued onward, this sense of calm persisted.

Back at home, late in the afternoon, I had to decide whether to go up to Nagi Gompa that evening to see Tulku Urgyen and Chokyi Nyima Rinpoche or wait until they came down the next morning. I decided not to intrude. The next day I telephoned Greg from my home. He was my colleague at the CIWEC Clinic, and also a student of Tulku Urgyen Rinpoche. He had been at Nagi Gompa when Tulku Urgyen Rinpoche died. He described the events to me.

Around two in the morning on that last day, Tulku Urgyen woke up and appeared sweaty and uncomfortable, although he didn't complain. It looked as if he were having a heart attack. He remained in bed that morning, propped up on pillows. That evening, he sat up and arranged himself cross-legged in a meditation pose. He stared into space, exhaled once, uttering the Tibetan syllable "Ah," and died. After a brief effort to resuscitate him, they allowed him to continue to sit upright in a meditation pose. His skin did not sag, and his face still looked alive. He remained like that for twelve hours. Then fluid was seen running from his nostrils, his skin suddenly began to sag, and he started to resemble a corpse. His body was packed in salt, still in the upright, cross-legged position.

As I listened to Greg, tears finally came to my eyes. I started crying, and Matthew, who was sitting in the living room with me, couldn't believe it. He had never seen me cry in his five years, and he thought I was just pretending, and he started to laugh. Then he saw that it was real, and he came over to me with concern on his face.

"I'm okay, Matthew. Don't worry. I'm just sad about Tulku Urgyen dying," I told him.

He put his hand on my forearm. "That's okay," he said. "We still have Chokyi Nyima." That struck me as an incredible thing for a five-year-old to say.

I drove my motorcycle out to the Ring Road the next morning to meet the truck carrying Tulku Urgyen's body, and all five of his sons, as they headed towards the monastery in Boudhanath. People lined the road, scattered at first, then forming a solid line that grew to multiple rows deep as we approached the turn-off to Boudhanath at Chabahil. The crowd had spilled into the street, and the large Tata truck had to creep along as people threw katas onto the truck one after the other, until it looked like it was covered with snow. People pressed their hands together in the namaste gesture and bowed, tears spilling out of their eyes and streaking their cheeks. I tried to maneuver my motorcycle through the crowd, but finally, I could no longer part the throngs of people, and I abandoned it by the side of the road and walked next to the truck. We were still two or three miles from the monastery. I was filming with a video camera, and I noticed that the mountains were clearly visible, the atmosphere starkly clear like it used to be. There wasn't a single cloud in the sky. *It's lucky to have such a nice day*, I thought.

In the days after Tulku Urgyen Rinpoche died, my meditation practice felt surprisingly easy. I could relax spontaneously into a state of awareness beyond thought. The improvement was so noticeable that I went out to see Chokyi Nyima Rinpoche to ask him about it.

"When a great master dies, his mind is able to mingle with the minds of his students for a period of time," he said. "It gives you a glimpse of how your mind can be with more practice."

"Wow," I said. "That really seems true." That explained the sudden feeling of calm and bliss when I was trying to relax when the beggar confronted me at the border.

"I've been wondering," I asked, "were there any special signs that appeared when Tulku Urgyen died?"

Chokyi Nyima Rinpoche replied, "When a great meditator dies, there can be signs that appear in the sky, or in the room where his body is kept. These signs consist of rainbows in an otherwise clear sky, or other lights and symbols that can appear." He paused. "But when the greatest masters die, there are no signs like that. Instead, the sky becomes completely clear and cloudless, with no pollution or dust."

"I've heard about the rainbows and other symbols, and I thought these were the ultimate signs of the passing of a great master," I said.

"These types of manifestations are still within the relative realm," said Chokyi Nyima Rinpoche. "Cloudless sky and clean air, free from dust, is the ultimate manifestation of the mind of a great meditator as it leaves the body."

"My meditation has been so much easier since he died," I said. I described to him my experience of bliss at the border while confronting the drunken beggar.

"Yes," he replied. "If you have a connection with a great master like Tulku Urgyen, then when his mind departs his body, it mingles with all of his students' minds. You can recognize your mind essence more easily for a while."

So, it hadn't been a coincidence that the mountains had stood out so brilliantly while I was filming, or that my meditation had gotten easier. The sky stayed completely clear and cloudless for three more days. On the evening of the third day, I noticed a tiny cloud appear over Shivapuri, where Tulku Urgyen had spent the last twenty years of his life. In my entire time living in Nepal, I had never seen such a continuous stretch of cloudless weather.

Before he died, Tulku Urgyen taught me what it means to practice nonmeditation. When you first start meditating, the day is divided into the time you spend in the meditation session, and the rest of the day, optimistically referred to in Tibetan Buddhism as "the time between sessions." As one's practice gets more natural and more stable, the distinction between a meditation session and the rest of one's time grows less. One can just let the mind rest in thought-free awareness, and operate from that state of mind, meeting people, answering questions, eating meals, and even sleeping. No longer practicing meditation in specific sessions, but still practicing continually, is called nonmeditation. In Tulku Urgyen's case, not only did his nonmeditation practice continue throughout his lifetime, but now we were seeing a sign of the power of his clear mind even after the death of his body.

Tulku Urgyen Rinpoche's preserved body sat in the main shrine room for forty-nine days. I went out two or three nights a week and sat in the shrine room doing meditation in the large hall with just a few other people, effortlessly experiencing the same calm awareness that I had been feeling on and off since Tulku Urgyen died. Finally, after seven weeks, Tulku Urgyen Rinpoche's body was placed in a specially-built stupa in the west courtyard of the monastery and cremated. All of the remaining living Tibetan masters in Nepal gathered to perform the cremation ceremonies. Hundreds of people crammed the balconies around the courtyard, while thousands more waited outside. Horns and drums and chanting filled the air continuously as the fire caught and grew hot enough to make my cheeks burn, even though most of the flames were held in by the brick stupa. A large column of black smoke rose into an empty blue sky.

THIRTY-SIX

All doctors want to make their patients better. In critical situations, we desperately want to save their lives. The safest long-term way to do this is to acquire a lot of knowledge, skill, and confidence, and to apply them when they count. But one can't know everything, and there may even come a time when confidence in one's knowledge can be one's downfall. Sometimes, when facing a difficult problem, it's better to be lucky than smart. It's also kind of scary to have to say that.

Here's an example. In the early 1990s, a forty-three-year-old British woman named Sarah came in with two days of fever and headache after six weeks of travel in India with her twenty-three-year-old daughter. They had just arrived in Kathmandu the day before. Her daughter had taken all her pre-travel vaccines, but Sarah had relied only on homeopathy. After ruling out malaria with a blood test, it looked like Sarah probably had typhoid fever. But she didn't want to take antibiotics if we weren't sure, so she waited two more days. Finally, feeling much worse, she started on an antibiotic called ciprofloxacin, the treatment for typhoid fever. That night she vomited for the first time, but her fever disappeared overnight.

The next morning, it was clear why her fever had gone. It wasn't because of the antibiotic. She didn't have typhoid fever. One look at her was enough to prove that. Her eyes were deep yellow, and her urine proved to be dark brown. She had hepatitis A. The disease causes fever, headache, and nausea for five days, and then the fever suddenly goes away as jaundice appears. Hepatitis A is a mild disease in children that confers life-long immunity, which is why it's not considered a health problem among people born in resource-poor countries. However, if you miss having it as a child, and get it as an adult, it's a severe disease. You are destined to feel sick for one or two months, with nausea, severe weakness, loss of appetite, and sometimes horrendous itching. Rarely, it becomes "fulminant" and can lead to coma and death. It was once prevented with gamma globulin shots every four months, but now there is a vaccine that is 100% effective at preventing the disease—if you take it.

There's no treatment for hepatitis A. All you can do is rest. That night, Sarah vomited again, and her daughter, alarmed, called during the night to say, "My mother isn't always making sense when she talks." I saw her first thing the next morning and was relieved to see that she wasn't confused, even though her speech and thinking were a little slower than they should have been. I ordered a blood test to determine how damaged her liver was.

Looking to be reassured by the test, I was alarmed to find that her liver damage was severe. She was becoming one of the rare travelers with fulminant hepatitis. There was a good chance that she would slip into a coma and die. Three of the five previous patients I had seen with fulminant hepatitis had died. Her best hope lay in being flown to Bangkok, where they have excellent intensive care. It was too late to get her on the one flight per day to Bangkok, but I contacted her evacuation insurance company to try to arrange her flight out the next day. Unfortunately, they didn't want to fly her to Bangkok, but instead to Delhi, which, in those days, offered little more than what was available in Kathmandu. I was waiting to talk to the insurance company again to try to change their minds when I got a call from a friend.

Bradley Connor was a gastroenterologist in New York and one of the top travel medicine doctors in the world. I looked at my watch—if it was 4:00 p.m. in Kathmandu it was around 6:00 a.m. in New York. What was he doing calling me so early?

He later told me that he had just gotten a sudden strong feeling that he needed to call me at that moment. We were planning on hosting a travel and wilderness medicine conference in Jackson Hole the following summer, and he did need to talk to me about that, but it wasn't urgent. In any case, at that moment, his call was a blessing for me. Gastroenterologists are the specialists for liver disease. We ran through the options, which were few, and he agreed that evacuating her to Bangkok was her best hope. Then he mentioned something I had never heard of. "Watch out for hypoglycemia," he said, referring to dangerously low blood sugar. I'd only ever seen severe hypoglycemia in people on insulin—I'd never encountered it in other conditions. The liver helps control sugar output for the body, and when it shuts down, sugar levels can fall to a dangerous degree.

Just as I got off the phone with Brad, Sarah's daughter appeared in the doorway of the office that the doctors shared. I invited her in. She sat down across from me.

"Is my mother going to be alright?"

That was a tough question to have to answer right at that moment. I was pretty sure that her mother was not going to be alright. But there was a chance that she could pull through, and there was no point in sharing my sense of dread with her daughter. Mustering an optimism that I didn't feel, I said, "I think she'll be alright." Was I lying? As Chokyi Nyima Rinpoche once told me, "Is it lying if you say something you think is true, and it turns out differently? If you say someone is going to die, because you think it's true, and they don't die, did you lie?" Maybe she *would* be alright.

"She's pretty sick," I told her, "but we're going to do all we can to make her better." Before I could worry about whether she believed me or not, a nurse yelled down the hall.

"David, come quickly! We need you."

I rushed the short distance to Sarah's room. She was unconscious and having seizures. These were classic signs of end-stage brain damage from liver failure. However, they were also signs of severe hypoglycemia. If Brad had not called me moments before, I would have resigned myself to the fact that she was dying from hepatic encephalopathy, and there was nothing we could do. Instead, having been made aware that she could be low on blood sugar, I ran to our pharmacy downstairs and grabbed an emergency bottle of 50 percent glucose, the strongest concentration of glucose that can be injected safely.

To get the sugar into her body, we needed to start an intravenous line. Sarah's veins had been thin and difficult to thread when she first came into the clinic—now her few good veins were no longer useable because we had used them to draw blood. Our nurse tried to thread a vein on her forearm, but she couldn't do it. I took over and tried threading one of the thin veins on the back of her hand, but the needle kept sliding off the side of the vein without penetrating. She was still seizing, her limbs flailing and shaking, and two nurses, using all of their strength, could barely hold her arm still. I gave up on one hand and started to move the tourniquet to the other arm just as the room plunged into darkness.

The electricity had gone out, as it frequently did at random times. The nurse grabbed the flashlight that we kept in each room just for this reason.

Sarah continued seizing, her eyes rolled up, her breath coming in harsh, loud gasps. The flashlight, with Indian-made batteries, cast only a dull light with shadows that made finding a vein even harder.

Then I remembered that Pavel Petrov, the Russian Embassy doctor, was downstairs seeing patients in our clinic. He took care of the Russian Embassy staff by day but came to our clinic one or two afternoons a week to practice alternative medicine, his true passion. He had told me, however, that he started his career as a pediatric oncologist—a child cancer specialist. Children with cancer need to have intravenous injections of chemotherapy regularly. He would have experience hitting tiny veins in a squirming arm.

Dr. Petrov was a big, handsome, gentle bear of a man, with a clean-shaven face and prominent jaw. Before 1990, he would never have been allowed to come to work in our clinic, but *glasnost,* the thawing of relations with Russia, had changed that. The nurse ran to get him. He came into the room and sat on the bed as a nurse held the flashlight and I struggled to hold Sarah's arm. After a few long moments, he managed to slip a tiny butterfly catheter into a vein. Pavel held her arm down while I carefully connected the full syringe of glucose to the end of the catheter and pushed the plunger.

Sarah instantly stopped seizing and woke up. She knew who she was and where she was. It was like a miracle. No, it wasn't *like* a miracle. I'd experienced a miracle. A miracle that Brad had called me, that Pavel was in the clinic, and that it truly was hypoglycemia and not end-stage encephalopathy.

I turned around and saw Sarah's daughter standing in the doorway of the room, her arms hanging limply at her side. I met her eyes. "That must have looked bad," I said. "But she's going to be okay now. Don't worry."

Delicately, I wrapped tape around the butterfly needle to hold it in place. I hooked up an intravenous bottle with more glucose, and we fed her sweet drinks. We transferred her to the Tribhuvan University Teaching Hospital where they had enough staff to stay up and watch her all night. But after a few hours of monitoring her, I knew she was going to be alright.

I drove her to the hospital in my car, and as I headed home through the deserted streets, I couldn't help feeling uneasy about what had happened. I could so easily have failed to save her. The extraordinary coincidence of Brad's call was difficult to explain. Why had he called at just that moment, so early in his day? I had been lucky. Better to be lucky than smart. However, I'd been studying Buddhist philosophy too long to just let it rest at that.

THIRTY-SEVEN

Chokyi Nyima Rinpoche discussed luck on many occasions. Luck is a term that describes the result, not the cause. It is defined in the dictionary as "good fortune, considered as the result of chance." It's also described as "a force that operates for good or ill in a person's life." However, as Chokyi Nyima Rinpoche pointed out, from a logical point of view, if luck is a force for good or bad, it still has to have a cause. If luck is said to be just the result of chance, it would mean that whatever happens to us is due to random circumstance. In this particular case, either a force had operated for this patient's benefit, or elset an improbable string of random chances happened to come together. Was it Sarah's good luck that she had survived? Or my good luck at not having to watch her die? Or was it both?

While the episode with Sarah was ultimately a marvel, it also shook my confidence. I thought I knew a lot about treating these diseases, but I had missed something critical. What other gaps were there in my knowledge that I didn't know about? My lack of knowledge about the risk of hypoglycemia in hepatitis was a gaping hole in my knowledge. The patch that plugged that hole arrived just minutes before I needed it. Which was cutting it a little close. I saw that as *my* good luck.

What about Sarah's luck? She was fortunate that she got sick after she came to Nepal, where she could seek care in our clinic. Nonetheless, without

Brad's phone call, she would have died, horribly and in front of her distraught and helpless daughter. We would have blamed her death on her decision not to take the hepatitis A vaccine. Was this just an example of how random life can be, or was it something more? That was the question I was grappling with.

I got home and got into bed with Jane, who woke up and asked me if everything was alright. I told her what happened. I was tired, but I couldn't go to sleep right away. I lay in bed thinking. The question of *why* things happen has fueled philosophy and religious debate throughout the ages. Sometimes things appear hopeless and turn out well. Sometimes things are going great, and there is a sudden catastrophe. I returned to the question of the force behind luck.

The physical world is ruled by a law of cause and effect. For an object to move, a force must be exerted. Each moment of existence is completely dependent on the moment before. Everything that we observe has a prior cause. However, in trying to understand our own lives, we are often unable to trace the cause of events.

Buddhist philosophy contains a belief in a law of cause and effect that impacts our lives. This is treated as a natural law, one that does not require the intervention of a higher being. The term for this law is "karma," which means "action." For every action that we take, physical or mental, a subsequent effect is generated. What makes this law difficult for us to observe, most of the time, is the fact that these subsequent effects are often delayed, spanning years or lifetimes, too long a time for us to make the connection ourselves.

Chokyi Nyima Rinpoche told me, "If you want to know why something is happening to you in the present, it's due to the things you did in your past lives. If you want to know what will happen to you in the future, look to your present state of mind." All of our actions stem first from thoughts that arise in our minds, so our state of mind is the key to generating karma. Only when our mind is resting in its natural state is karma not generated. Our natural state is enlightened, beyond karma. Good karma results in less suffering and more favorable conditions for spiritual practice, but the ultimate goal of practice is to transcend the level of existence that is driven by karma. Even with good karma, wherever we are born will still be subject to the four sufferings of birth, old age, sickness, and death. If we can transcend karma, we can then act for the benefit of all other sentient beings with profound compassion and wisdom. Those two qualities are intrinsic to our natural state of mind. Since people cannot rest continually in their natural state until they have practiced for considerable time and achieved stability, we are encouraged to consciously cultivate virtuous thoughts and actions and avoid causing harm to others. That's why His Holiness the Dalai Lama said, "If you can't help people all the time, then at least refrain from hurting them."

"The main problem with understanding karma," Tulku Urgyen taught me, "is that the effects of our actions are delayed. If karma happened instantly, there is no question that everyone would behave perfectly. Every negative action would cause instant suffering, and every positive action would bring great joy and happiness. It is because the effects of karma are delayed that we can't see the connection."

He went on to say that every thought or action produces a consequence in our mind stream. It is like a seed that is destined to germinate and grow at a later time. Just as each blossom produces a seed that can only grow into that particular flower, a discrete thought or action produces a seed that can only ripen in one way. And like a real seed, it can only germinate when the circumstances are right, such as when it encounters the right amount of soil, moisture, and light. Once it starts to grow, the seed has no choice but to grow into the flower it is destined to be. Just as a tulip seed cannot produce a cactus plant, a virtuous action cannot result in future suffering.

It seems that "luck" is just a word we use to describe circumstances we can't otherwise explain. Karma is a word that can help to explain why good things and bad things happen in our lives. But understanding karma is not easy. Chokyi Nyima Rinpoche told me that the Buddha was asked to explain karma, and he replied: "I teach about emptiness, which is difficult to understand. However, compared to emptiness, karma is *really* hard to understand."

The advantage of *trying* to understand karma—or any explanation for why things happen the way they do—is that when painful events happen, we are in a better position to accept them and deal with them, like the Tibetans who shrugged off their twenty years of suffering at the hands of the Chinese. The world that we are born into—pleasant and enjoyable, or harsh and difficult— may be the result of our actions in past lives. How we steer our current life will help determine the world that we inhabit in the future. Moment by moment we fashion our future, which is why Buddhists learn to be extremely careful both with their behavior and in monitoring their mental state. If, perhaps, in a past life we have been conscientious in wanting to help other people, the right message could arrive in some future life—at exactly the right moment—to help save someone's life.

How did I end up living and working in Nepal? Was it because I started reading about Everest expeditions at age twelve? Learning to climb mountains a year later? The lecture in medical school? The doctor during my internship who sent me a brochure about a mountain medicine course—

the first one ever offered in the U.S.—that led me to meet Peter Hackett and get appointed to work at Pheriche? The inability to choose a specialty and settle down to medical life in the U.S.? The vision that I had in the hot tub at the Hotel Vajra that smoothed the way for me to decide to move to Kathmandu? Even after I moved to Nepal, there was a small event that could have upended everything.

Two months into my life in Kathmandu, I drove my three-year-old white Toyota Corolla station wagon over to Pokhara, a five-hour drive, and went trekking for two weeks up to the Annapurna Sanctuary. Driving back, I was cruising downhill into the Kathmandu Valley, traveling about thirty miles an hour as I approached a tiny village. I slowed down when I saw people by the side of the road. Just as I drew near the first houses, a soccer ball rolled in front of my car. Seconds later a three-year-old boy darted into the road after it, and then froze as he saw my approaching car. I slammed on the brakes, the brakes locked up, and I slid helplessly toward the little boy. The car slowed but continued its slide toward the child, getting so close that I could no longer see him over the front of the hood. All the people of the village, in second story windows and on the street, were frozen in a tableau of horror. I wasn't certain whether I had hit him or not. Then, as I watched, the people suddenly relaxed and went back to what they were doing, and the child trotted after his ball.

I was shaken by the near miss, but as the villagers appeared unconcerned, I finally drove on. I later calculated that if I had reacted two-hundredths of a second slower I would have killed the child, which would have meant my automatic expulsion from Nepal—if I hadn't been beaten to death by the villagers. Although Nepalis are some of the gentlest and most easy-going people one can meet, they can occasionally be triggered into mindless mob violence. This tendency toward vigilantism is even recognized by the law. If you hit a child—or worse, a cow—it is considered okay to keep driving until you reach the nearest police post and then turn yourself in to avoid being killed at the scene by an irate mob. This was a fact that I learned only years later.

In any case, in a length of time that is fifteen times less than the blink of an eye, I was able to stay in Nepal. Was that luck, karma, or just good reaction speed? Even though I often felt lost and irresolute, in retrospect I can see how seemingly unrelated events all conspired to help compel me to Chokyi Nyima Rinpoche's monastery. Where, you'll remember, he came out of his door holding a statue he had been waiting to give to me.

THIRTY-EIGHT

In addition to all the karmic occurrences that seem to have steered my life, there was the mysterious connection between my romantic life and my spiritual life. Whether you see this as karma, or just coincidence, depends on your view. It was always odd, meeting two Canadian women named Jane in the same week, in Kathmandu. It wasn't just their names that were the same, but (in case I didn't make the connection just from their names) they were born in the same city, had the same hair and eye color, and both used their middle name as their first name. If the first Jane's role was to finally get me to address my "romance as religion" belief system, what was the role of the second Jane? And why was it necessary for me to meet her at nearly the same time?

I've now had half my life to contemplate this question, and I still don't have a conventional answer. The coincidences are too great, and the outcome, a lasting and happy marriage, is difficult to write off as "well that's just how it happened." Bedazzled as I was by the first Jane—a model not only of beauty but adventure, humor, and fun, I still found that the second Jane (my future wife) lingered in my mind in a positive way for years, yet not in a way that made me think of trying to find her. Later, when Chokyi Nyima Rinpoche told me that I would get married someday, it never occurred to me that I had already met the woman I would marry.

The way I've come to think about meeting the two Janes is that my two options for romance became two points on a spectrum at that moment. Both types of relationships—sudden and overwhelming (as usual) or gradual and warm and trusting and loving (but never yet experienced)—appeared at the same moment. My mission, if I chose to accept it, was to find out which type of relationship was more likely to lead to lasting happiness. At the time it happened, I was unable to see it that way; my propensity to equate sudden passion with lasting love was too strong. The relationship with the first Jane, in conjunction with meeting Chokyi Nyima Rinpoche, started me slowly on a new path. How long would it take for me to be able to look at love in a new way?

As it turned out, it was four years. The second Jane arrived back in my life at almost the exact moment I was prepared to be with someone like her. I remembered her company as a memorably nice distraction in the dizzying aftermath of meeting the first Jane, but after our nice day together driving out of town for lunch, we had not exchanged addresses or phone numbers, and as a result, we didn't have any contact with each other for the next four years. She even came back to Nepal once during those four years—with her boyfriend—and didn't try to get in touch with me.

I needed those four years to come to grips with my approach to romance, and the firm grip that romantic love had on my sense of happiness. I didn't have another serious relationship during that time. I knew what I needed to do, to try to become more stable within myself, and not project my happiness onto another person based on their attractiveness to me. But despite that dawning recognition, the goal remained just an intellectual aspiration. I still felt that only an instant, total attraction could trigger what I thought of as true love. True love, as I experienced it, arrived as a physical sensation—a pit in my stomach, a slight difficulty in breathing freely, followed by an obsessive interest in the details of the woman's physical appearance. The bulge of a breast, the curve of a neck, the fineness of the skin, a grace of movement. Without these qualities, it didn't feel like "love." When the feelings were reciprocated, I felt transcendence. Even when I had been repeatedly bruised from past affairs, I couldn't recognize any other way to get involved with someone. Try as I would, the concept of gradually falling in love, of moving from friendship to love, eluded me.

I was stuck in a loop. The intense loneliness I experienced in between these affairs could only be assuaged by an equally intense sense of attraction when I started a new one. If I felt only a mild degree of attraction, I still felt mildly lonely. But as the years went by, Chokyi Nyima Rinpoche's teachings were affecting me. His influence and my daily efforts at meditation were helping me feel more content, and feeling more content meant feeling less lonely. For the first time in my life, I was able to at least imagine the possibility of being happy if I lived alone. The concept took a firmer shape during a casual Saturday morning teaching session with Chokyi Nyima Rinpoche. He sat with a group of seven students.

"Some people come to me, and they say, 'Oh, Rinpoche. I'm so lonely. I need to meet someone. What can I do?' And then other people come to me and say, 'Oh Rinpoche, I'm married but now I'm not happy. I don't know what to do—whether to stay together or leave. What can I do?' It's like this a lot—some are unhappy because they are lonely, some are unhappy because they are with someone. What is the main problem?" He paused, waiting for someone to volunteer an answer. No one spoke.

"You need to learn how to be content. How to just be happy. That is the key."

I felt like he was speaking mainly for my benefit. I realized what he was trying to say. It is possible to be unhappy alone, or unhappy in a relationship. The trick was to learn how to simply be happy within yourself, without depending on some outside situation. That is how it could be possible to be happy in or out of a relationship. *Now you know where to look for happiness.* It's all within yourself. But how does that work?

What prevents us from being content within ourselves are the disturbing thoughts and emotions that we experience. We generate a constant string of opinions about our life: *I like this, I don't like this, I don't care about that.* We get attached to those opinions and feel that if we can get the thing we like, we'll be happy, and if we can avoid the thing we don't like, we'll also be better off. And maybe we can distract ourselves from feeling bored when we don't care about anything. Our life plays out like that, always waiting to see how we are going to feel, and never sure what that will be. Even when we get what we want, we don't stay permanently happy. What Chokyi Nyima Rinpoche was emphasizing is that we can learn to just be relaxed within our mind and be able to relate to our world from a place of stability. That was the primary purpose of meditation practice.

I had worked hard on taking that advice to heart. And I think that is the main reason that I could finally see the second Jane, my soon-to-be wife, clearly as a lovely, engaging, thoughtful, adventurous, and fun person, and not just as an object of attraction that could fulfill some need within myself. I hadn't felt floored when I met her, but I had been sufficiently attracted to keep her in my mind for four years. Now that we have been married for many years, how has that played out?

Jane has so many remarkable qualities. She has such confidence in her people skills—she just genuinely likes people, starting with her own family, and radiating out in wide circles. Everyone who meets her likes her. That's an incredible thing to be able to say. She treats everyone the same.

Jane and I were married before either of us met the other's parents. My parents had always made it clear that they wanted me to marry a Jewish girl. When I was in high school, they didn't even want me to date a non-Jewish girl. Somehow, I was only attracted to non-Jewish girls. This created tension when I occasionally brought a girlfriend home and experienced their lukewarm reactions.

A month after our wedding in Kathmandu, we arrived in Portland to meet my parents. It happened to coincide with their fiftieth wedding anniversary, which they were celebrating with a large party at a downtown hotel. Jane would be thrown into the full mix of my parents' friends. It turned out, however, that while I had had a succession of girlfriends and affairs with women from Canada, Jane had a more-than-casual succession of Jewish boyfriends, and even a previous Jewish husband. She experienced my parents' wedding anniversary with the enthusiasm of someone who had suddenly found themselves living in a Woody Allen movie. She loved it.

And they loved her—immediately and unreservedly. My mother later told me that while they would have preferred that I married a Jewish girl, I couldn't have done better than Jane.

Jane and I have talked about what has made our relationship work. Foremost is a sense of trust. We both felt confident that what we saw was what we were going to get. Not much sense of undercurrents, or hidden needs. No strategizing. We travel together particularly well, with a similar sense of problem-solving and taking things in stride. We're comfortable in rough teahouses in the Himalayas, or our favorite hotel in the world, the Mandarin Oriental in Bangkok.

Just as Jane is equally comfortable in both these settings, her looks are also easily adaptable. She can dress up or down with ease and is unselfconscious about her looks. And even though I've been extolling the first Jane's beauty, my wife, Jane, is and always has been, very pretty. Sometimes I look at her and just think that I'm really lucky to be around her. And I still feel that way after more than thirty years.

Before Jane agreed to marry me, she wanted to make sure that I was willing to have a child. Matthew arrived right away, and I thought that was that. It never occurred to me that we would have a second child, but it had occurred to Jane. When Matthew was approaching three, she told me she wanted to have another baby. Not yet imagining what I was up against I said, "You know, I'm really good with just having one," and I thought that would settle it. But I was naïve. I was trying to keep my life as simple as I could, given all that I was already doing. I also wanted to focus on my Dharma practice as much as I could.

Jane wasn't at all ready to capitulate, however. This period created the only real tension that we've experienced as a couple. The impasse was great enough that we sought marriage counseling. We met with an Australian counselor whose husband worked on an aid project in Nepal. She was very pleasant, and we each got to present our point of view, but the net result was a confirmation that we both had pretty fixed attitudes on the topic. However, the counseling sessions finally made me realize *how* fixed Jane's attitude was. I began to feel that I was fighting a battle that I wasn't destined to win. It was far more likely that I could adjust to having a second child than Jane could reconcile herself to just having one.

After agreeing to go along with the program, however, it wasn't happening.

Jane was forty-four by then and getting pregnant was not only more difficult but the chance of having a baby with a problem was greatly increased.

We agreed to consult Chokling Rinpoche, Chokyi Nyima Rinpoche's younger brother, who lived one floor below him in the monastery. Chokyi Nyima Rinpoche was the head of the monastery, but Chokling Rinpoche oversaw all the rituals and led all the pujas that they performed. He was also known for the accuracy of his divinations, or *mos*. Being able to predict the future is not something that most people believe in.

I don't know how it works. I do know that the minds of my teachers are far clearer than ordinary people, and that clarity may allow them to see things in ways that we can't imagine. A *mo* is a way to try to determine a course of action—deciding which would be better, doing this or doing that, finding out whether taking a particular course of action would turn out alright. Tulku Urgyen Rinpoche had done a *mo* to determine whether the clinic would be allowed to stay in Nepal or not. I had learned that it was best to be very careful before asking for a *mo*, as one needs to be prepared to hear the answer, whatever it may be. I'd also seen my teachers decline to do a *mo* for people in certain circumstances.

Chokling Rinpoche came across as a bit shy and withdrawn, although he was just as kind and attentive as the other lamas. He was a bit rotund, with a small mustache, giving him a kind of innocent look that belied the powerful reputation he had for performing rituals. We sat on the floor in front of him and asked our question.

"We would like to know if Jane can still get pregnant, and if she can, would the baby be okay?" He nodded and reached for a small, dark, carved box with slightly asymmetric dice in it. He rolled them out on the table, scooped them up, and rolled them again. He then consulted a text laying nearby. He looked up and said, "Jane can get pregnant, but the baby would not be okay." We asked him what would be wrong with the baby, and he said, "Physically okay, but mentally not right." Our biggest concern had been having a baby with Down's syndrome, and it sounded as if this might be possible.

That's that, I thought, relieved.

I turned to Jane to see how she was taking this news, but it seemed to energize her. "Can we adopt a baby, then?" she asked. *Wait!* I thought. But Chokling Rinpoche was already responding. "Yes. But before you choose which baby to take, you need to check with me. I'll see whether there is a good connection between the baby and yourselves."

Jane walked out happy. She had harbored a desire to adopt a Nepali girl ever since her first visit to Nepal, fifteen years earlier, when she saw a young Nepali girl and fantasized about adopting her, even though she was not yet even thinking of having children. She secretly nurtured that vision all those years but thought it would never come true. Suddenly, it looked like it could become a reality. I realized that I was resigned to having a second child, which sounds bad, but I gradually warmed to the idea and knew it was the only way that Jane could be happy. *And maybe it will be wonderful*, I told myself.

Because we were living in Nepal, we were able to meet pregnant women who knew they couldn't keep the baby for various reasons. We put out the word that we were looking for a child to adopt at birth. We were introduced to one pregnant woman, but when we asked Chokling Rinpoche about it, he said the baby was not the right one for us. We met a second woman, six months pregnant, and when we asked Chokling Rinpoche, this time he said it was a good match, and that we should go ahead with our plans.

First, however, we needed to check whether the baby was a boy or a girl.

Under Nepali law, if you already have a child, you are required to adopt a child of the opposite sex. No one seemed to know the origin of the law, but perhaps because Nepalis favor having male children, they thought that foreigners would only adopt male children if they didn't have this law. We needed to get an ultrasound, which was our first photo of our future child. It's a girl!

The story of our daughter's biological mother is moving, and we have remained in touch with her, and she and our daughter have met several times in Nepal. I would like to share more of this story, but I want to respect the privacy of my daughter and her birth mother. Our clinic took over the prenatal care of the mother, and in the week before the baby was due, the mother said that she was feeling less fetal movement. The obstetrician could detect that the baby's head was not engaged as it should be and suspected that the umbilical cord was wrapped around her neck. She said we had to do a Caesarian section the next morning. I went in to watch the surgery, and when they cut open the uterus, the umbilical cord was wrapped one-and-a-half times around the baby's neck. If the mother had been allowed to go into labor, the baby might have died.

Instead, I was handed a wet infant girl; I took her over to the examination table myself, dried her off, looked her over, and wrapped her up. I walked out into the cold January air to introduce her to Jane and four-year-old Matthew. We stood around for a while, and when we realized that there would be no further checks or paperwork, we drove home with our daughter.

The house staff embraced her as one of their own. Whereas with Matthew, they spoke to him as an infant in English, they spoke to the new baby in Nepali, and called her *Nani*, which means "baby girl." It took us ten days to come up with a name for her. We searched for a name that would straddle her Nepali background and her Western future, giving her some choices when she was older. We came up with Anna Tara; Anna because it's a nice name, and Tara in reference to a female Buddhist deity. She was a lovely, strong-willed child, who grew up to be a lovely and determined young woman. Thwarted in her desire to play soccer by successive anterior cruciate ligament tears in each knee at age fourteen and fifteen, she took to Nordic ski racing as a consolation prize and ended up third in the state of Wyoming in her senior year. She's proud of her Nepali heritage, and even feels that she may have had a genetic advantage over her rivals in ski racing. Her birth heritage is Tamang, an ethnic group notorious for their hardiness.

We left Nepal when she was two, and we didn't realize that she had no memories of Nepal when we talked to her about where she was from. We would read her books about adoption, but she wasn't very interested and didn't seem to relate them to herself. It was clear that she knew she looked different than us, but that didn't seem to bother her. When we told her she was Nepali, she just seemed to accept that.

When she was five, we took her back to Kathmandu for the first time. After a couple of days, she stood on a street corner, looking around her, and had a moment of bursting insight. Having finally absorbed seeing so many people who looked like her, and not like us, she suddenly blurted out, "I get it. I'm Nepali." A pause. "And I'm American. And I'm adopted." And that seemed to settle it for her.

A short time later, back home in Wyoming, she again tried to prove she understood the concept. We had gone to choose a Labrador puppy from a litter of ten. Eight of the puppies were black, but two were chocolate brown. Anna Tara stared at the litter and said, "Look! Those two are adopted."

THIRTY-NINE

It was a thought that had been gestating for several years: *maybe we should move back to the U.S. one of these days.* We had been spending our summers in Jackson Hole, Wyoming, since I married Jane. Then, in 1993, we purchased a small lot in the tiny town of Kelly, about fourteen miles northeast of Jackson, within Grand Teton National Park. Land in Kelly almost never became available. We had caught wind that a seven-lot parcel of land would be listed the next day, and we quickly formed a group of three friends who managed to make a bid on the land before it was even publicly for sale. We ended up with two of the lots, which totaled 100 by 150 feet.

We still weren't sure if Jackson Hole was the right place for us. Having the land was like an insurance policy. If people asked us, "When are you going to leave Nepal?" we still said, "In a couple of years." But we said that every year.

Kathmandu was growing in population at an extraordinary rate. It was now a city of almost a million people, and it seemed that you encountered most of them on the roads during the day. It was getting harder to get outside and get some exercise. Ten years earlier I had found that a lap around the Ring Road was one of the best bike rides in the world. It was a seventeen-mile loop with four moderate hills, phenomenal views of the Himalayas, rolling past rice paddies and small villages. There was almost no traffic in those days. Now it was impossible to consider riding a bike on that route. The road was choked with smoke-belching diesel trucks and buses. Apartments, houses, and shops had completely engulfed the Ring Road. Air pollution in Kathmandu Valley had increased to the point that it was rare to get a clear view of the Himalayas.

In 1993, I hired Prativa Pandey to work at the clinic. She was a remarkable Nepali doctor who had been born in Kathmandu at a time when almost no foreigners had ever visited the kingdom. At age sixteen, she had already started medical school in Delhi. She did her internal medicine residency in the U.S. and then worked for eleven years in Boston as a clinical instructor at Harvard Medical School. She needed to move back to Nepal to help care for aging parents. She heard about our clinic from a doctor in Boston.

Prativa grew into the perfect person to replace me as Medical Director. We had finally solved the problem of permission to run the clinic by becoming a licensed nursing home with foreign investors. Operating within the Nepali system required skills that perhaps only a Nepali could have. Her presence at the clinic was another step toward allowing me to think about leaving Nepal.

In 1996, we began to say, "We'll leave in two years," and meant it. We had decided to move to Kelly. We couldn't resist living in a place with spectacular beauty and wild animals all around, and a community of friends similar to those who lived in Kathmandu. The surprising thing about Jackson Hole was that everyone knew where Nepal was, and most of the people we met had been there. My fifteen years in Nepal made it difficult to consider moving back to Portland, Oregon, for example, where few people had heard of Nepal or knew where it was on a map. Having made this decision, however, I still had to figure out how I could earn a living in Jackson.

I decided that I didn't want to start a family practice and work full-time seeing patients. I had another plan, one that I had fostered for more than eight years. Meditation and spiritual practice had allowed me to be much more compassionate with my patients, and I had started to dream of inviting Chokyi Nyima Rinpoche to the U.S. to teach a group of non-Buddhist doctors and nurses about how it is possible to train in compassion. My plan was to put on the conference, tape record the teachings, and use the transcripts of the recordings to create a book called *Medicine and Compassion*. But none of that would earn a living.

That piece of the puzzle fell into place when I was hired to work for a company called Shoreland that produced expert travel medicine information for health professionals. The salary would allow me to live in Kelly without having to work in family practice, and to have some control over my free time.

For Jane, the transition was back to her world of Exum Mountain Guides and the skiing world she had generously been willing to set aside to live with me in Kathmandu. Skiing was her family religion, and she had remained faithful. She loves to make turns on snow, whether climbing up under her own power for three hours to find untracked powder in the backcountry, or at Jackson Hole Mountain Resort, one of the best ski areas in the world. In the summers she hiked and climbed, going on marathon twenty-mile hikes in a day through the Tetons, or going with one of the Exum Guides to the top of the Grand Teton. She's climbed the Grand about seventeen times.

The time had come. It was late in the afternoon of the last day that I would spend in Kathmandu as an expatriate. We were staying at a friend's house, having sold off or packed up all of our possessions. The next day we would drive to the airport and my fifteen years of living in Nepal would be over. I drove by myself to the house where I had lived for eleven of those fifteen years. It was a little worse for wear after that time, but I could say the same about myself. The walls had water damage in places, and a few chunks of plaster had peeled off. The electrical wires, stapled to strips of wood on the walls, hung loose in places. Our books, clothes, trekking gear, and toys had been packed into large wooden crates. I had grown attached to a handmade wooden desk that I had used for fifteen years and decided to ship that home as well. Earlier that day the crates had been picked up and loaded onto a truck.

I stepped outside and walked around the backyard one last time. In one corner rose a row of tall pine trees, on whose branches groups of noisy spotted owlets would roost, and in the higher branches sat brain fever cuckoos, with their semi-psychotic ascending calls. There was a magnificent fan palm in front of the pines. Bamboo grew in tall clusters by the gate. At the moment, jungle mynahs flitted in and out of the large bougainvillea tree that grew across the front of the house, and a noisy flock of rose-ringed parakeets screeched past the treetops. The landlord had sold the house, and the new owners were going to divide the lot and build two new houses in the backyard for his sons. I would never again see it like this.

I got in my car and drove up the brick driveway through the gate. I turned right and drove down the long lane past the French Ambassador's residence and right again at the Batbatini intersection.

When I had first moved to this neighborhood, I'd bought refrigerated items at a tiny storefront called the Batbatini Cold Store. It earned the designation "cold store" based on having a single refrigerator. Now the entire block was taken up by a five-story department store owned by the same people. I turned left and drove past the little stone Ganesh shrine, streaked with red powder, still jutting improbably into the roadway so that cars had to swerve around it. I drove past Mike's Breakfast, and around the algae-filled pond called Nag Pokhari that had a cobra-headed statue emerging from the middle of the water. I ascended a slight hill up to the Royal Palace.

Just then a shadowy flash of silver-white caught my eye. It was the same elusive phantom that had remained a mystery to me all those years. I had seen it many times over the years, and each time it kind of freaked me out. This time my eyes moved fast enough to catch a fleeting sharp view of what it was. I saw a tight formation of five large white birds, wings cocked backward, coasting, and dipping for a brief second before they turned and disappeared.

I looked up the birds in *Birds of Nepal*. They were night herons, white on their bellies and dark on their heads and backs. They roosted during the day, then flew out at dusk in small groups to hunt for food. Because they were grayish black on top, they were nearly invisible at dusk. But when they turned and caught the fading light at just the right angle, their bright white feathers were illuminated for an instant. Then they swooped again and were gone.

You go through life getting glimpses of truths, unable to recognize them for what they actually are. And then, suddenly, you can.

Jackson Hole

FORTY

Compassion is a quality that is said by Buddhists to be part of our very nature. As a result, it is possible to meet people who exhibit great compassion without being overtly spiritual. Just what the limits of that compassion might be can occasionally reveal themselves in our ordinary lives.

It was my third winter in Jackson Hole. I had flown down to Breckenridge, Colorado, to teach at a winter wilderness medicine course. Afterward, I drove down to Boulder and visited my friend Elliott, who had moved away from Nepal two years before I had. I drove from Boulder to the Denver Airport in plenty of time to catch my flight, checked in, and got my boarding pass. In the terminal, I used the extra time to shop for some presents for Matthew and Anna Tara. When I went to the gate, they told me that they had closed the flight due to weight restrictions flying into Jackson, and I wouldn't be allowed to board. The altitude in Jackson, over 6,500 feet, made it difficult to land when the weather was warm, but I had never heard of closing the flight for weight in the winter. However, they told me there was another flight in an hour, so I would still get home that night. I was just disappointed that I wouldn't get home before the kids went to sleep.

I boarded the next flight, an Airbus 319, which was not very full. While passengers were still loading slowly, I heard a woman say, "Are you alright, sir? Are you alright?" I turned around and saw her gently shaking an older man who appeared to have passed out in his seat, a couple of rows behind me and across the aisle. I immediately got up and went over to him and felt for his carotid pulse. There was no pulse; he was in cardiac arrest.

I unbuckled his seat belt and dragged him from his seat out into the aisle where he could lay flat. I tilted his head back so that he would have an airway, and reached in to remove his false teeth, which had already shifted. I started chest compressions. I had just read an article written by doctors in Seattle that demonstrated that chest compressions alone can be as effective as chest compressions with mouth-to-mouth breathing. A heavyset ground crewman ran in and said, "I'm trained in CPR!" I let him take over the chest compressions, and I went to the man's head, cradling it and tilting it back so that I could see that air was moving in and out of his throat. A flight attendant brought a breathing mask and a bag, but the mask was unable to form a seal over his toothless mouth, so we just kept going with chest compressions alone. There was no automatic defibrillator on the plane.

When I first realized that the man had arrested, I felt a brief pulse of anxiety. I had never faced an out-of-hospital cardiac arrest before, and it had been many years since I had managed a cardiac arrest in a hospital. Then I reminded myself that this is what I had been training for all my life, both in the medical skills, and the sense of compassionate concern that made me want to help. A deep calm settled over me as we worked on the patient. The woman who had noticed his arrest knelt on the floor beside me and held his hand. I glanced over at her. She was profoundly attractive, with long black hair gathered behind her head. Whatever it is that makes a face look sweet, she had it. She had a gentle manner as well, and she began speaking to the man in a wonderfully calm and matter-of-fact voice.

"You'll be alright. Don't worry. We're here. We'll help you."

I remember thinking that another doctor might have been irritated by these seemingly inane remarks made in the face of a medical emergency and shooed her away. Instead, I found her presence comforting. I had never encountered any layperson who felt so confident offering comfort to an unconscious patient in such an extreme situation.

The man himself appeared calm, even in near-death. He occasionally gasped, which made me doubt whether he had actually arrested, but he never had a carotid pulse. He even blinked a few times. His pupils remained small and reactive. These were all signs that our efforts to get oxygenated blood to his brain were working.

I had checked my watch when it all started. Twelve minutes had gone by. The chance that administering an electric shock will bring a patient back to life decreases dramatically after the first six minutes. The flight attendants had little to offer, and one was in the front of the plane crying gently (I found out from her later on that she had just experienced a family tragedy herself). Finally, the emergency medical technicians from the fire department, decked out in bright yellow vests, strode onto the airplane. They walked casually up the aisle, looked down without expression, and walked out without saying anything.

What the—? Then I realized that they must have first wanted to confirm that there was still a patient, and that he had really arrested. They came back, and without a word, lifted him by his arms and legs and dragged him out of the plane. I followed along. They had gone out to set up their gear in the jetway where there was more room to work.

They were professional, if detached. They started an IV, hooked up the monitor, and confirmed that he was in ventricular fibrillation, a fatally chaotic heartbeat that doesn't pump any blood. They shocked him, and a normal heartbeat returned...for a moment. Then he was back into ventricular fibrillation. They gave some drugs and shocked him again. When he did get a heart rate on the monitor, there was still no pulse. This is a sign that although the heart can be stimulated electrically, it can't pump. They kept trying new drugs, then re-shocking him. They were unable to achieve a stable cardiac rhythm that could pump blood. After thirty minutes, if I had been in charge, I would have called off the efforts. There had been no real response, and there was nothing left to try.

However, I wasn't in charge, and the EMTs were bound by protocol. They couldn't declare someone dead in the field. They had to continue CPR and take him to the nearest emergency room. They brought in a stretcher, lifted him onto it, and secured him to it with duct tape so they could carry him down the steep stairs from the jetway to the airfield where the ambulance was parked.

After they took off, people asked me if I thought he would make it. I had to say that I thought not. Some people wept. I talked to the woman who had held his hand. She was with her husband, both in their early thirties, and flying to Jackson to see if it would be possible to live there. She exuded the same sense of calm that she had expressed while trying to comfort the man we were trying to help.

The flight took off and I arrived home late that night. I thought about the event often. If I hadn't been bumped from my first flight, I wouldn't have been there to help. I'm sure that my presence kept things much calmer than they would have been with no strong leader. I often thought about the remarkable young woman. I later told my father that I was glad I was there, and he said, "What difference did it make? He died."

A few weeks later I was opening my mail late at night after a busy day.

There was a letter from United Airlines offering me a $100 flight coupon for having helped on the plane. It was difficult to know how they set these values—I had received a $300 coupon just for being bumped from my earlier flight. I read the accompanying letter, thanking me, etc., when I suddenly felt a chill. They said that the patient was alive and doing well! I couldn't believe it. It made no sense.

The next day I called the airline and spoke to the woman who had written me the letter. She said that the man had apparently recovered in the hospital, and they had even flown his family out to be with him. That detail made it seem real. However, I was still having trouble understanding how it could have happened. She didn't know any other details, but she gave me the number of someone in Denver who might know. That person never returned the several calls I made to him. To this day, I'm not sure if he survived, but I tend to believe that he did somehow. Why would she have written that if he hadn't? And whenever I think about it, I somehow attribute it to the kind woman who held his hand and reassured a dying stranger. Her gentle presence was as if an angel had been there to look after him. If this had been a movie, the director might have included a parting shot of a stray feather peeking out from under her jacket in the back.

Or, as Hemingway wrote, "Isn't it pretty to think so?"

FORTY-ONE

How does the last day of your life begin? Like any other, if you're not already sick. You wake up and then, if you're like me and able to work mostly at home, you try to decide what to do that day. Should I stay home and work on this book? Or should I join Jane and our friend John to go backcountry skiing on Teton Pass?

I know I left you hanging at the end of the prologue. I now want to back up a little bit from that cliffhanger and fill in more detail.

Ten inches of fresh powder overnight pushed my hand to go out skiing. It hadn't snowed in about ten days, and backcountry skiing is about experiencing the pleasure of untracked fresh powder. I got my gear together, bringing extra clothes to deal with the -10 F temperature. We had to take a detour out to the ski resort at Teton Village because Anna Tara was skiing with her school that day and had forgotten her helmet. By the time we made the extra drive, I was hungry and stopped for an espresso and a cold ham and cheese croissant.

Up at the pass, we found a place to park right away, which doesn't always happen, and I was unusually efficient at getting my boots on, grabbing my skis, and heading up the trail. For perhaps the first time that I had skied with Jane and John, I was in the lead and feeling good. My fingers, which often start feeling cold by the time I get my skis on, still felt warm.

The track was not steep as we started out and I strode along easily, occasionally hitting the snow at the side of the track with my pole just to see how much light powder had fallen. I began to notice a slight aching in the backs of both upper arms, like a muscular soreness that could have come from doing a lot of pushups. Except that I hadn't done any pushups that week. It was curious, but as I continued along, the ache moved to my left side, and up my chest into my neck. Not severe, but a noticeable aching. At the same time, I could feel a kind of burning discomfort in my stomach, which I attributed to the espresso/croissant combination.

I like to think that I'm the kind of person who can face reality, so I considered whether any of these symptoms could be caused by a heart attack. It would be unusual to have aching in both arms, although aching in the left arm and chest is common. The chest pain associated with a heart attack is usually slightly left-sided and described as more of a pressure that makes it hard to breathe than a burning discomfort like I was experiencing. Still, I had no other good explanation for what was going on. I continued to skin up the track, with John and Jane behind me. They had connected with three young women who were skiing here for the first time, so they started giving them some pointers as to where to go. I began to slow down, feeling slightly short of breath as the stomach pain became more insistent. They went by me, engaged in chatter, and I didn't say anything.

I had passed a cardiac stress test eighteen months earlier. I had ridden my road bike an average of fifty to a hundred miles a week all summer, sometimes going for fifty-mile rides in a day. Although I knew that neither of these facts precluded having a heart attack, it was still somewhat reassuring. I kept going.

By now, I had crested a small hill and skied past a large electrical transmission tower. I started into the woods. I was now becoming genuinely uncomfortable, and just hoping that the pain would somehow magically stop and I'd be okay. I found myself all alone on the trail, but I carried on, hoping I'd start to feel better, until suddenly I couldn't catch my breath. I was panting sixty times a minute trying to move enough oxygen into my blood and failing. The rapid breathing took all of my strength, and I was no longer strong enough to stand up. I fell over into the deep, soft snow at the side of the trail.

Jane and John were around a corner and out of sight. They likely wouldn't worry about my lagging behind until they got to the downhill portion. There are a lot of reasons for falling behind—just being slow, having trouble with a binding, having to stop to put on or take off more clothing. I was known for doing all those things. Except this time was different. I was completely stranded and helpless. But not yet completely beyond denial.

Which must have been why, when a couple skied by at that moment and slowed to check on me, I refused their help, giving a thumbs-up gesture that belied my actual situation. It was a reflex at the time: if I admitted I needed help, it would mean I was actually in trouble, and I wasn't ready to face that yet.

Instead, I was alone again. Gasping for air. Fighting the pain in my stomach. I knew I had to try to reach Jane on her cell phone. Cell phone coverage on the pass is spotty, and we usually turned off the phones to save the battery. Had she done that yet? I dialed her number.

I've already described how I called Jane and she came back to find me laying in the snow. I still felt like the best thing was to try to get back to the road. But I wasn't physically capable of moving myself at that point.

The arrival of the physician's assistant at that exact moment may well have saved my life. His name is Dave Saurman, and he deserves a mention here. I remain immensely grateful for the calm and kind way he took charge of the situation and initiated the rescue. Suddenly I was able to drop the denial and admit what was obvious to everyone around me: *Yes, I'm having a heart attack. That explains it. I need to get out of here.*

Jane stood above me, and I could see her outlined against the white sky. As she called 911, I worried that the dispatcher might be skeptical and want her to explain why she thought I was having a heart attack. Even if they decided to send help, I wondered if the dispatcher could figure out where we were. However, the dispatcher immediately knew what to do. We had seen the rescue helicopter an hour earlier lifting out two snowboarders who had been stuck overnight on the pass. It turned out that the helicopter and the rescue crew were still at the base of the pass and ready to go.

The aspirin arrived with a well-prepared first aider, which may have also contributed to my surviving. He had to place the aspirin in my mouth himself, as my arms were pinned at my side in the tubular space blanket that had been stuffed with spare jackets.

I was on a thirty-degree slope, with soft, knee- to thigh-deep snow. With their skis off, the rescuers postholed in the deep snow. The slope was too steep for the helicopter to land where I was, so they were going to have to carry me across the slope. The steepness of the grade, along with the deep snow, made it extremely difficult to move me. There was no stretcher available. Dave Saurman phoned back to a friend who was at the parking area on the pass and asked if he could get some more skiers to come and help. Without any further information than "There is a man who might be having a heart attack," about twenty skiers put their skis on and headed out to help. That's Jackson Hole for you.

Ensconced in the space blanket with people standing above me, I couldn't initially see the helicopter when it came overhead. I heard the *thwump thwump thwump* of the rotors and caught a brief glimpse of the helicopter as it hovered briefly above us, and then pulled away to a flat area about a half-mile back towards the road, where it waited for us. That's when one of the rescuers made the comment about needing to stamp out a platform in the snow in case I needed CPR. Rather than being distressed to hear him talk about that, I first had the strange reaction that it would be distasteful to have people do CPR on me. That's the moment that I realized that I could die any second, and it was time to start thinking about how I would want my mind to be if that happened.

I realized that my situation was all or none. Either I would die suddenly on the pass, or I would survive. The moment of death is of critical importance in Tibetan Buddhist training, but we like to think that it will happen at some distant time in the future. Now that moment had suddenly arrived; it was time to apply my training.

I was still shivering uncontrollably, but I didn't feel like I was suffering from the cold. My hands and feet were fine. The rescuers were still trying to figure out how to move my two hundred twenty-pound body across the snow to the waiting helicopter.

The first person from search and rescue arrived carrying a tarp. Ski poles rolled along the edges formed handles that the squad of volunteers could grasp. The situation was still problematic though. The rescuers on the uphill side had to bend way over, while the downhill volunteers had to try to lift me up to their waists, all the while floundering in the deep snow. They could go only a few steps before they had to set me down and regroup.

However, I stopped paying much attention to their efforts, as appreciative as I was. I began to focus on what would happen if I died. I thought about my family—Jane was still there, although outside the scrum of rescuers and I couldn't see her. Anna Tara was skiing at the resort, and Matthew was at school in Olympia, Washington. I thought, *If I don't die, I'll still get to be with them, just like before. If I do die, I'll never see them again.* So, in terms of things to worry about, I chose to think about where I might be headed, rather than what I might end up missing.

I began reciting a phrase that I often repeated to myself. I had even practiced saying this in the brief moment that I was still conscious after I was given an anesthetic for minor procedures, in case I died during the operation. I thought that, at the very least, if I died suddenly, it could be with a virtuous thought on my lips:

May all sentient beings be free from suffering and the causes of suffering
May all sentient beings be happy and have the causes of happiness
I will attain enlightenment for the benefit of all sentient beings

I kept saying it softly to myself, over and over. I decided that it would be a good idea if I tried to meditate, to rest my mind in the recognition of mind nature, if I could. Every minute or so, the rescuers—who couldn't see me at all inside the space blanket tube and tarp—leaned in and asked if I was okay—which really meant, was I still alive. I'd say, "I'm good," but it didn't disturb my concentration. I felt surprisingly relaxed—no thoughts of the past at all, and only thinking about what I could do to focus on the moment of death, should that occur.

The summer before, I had been taught the *phowa* practice by Chokling Rinpoche in a seminar at Gomde, California. Phowa is the practice by which a dying person can eject their consciousness in a positive direction, out the top of one's head, and thus avoid a negative rebirth. A sign that one has assimilated the practice, during the teachings, is that a tiny hole opens in the top of one's scalp, over the central channel. An experienced lama comes around when he senses you might be ready and finds the hole and inserts a stalk of *kusha* grass into your skin, leaving it sticking out from your head. Kusha grass grows tall and thin, like wheat. It's been used for millennia in sacred ceremonies. On the first day, doing the practice, I felt a tingling in my scalp right over the central channel. On the second day, the assistant lama came over, took a close look, and inserted a stalk of grass into a small hole which had opened up in that space. The stem went in deep enough that the stalk of grass stayed in my head until I eventually pulled it out about an hour later. There was no pain, and no bleeding.

It would be possible to be skeptical about this process, so I paid close attention as the lama went around and searched for the open holes. If the hole is not open, it's impossible to just stick a stalk of grass into a person's scalp, especially without causing any pain or bleeding. By the fourth day, all ninety people who had attended the seminar had been able to open the tiny hole.

Now that my death might be imminent, I thought about getting ready to practice *phowa* but decided to leave it as a last resort, if I felt stuck in some way. I realize that these thoughts, while facing the real prospect of dying, may sound strange. I have to admit that I was surprised to find how clearly my mind was dealing with the situation.

Tulku Urgyen Rinpoche told me many times that it's best, if possible, to die while resting in the recognition of your mind, so this is what I focused on, leaving *phowa* on the back burner. He also said that it would be good to try to visualize one's teacher at the moment of death, as thinking of the teacher would remind one of the teachings. Whenever I meditated near Tulku Urgyen Rinpoche, my recognition of mind nature was always clearer and easier to attain, so now I attempted to conjure up a vision of him in my mind, trying to see him in his red robes, sitting cross-legged in his room at Nagi Gompa, where I had so often visited him. While I was thinking of this, a vision of him suddenly appeared, but not the one I was trying to imagine. He was in the sky, standing, wearing a thin, loose-fitting robe that initially was tan but turned sky blue as I watched. The vision remained very stable in my mind. The sky, which in reality was cloudy and snowing, now appeared clear and blue. He just stood there and didn't say anything.

The next step would be to try to merge my mind with his, to open up to his spacious awareness and try to allow the same awareness to occur in my mind. Rescuers continued to ask me if I was okay, and I'd respond, but the vision didn't shift. I started feeling as if I was floating towards the vision, just in my mind. I didn't feel I was leaving my body, but I was definitely drifting towards the vision; a feeling of utter calm and peace suffusing me, no thoughts of the past, present, or future. I felt sure that when my mind reached his, I would die, but peacefully and unafraid.

And then I heard myself say, almost apologetically, "But if it's okay, I wouldn't mind sticking around for a while." It was like I was hesitant to bring it up—like I didn't want to rock the boat. Things were going pretty well, considering that I thought I was about to die; I don't remember consciously forming that thought, it just appeared. But there it was. I remember saying to myself, too embarrassed to say it out loud, wondering if it was true or just an excuse, "Maybe I can still be of benefit to someone."

There was a pause. My gentle floating feeling towards the vision stopped, then reversed. I was moving away, back towards where I actually was. The vision faded.

"How are you doing, Doctor Shlim?"

"I'm good."

The tarp lurched me along the ground. Step-step-step, pause, set me down. The rescuers were focused, calm, and strong, and I deeply appreciated their compassion. They were scared, I later found out. They *really* didn't want to see me die.

I remained calm, but more in touch with my situation. A sled finally arrived with additional members of the search and rescue team who had skied in. They had oxygen, and the flow of enriched air slowed my breathing and made me feel warmer. I remembered that I had the only keys to our car in my pocket, and I reached down to get them and give them to Jane, who would have otherwise been stranded after I left.

I was surprised to find out that I would be sitting up in the helicopter for the short flight to the hospital in Jackson. The paramedic sitting across from me took my arm and started an intravenous line in the back of my hand. I hadn't ridden in a helicopter since the last time I rescued a trekker in Nepal. I had flown dozens of rescues in my fifteen years there, swooping in to pick up the ill and injured, taking them from a desperate situation in a remote Himalayan valley to safety, comfort, and medical care in Kathmandu, usually only about an hour away. Now it was my turn.

Six minutes later, I landed on the roof of the hospital and was transferred to a gurney. I briefly worried that they might cut my ski pants off (it's not easy to find good ski pants), but this was Jackson Hole, and the nurses unbuckled my heavy ski boots and got me undressed without giving it a thought. The young ER doctor was alarmed by my EKG: "You've got tombstones!" he blurted out, and then appeared embarrassed at using the black humor term for a distorted wave that goes straight up, rounded at the top and straight down again. Like a tombstone. The meaning is clear—these tombstones only appear in the worst kind of heart attack, one that often doesn't end well.

I could see the monitor from where I lay. And then it struck me: the pattern on the monitor looked exactly like Tulku Urgyen's EKG twenty-eight years earlier at the moment he was having his heart attack. That thought gave me a sudden sense of recognition and a smile. My incredulity at that time that he could be having a massive heart attack without fear had led me to explore how that might be possible. And now I was experiencing the exact same heart attack—the widow-maker—without fear, and having had Tulku Urgyen Rinpoche appear to me in a vision when I really needed him. Although I had several more hours to go to get transferred to Idaho Falls and undergo coronary catheterization and the placement of a stent, I still didn't feel afraid.

The weather was too socked in for the helicopter to fly me back over the mountains. Jane flew with me in a fixed-wing plane to Eastern Idaho Regional Medical Center. My chest pain had eased up in the ER in Jackson after getting a clot-dissolving drug, but that wore off en route, and my chest pain returned. The ambulance from the airport to the hospital in Idaho Falls turned on its lights and sirens and ran me to the emergency room.

Later that night, after receiving two stents to hold open my left anterior descending coronary artery, I rested in bed in the comfortable coronary care unit. My recurrent thought was wishing I could be in Chokyi Nyima Rinpoche's chambers, just sitting and watching him—as I had done so often—greet a long line of visitors requesting advice or blessings.

I had a private room in the coronary care unit, and the nurses and doctors could not have been nicer to me. After only three nights in the hospital, I was discharged home. I was sitting in the car while Jane drove me back over Teton Pass to Jackson when a newspaper reporter from the local paper reached me on my cell phone. I had been front-page news after my rescue, and he wanted to know how I was doing. It gave me the chance to express my gratitude to my rescuers, a fortuitous combination of volunteer skiers and trained search and rescue personnel. The selflessness with which the skiers threw themselves into my rescue had touched me deeply. I said, "I'm very lucky. One bad thing happened that day, and then a lot of good things happened after that."

I managed to call Chokyi Nyima Rinpoche the next day and have a brief phone conversation. He told me that the entire monastery had chanted three days of prayers for me as soon as they heard that I was in trouble. Despite a poor phone connection, he was very reassuring. "Don't worry," he said. "Everything will go smoothly now."

I slowly recovered my strength. At first, I could only walk out from my house on the snow-packed roads for five minutes at a time, but each day I walked a little further, getting to the bridge over the fast-flowing Gros Ventre River that runs through our small village. When I turned around, I could see the Teton Range illuminated in bright relief against often clear blue skies.

Just three weeks after my heart attack, Jane drove me down to Park City, Utah, to give a previously planned talk at the Wilderness Medical Society winter meeting. It was a reunion of old friends among the faculty, including Peter Hackett. Since my friends were of a similar age, they asked a lot of questions about how I happened to have a heart attack. I had a hard time walking up even small hills, and when I gave my talk, I needed to hold on to the lectern for balance.

I wanted an opportunity to talk to one of my teachers in more detail about the experience I had on the pass. To my great surprise, Phakchok Rinpoche e-mailed me and asked if I wanted him to stop in Jackson Hole on his way to visit some relatives in Minneapolis. It had been three months since my heart attack. He is the son of Chokling Rinpoche, and the nephew of Chokyi Nyima Rinpoche. He was thirty years old, but I first met him when he was five years old. He'd already been recognized as a reincarnate lama and was wearing robes. He'd crawled into my tent while I was camping at Nagi Gompa during a retreat with Tulku Urgyen Rinpoche and hung out comfortably for a while, looking at my things. He hadn't learned English yet, and I didn't speak Tibetan, but I'd thought the visit was significant enough that I'd taken a photo of him. At age twenty-two he finished his formal Buddhist education and started to travel to teach. Jackson Hole was one of the first places he taught. He had come every year for the past six years.

When he arrived, April was underway and winter was losing its grip, with gray patches of sagebrush poking through the aging winter snowpack. He stayed at my house and listened to my story with great interest. He's an utterly unique Tibetan Rinpoche—fluent in English, with a large, fluid body and a malleable face that serves him well as he imitates people in various stages of happiness and distress to illustrate his points. He's kind, but strong, and says what he thinks. When I described my heart attack experience to him, he treated it very matter-of-factly, stating that many practitioners have had this type of experience as they approach their death. The fact that I had a vision of Tulku Urgyen Rinpoche derived from a strong karmic connection, as well as the efforts I had made to practice. He also picked up on the fact that the seemingly casual thought I had while approaching my moment of death ("But if it's okay...") had saved my life. If that thought had not arisen, he said, I would have died. Instead, it showed that I valued this precious human life and thought that I could still be of benefit to myself and others by being here.

Years later, Mingyur Rinpoche, the youngest brother of Chokyi Nyima Rinpoche, described in his book, *In Love with the World*, his much more elaborate experience of near-death. He came close to dying of severe gastroenteritis while pursuing his dream of becoming a wandering beggar. He was so sick that he felt certain that he was going to die—in fact, he was sure he had died. Then he wrote, "What happened next is hard to relate. I did not decide to come back. Yet I came back. This did not happen independent of choice, although I cannot say who directed the change." I could relate to this statement, as I still wasn't sure how my faint "But if it's okay..." comment had arisen.

Phakchok Rinpoche went on to tell me that, in my case, the prompt availability of rescuers and the helicopter was a direct consequence of my rescuing trekkers and climbers in Nepal. "This is the way karma works," he said. "If you rescue people and save their lives, then when you need rescue, it can happen more easily." Although I faced a long, slow recovery from the heart attack, and the fact that I may never recover completely, I couldn't help feeling that the experience was a valuable preview of what I would have to face someday. When I said this to Phakchok Rinpoche, he agreed completely. "Oh yes. You are fortunate. An experience like this is worth a lot of meditation."

So how do I feel about what happened? I had no idea that I would react the way I did during the life-and-death drama on the pass. Just three days earlier, I had been teaching my weekly Tibetan Buddhism class in Jackson Hole and talking about impermanence and how it can arrive without warning at any time. And I remember feeling uneasy, as I always subtly did when I talked about the uncertainty associated with impermanence. And then impermanence arrived! What I've described is the thought process I went through, and the way I felt. I think the most important thing that helped me was having confidence in what would happen if I died, and what I needed to try to do. It focused my mind in a positive way that couldn't have occurred if I was terrified of the unknown.

If—or more accurately *when*—this happens again, I don't know how I will react. Looking back on the experience, I feel like I can encourage others who may not feel they are ready to die; I can also attest that if they have some spiritual training, it may kick in even if you previously thought you were not ready.

I recounted my story to Lama Tashi, the grown-up young Tashi that I traveled to Tibet with in 1987. He gained a lot of wisdom over the years and spent nearly two years as a wandering mendicant in Nepal, India, and Bhutan, traveling part of the time with Mingyur Rinpoche. We met up at the Yak and Yeti Hotel in Kathmandu five years after my heart attack. He said, "When the time comes for you to die in the future, don't think about what happened during this near-death experience. Don't try to re-create what you already went through, but just try to experience dying freshly in the moment that it happens, based on all your training."

Jane and my two children were, of course, happy that I was still with them. I think they would have been able to cope with my death, but we are a close family, and we are glad to all be together. They knew how close I had come, but they didn't dwell on it now that I was okay. When my friends came to see me after my heart attack, they first asked me how I was feeling. Then they wanted to know if my cholesterol level had been high, or whether I'd had any symptoms earlier that I had ignored. My cholesterol level was, in fact, below normal, and I hadn't experienced any warning symptoms.

I recognized what they were doing. I'd seen it after every mountaineering accident that I had been close to. First, people wanted to know what happened when someone got killed climbing or skiing. Then they tried to determine *why* it happened. Did they not check their knots? Did they rappel off the end of the rope? Could they not have foreseen the avalanche danger? Although they wanted to learn from what happened, the sub-context was trying to reassure themselves that it wouldn't have happened to them. They wouldn't have made that mistake. When you engage in dangerous sports, you always know that something bad could happen. The worst accidents, in terms of hearing about them, are the ones that had no obvious mistakes. It meant that *just doing the activity* was the risk itself. It meant that by just being out there one could get killed.

Life is like that, too, but we don't like to be reminded. Just by being alive, it's possible to suddenly die. That's why my friends were looking for a reason. Some reason why it might not happen to them in the same way.

This fear of dying or coming close to dying is so strong that my friends just assumed that I must be traumatized by going through it. But I hadn't experienced near-death in that way. I attribute that to years of thinking about dying, training in meditation, and being inspired by the examples of lamas that I met who had died.

I ran into a friend at the grocery store whom I hadn't yet seen since my heart attack. He asked me if I had been terrified about dying up on the pass.

"Not really," I told him.

"Are you taking Zoloft now to deal with the experience?" he asked.

"I didn't die," I replied. "I might have needed Zoloft if I had died." He shot me a puzzled look.

From my point of view, not only had I not died, I had an amazing experience. If I had died, I might have had to face a lot of uncertainty and loneliness in the intermediate state after death. Which would have made taking Zoloft (an antidepressant) more appropriate (if not actually physically possible).

"Just kidding," I said.

FORTY-TWO

The day I came home from the hospital after my heart attack, I went upstairs to my office over our garage. The large room is filled with the many statues and sacred paintings that I accumulated while living in Nepal. I went to my shrine and picked up the statue that Chokyi Nyima Rinpoche had given me at the moment I met him and touched it to my forehead to receive its blessing. It was the one antique statue that I owned. All my other statues were new when I purchased them or received them as gifts. Since it was old, it likely had a history, and I didn't know what that was, or why he picked that particular statue to give me when we first met. During the years I spent around Chokyi Nyima Rinpoche, I saw him give away statues to other people, but they were always new. When I asked him about the statue, he would deflect the question with a shrug and say that he just happened to have it around at the time.

However, three years earlier, Chokyi Nyima Rinpoche had come to stay at our house in Jackson Hole for a few days. While he was there, I showed the statue to him and asked him about it once again. This time he said, "When I first heard you were coming to meet me, I knew that we had a deep connection from our past lives. I knew I needed to give you something, and it needed to be something old to symbolize that old connection."

The summer after my heart attack, I met Chokyi Nyima Rinpoche at his retreat center in northern California, which he visited once a year for ten days. I've been involved in running the retreat center, called Gomde California, since it was founded in 1998. I'm currently the president of the center. It was my first chance to talk to him in person about the experiences I had during my heart attack. He reaffirmed what Phakchok Rinpoche had told me, and similarly didn't treat it as that big a deal.

As we talked, I felt so close to him, a kind of love that is difficult to describe, a feeling that is based not on desire, or expectation, but on respect, devotion, and gratitude. I had come to realize that my love for him was able to be so pure because it was simply a reflection of the unconditional love that I constantly felt coming from him—toward not only me but everyone he knew. Knowing what my life was like before I met him, I realized once again how lucky I had been to live so close to him for fourteen years, to be able to go to him over and over again with questions, to hone my beliefs and my practice in a one-on-one apprenticeship that I was extremely fortunate to attain. That relationship could not be reproduced for either of us these days. His life is so busy—the monastery has grown from eighty monks to over five hundred. He has thousands and thousands of students from all around the world. He started a Buddhist university in Kathmandu that offers, for the first time, an authentic education in Tibetan Buddhist philosophy and language to foreign students. When I visit Nepal each year, I feel fortunate when he can carve out even fifteen to thirty minutes in which we can be alone and talk.

We sat in a comfortable silence in his rustic small house at the retreat center. The statue had once again been on my mind, and I wanted to ask him about it one more time. I still felt there was something more to it. I reached over and touched his forearm, a gesture that acknowledged that I was about to push a boundary, and it was okay if he didn't feel like answering. "Rinpoche, I still have some feelings about that statue you gave me when we first met," I said. "I keep thinking there is something more you could say about where it came from."

He did not answer right away, as if weighing a decision. Then he said, "It came from my monastery in Tibet." I may have still been emotional from my heart attack, but tears flowed from my eyes, and my hands went to my face. I covered my eyes briefly to wipe the tears away with my palms. When I looked up, Chokyi Nyima Rinpoche had lifted his glasses and was wiping tears from the corners of his eyes, the first time I had ever seen him cry. He reached out his arms and we embraced, and I sat back.

"It belonged to my predecessors," he went on, referring to the previous reincarnations of the head of his monastery in Tibet, of which he was the latest. "I don't really know how old it is," he added. The magnitude of what he was telling me began to sink in. If it had belonged to his previous incarnations, it could be well over a hundred years old.

Chokyi Nyima Rinpoche was eight years old when he fled Tibet. He had been recognized as the reincarnation of the head of his monastery when he was eighteen months old, and his mother and younger brother had moved there a few years later so that he could begin his training. His father was serving as the attendant to the 16th Karmapa, the head of one of the four main lineages of Tibetan Buddhism in Tibet. In 1958, as the Chinese began to cement their hold on all of Tibet, the Karmapa took Tulku Urgyen Rinpoche aside and told him that he must leave Tibet to save his life. Tulku Urgyen said that he wouldn't leave without the Karmapa, but the Karmapa insisted and said not to worry about him, that he would leave later and be safe.

Although Chokyi Nyima Rinpoche and his family were in a more remote part of Tibet, it became clear that they would need to flee as well, as the Chinese were looking to arrest or kill all the reincarnate lamas. They had to sneak across Tibet, avoiding Chinese troops, for two weeks to get to Bhutan to join Tulku Urgyen Rinpoche. This small statue had ended up with him in Kathmandu, and I imagined that it was a treasured possession, one of the few icons of his past life in Tibet. The Chinese destroyed his monastery, and most of the remaining statues, after he left. Yet Chokyi Nyima Rinpoche decided to give this particular statue to me, *based on just hearing my name.* He emerged from his chambers *already holding the statue* to prove that he had sensed this connection before we met.

If he had given me the statue later, it could have been seen as a special reward for my volunteer service. Even if he just wanted to give me something to thank me for my intention to help, he could easily have given me a newly made statue, which are manufactured by the thousands by craftsmen in Kathmandu. What he had just revealed about the statue confirmed beyond a doubt that Chokyi Nyima Rinpoche had been waiting for me. And when he heard my name, he reached for one of his most precious possessions to give me to affirm our prior connection. He just didn't tell me that until he felt the time was right. About thirty years later.

My secret fantasy during my first trip to Nepal—my wish to be singled out at a Tibetan monastery and brought inside to receive special teachings—had come true. That self-conscious, almost embarrassing yearning that I felt outside the Thyangboche Monastery had a genuine basis. I just didn't realize I was standing outside the wrong monastery.

FORTY-THREE

I traveled a lot after moving to Jackson Hole. I spoke often at travel medicine conferences and received invitations to give talks on medicine and compassion. I often flew twice a month or more throughout the year. My travels took me around the world, to Europe, New Zealand, South Africa, Singapore, Vietnam, and Peru, in addition to our annual visits to Nepal and...Bhutan.

Bhutan had begun to figure prominently in our lives. Starting in 2005, we agreed to host a Bhutanese exchange student in our home, a fifteen-year-old girl named Thinley. Within a couple of years, we were hosting her two younger sisters, Megom and Tashi Lam, as well. Their parents are extremely interesting—the father, Tashi, was the first PhD wildlife biologist in Bhutan and helped create the national park system there. He did his master's thesis on the four pillars of Gross National Happiness, the guiding principles of development in Bhutan. He then went on to pioneer electric cars in a country that has an excess of hydroelectric power but must import all of its fuel. The mother, Kelzang, is a remarkable woman from a remote village who got a master's degree in education in the U.S. The daughters continued to live with us on and off for ten years as they finished high school and college, and the parents visited often and stayed with us. Sometimes we had nine people staying in our house. We've visited the family in Bhutan many times. I feel like we are so close that we are a blended family. In addition, it was great that

Anna Tara could grow up with Himalayan sisters.

Bhutan is remarkably different from Nepal, despite being nearly adjoining. The country is officially Buddhist and their language is derived from Tibetan. The population of Bhutan is just over 750,000, compared to over 29,000,000 in Nepal. Tourism is strictly regulated in Bhutan: every tourist must sign up with a travel agency and have a guide the whole time. One can't just go and hang out in Bhutan—unless you have a connection to someone.

Our family went from two children to five, and it was all made possible by Jane's love and energy and wisdom in dealing with children. I enjoyed the added dynamics of all the kids, but my focus was on trying to promote medicine and compassion while still practicing travel medicine. And occasionally, I was called upon to combine my focus on Buddhism, compassion, and medicine in a new way.

In the fall of 2015, I had just landed after flying back from California, where I had given some talks on compassion to a group of doctors from the Palo Alto Medical Foundation. When I turned on my cell phone, I saw that I had a voicemail from someone I didn't know, asking me to call her about seeing a patient who was dying of ovarian cancer.

The patient had asked for me. Since moving back from Nepal, my medical practice had been limited to seeing patients before or after travel. I had seen this woman, whose name was Susan, a year earlier when she was preparing for a trip to Nepal. She had been treated for ovarian cancer, and was in remission, and wanted to travel to the Himalayas. She was forty-four years old and single. As I was traveling to Nepal around that same time, there had been a chance that we might meet up in Nepal, but it hadn't happened, and I hadn't heard from her until then. Her cancer had returned, rendering her situation irreversible, with cancer throughout her abdomen and bones. She was receiving intravenous narcotics to control the pain.

She had no one to care for her in Jackson. She was in the hospital but was about to be discharged home to die. Except that she had no home at the time. She had a mother, a thousand miles away, but when she called to let her know what was happening, her mother was unmoved, and just said, "Good luck," offering no assistance. Through a friend of a friend, she ended up being able to go to a nice house.

I went straight from the airport to the hospital. Susan was drowsy from her drugs but knew who I was and was grateful that I had come. She asked for me because she knew she was about to die and wanted "something Buddhist." I sort of knew what she meant but didn't know what I could provide. The patient wasn't a practicing Buddhist and had not been to any of my classes. But as she was days away from an inescapable death, she had an instinct that there was something in Buddhist teachings that might make it better for her. What could that be?

I talked to her a little that night but wasn't sure what to offer. She went to the friend's home the next morning, and I went to see her there. I gave her a sacred blessing substance called *mendrup*, which came directly from Chokyi Nyima Rinpoche. Mendrup consists of small, irregularly shaped black particles that look like large coffee grounds. They are put in the mouth and chewed, and have an earthy, slightly charred, pleasant taste. They are compounded from many sacred non-toxic substances and then blessed for months on an altar. I've already described the sense of power that I felt in person at sacred sites; it's possible to imagine that these pills somehow embody that power so that it can be passed onto someone wherever they are. When given to a person just before dying, they are said to have a very favorable influence on their karmic journey through the intermediate state.

"I want something Buddhist," she once again asked. The next day I brought a few things and performed the Medicine Buddha practice next to her bedside, chanting from a text and ringing a bell. This particular practice helps promote healing, both physically and mentally.

Then I leaned over to her and spoke directly into her ear. "It's okay to let go. Let go of everything. Your feelings about your mother, all of it. Just relax and let go. Buddhists spend their whole lives practicing so that at this exact moment they will be able to let go and just relax peacefully. If you can do that now, you will have achieved as much as any Buddhist practitioner would have achieved. Just let go."

She nodded slightly. She looked at me. She had pretty blue eyes, and they were still clear. She had lost her hair to chemotherapy, but wore a surprisingly stylish, bright scarf around her head. I smiled encouragingly. Then I went home, promising to see her the next morning. When I arrived the next day, around 8:00 a.m., I was told that she had died at 4:30 a.m., peacefully.

I went in to see her. Her face was relaxed, her limbs supple; there was no rigor mortis. Her skin was still flexible. These were good signs. The woman looking after her told me, "She had been waking up the last two nights around four-thirty a.m., screaming and crying, nearly hysterical, and I would have to hold her til she calmed down. Last night she didn't wake up. She just died peacefully."

She had let go. Letting go is the key, and you can start working on that at any point in your life. The more you practice while you are healthy and things are going relatively well, the easier it will be to do when it comes time to die. Letting go is not the same as giving up. Letting go encompasses the recognition of impermanence, that everything changes, and at some point, our lives will end. We don't like to think about this—we actually hate to think about this—but it's true. Coming to grips with impermanence while things are going well is much easier than confronting it all at once when it arrives unexpectedly.

Susan's death is also an example of how one can gain spiritual insights up to the last moments of one's life. If consciousness does continue past the death of the body, entering that phase with acceptance and lack of fear can set you up to have an easier time after you have died. The mind that we have in the intermediate state is the same mind that we have now. A stable mind while we are alive will be a stable mind after we die. Arriving in the intermediate state with knowledge and confidence about what to do is like landing in a strange land having already studied the guidebook. Without that, it can be frightening and disorienting; with preparation, we can find our way to a favorable rebirth and continue our spiritual journey. Entering that phase with confidence is the goal of the long-term practitioner.

FORTY-FOUR

As I gained experience with Buddhist practice in Kathmandu, I noticed that I was changing as a physician. I was becoming more patient, more kind, more skilled at discovering what was really troubling a patient beyond the symptoms that they came in with. I was able to convey a kind, nonthreatening presence, and the patients' tears came more easily as they were able to tell me what they were really worried about.

Since compassion is the essence of Buddhist training, both the method and the goal, I felt that Chokyi Nyima Rinpoche was responsible for these changes in me. He showed me that there are ways to train one's *capacity* for being compassionate, not just to think about wanting to be more compassionate. As the capacity for compassion increases, one's compassion becomes more stable—able to be present for more of the working day. It becomes more inclusive, able to be applied to difficult people, or people that we may not immediately like. Most of all, it becomes more effortless, not requiring as much of a conscious struggle to gear up for each patient. In our Western culture, the phrase "effortless compassion" might appear to be an oxymoron, but the Buddhist understanding of the origin of compassion allows that phrase to seem like an achievable goal.

To Tibetan Buddhists, compassion is our basic nature. It's not something that has to be added on or cultivated. Our thoughts and emotions obscure our compassion. Whenever we are thinking about ourselves—our own concerns, hopes, and fears—we are not experiencing compassion. If we can let go of this constant thought activity, for even just a moment, our innate compassion can emerge. As a physician, when I walk into a room with a patient, if I can let go of all the thoughts that are spinning in my head at that moment and focus on my desire to help, what the patient feels is my compassion—in a very genuine way. Training in compassion is training to let go of those things that obscure our compassion.

For many of us, empathy is the tool we use to relate to how others are feeling. By being able to share in their fears and pain, we can be more sympathetic to their plight. But empathy has its limits—the more we share in the pain of our patients, the more painful it can be for us. If we are going to open up to their suffering, we also need a way to let go of those feelings when we walk away. For many of us, how much we hold onto the pain of others when we are caring for them is a measure of our own compassion. If we are going to let go of those feelings when we walk away, it may feel like we need *permission* to do so. As Chokyi Nyima Rinpoche said, "If holding onto the feelings of your patients when you are not with them would benefit them, then you should do it. But since it doesn't have any benefit for them, and only hurts yourself, why do it?" Instead, we can gain the freedom to open up our empathy when we are with people who need our care, knowing that we can let go of it safely when we move on. This keeps empathy from gradually wearing us down or forcing us to relive those feelings over and over after we've gone home for the night.

Where does compassion originate within us? Is it something that was genetically encoded as we competed to exist as human beings? Has it been placed in us by a compassionate God? Is it something that we learn as children? Or is it something intrinsic to our basic consciousness? Let's just agree, for the moment, that it is something intrinsic. Where does that come from?

The Buddhist concept of mind is that it has always existed. It is an awareness beyond thoughts, filled with limitless compassion and wisdom. We're not in touch with this incredible inner quality due to the negative habits we have acquired along the way. As a result, we take rebirth in an endless cycle that leads to suffering. We have the antidote to all that suffering already within us, and thus the essence of Buddhist philosophy is how to recognize that nature and stabilize that experience. If we can stabilize it completely, we can transcend the cycle of suffering, and be able to help others do the same. The experience of recognizing one's own mind nature—as taught by Tulku Urgyen Rinpoche—is the key that unlocks the door to our ultimate wisdom and compassion. But even short of resting in mind nature, any effort that we make to decrease our attachment to our thoughts and emotions will allow our natural compassion to grow.

The less we are distracted by disturbing thoughts and emotions, the easier it is for us to react compassionately. Training in compassion is just training in how to maintain a relaxed, aware mind, while being motivated by the desire to help others. As our mind becomes less attached to its inner constant chatter, as we tame our negative emotions, our natural compassion expands. The compassion that flows from our basic nature is what Tibetan Buddhists refer to as "nonconceptual compassion." It is always present, always ready to act for the benefit of others—vast and effortless. This is how meditation practice can lead to an increased capacity for compassion.

As I recognized the benefit of training in compassion in my own medical practice, I became interested in trying to share this insight about compassion with other Western doctors and nurses. Tibetan Buddhist concepts on how to train in compassion had never been presented to a Western professional audience before. I felt that these ideas needed to be presented by a genuine Tibetan lama, the way it had been presented to me. To do this, I would need to organize a medical conference with Chokyi Nyima Rinpoche as the only speaker. I dreamed about putting on the conference for ten years, but I was unable to make it happen until I moved from Kathmandu to Jackson Hole.

Focusing on an audience of doctors and nurses whose work required a constant need for compassion made sense. They could leave the conference and immediately put the teachings into effect with their patients. Is it possible, however, that the teaching of compassion could have an impact on the overall world? Can compassion serve as an antidote to the increasing hostility of the political divide, the wars, terrorist attacks, racism, environmental destruction, and greed that are flaring so rapidly in the world these days? Can deciding to train oneself in compassion make any difference in the world? It's a valid question, which is why, when Chokyi Nyima Rinpoche came to Jackson Hole in 2000 to teach the first course on Medicine and Compassion, he appeared to pull off a little feat of magic to remind us that training in compassion could serve a larger purpose.

Jackson Hole was on fire. In every direction. I could see the flames at night burning at the base of Mt. Moran in Grand Teton National Park, and the smoke rising from the Gros Ventre Mountains and from south of town. The fires were not close enough to our house for us to feel immediately threatened. The bone-dry summer had gone without even a millimeter of rain for months, and the fires there were echoed by fires across Montana, Idaho, and into Washington. Chokyi Nyima Rinpoche was flying in that week to teach the first Medicine and Compassion course. His students in Nepal had contacted me to ask whether it was even safe for him to come. Discouraged firefighters, resources depleted from constantly battling so many fires, announced that they were giving up on putting them out. They predicted that only the winter snows, still two months away, would finally put the fires to rest.

As I drove the short distance from my house to the airport to meet Chokyi Nyima Rinpoche, it started raining. I initially thought, *It's a shame that it's raining on his first visit.* Then I realized that this was great; it was just what we needed. And then I got suspicious. I asked his translator whether Rinpoche had done anything to cause this rain to fall. He told me that Rinpoche had performed a ceremony to help bring rain to the region. When I turned to Rinpoche and asked whether this was true, he gave me only a brief, noncommittal smile, and a shrug.

The rain continued for three days. The fires that had been burning around Jackson Hole all came quickly under control, as did most of the other fires in the west. Rinpoche didn't say anything about this good fortune while addressing the conference-goers, except to refer to it in a beautifully oblique way:

> These days, a lot of forest has been on fire in the United States, and now the rain of compassion is falling, which is quite wonderful. Now it is not just talk, but in actuality the forests burning from the fire of anger are being subdued by the rain of compassion. The gentle rain of compassion is putting out the fires of anger.

That's all he said about the fires. But his unspoken lesson was profound: no matter how fierce the fires of anger are, they can be subdued completely by rain. Each of us may only have the capacity to become an individual drop of rain, and when a single raindrop falls on a forest fire, it can't do much by itself. But enough drops of rain can subdue even the most raging forest fires, and by analogy, the fires of anger on our planet. And even if an individual raindrop can't do much by itself, it also doesn't disappear. It evaporates and returns to the sky, where it can fall again as rain, thus creating an endless cycle of compassion.

The experiment as to whether a Tibetan lama, teaching in translated Tibetan, could connect with non-Buddhist Western health workers was a success. His compassionate wisdom moved the audience, who recognized his uncanny ability to describe the problems that they faced at work and to suggest solutions. His teachings validated their intuitive feelings about the value of compassion.

I put on a second conference in 2002 and spent four years transcribing and editing the teachings into a book. Presented in simple, non-Buddhist language, the book distills most of what I learned in my fifteen years in Nepal. Published by Wisdom Publications in 2004, it has been continuously in print since then, with translations into German, Spanish, Catalan, Italian, Chinese, and soon, Russian and Czech. A ten-year anniversary edition came out in the spring of 2015. The title is *Medicine and Compassion: An American Doctor and a Tibetan Lama on How to Provide Care with Compassion and Wisdom*.

Since the book was published, I've traveled all around the world giving lectures on the possibilities of training in compassion. I feel like I've been sowing seeds, planting new ideas into Western thinking about how compassion can be made more stable, vast, and effortless, and along the way prevent burnout and compassion fatigue. Doctors get better at medicine in the years after they finish their medical training, but their compassion often feels like it wears out over time. If doctors and nurses started training in compassion at the same time they started their medical training, their compassion could gradually grow more expansive and stable as their careers progressed, allowing them to experience their profession in a whole new way, and inspire the younger people they are mentoring to try to do the same.

FORTY-FIVE

It started off not so bad.

"Matthew's had a seizure. They're taking him to the emergency room," said Jane, after fielding an early morning phone call. Matthew was still living with us, and he had left at six in the morning to drive to his job at a rental shop at the ski resort. It was now eight a.m.

Matthew had had seizures before. It's bad, but he wakes up and then we take him home. He hadn't had a seizure in a long time. He was twenty-three years old.

When we got to the ER, the doctor said Matthew was still unconscious, and he wanted to get a CT scan of his brain. He had a small cut on his scalp on the right side. His seizure had made him fall, and he'd hit his head on the cement floor where he was working. I looked at the laceration—not very big. He should be okay.

Fifteen minutes later, it was clear that he was not okay. The scan showed he had arterial bleeding inside his skull—an epidural hemorrhage. He needed immediate brain surgery, but that wasn't available in Jackson. He had to fly to Idaho Falls. The weather again was too socked in over the mountains for a helicopter. It wasn't even certain that a fixed-wing plane could fly here from Idaho Falls.

Time is of the essence with an epidural hemorrhage. The majority of people who survive get to surgery within two hours of their injury. It had been an hour and a half already.

I had never called Chokyi Nyima Rinpoche before to ask him to say prayers for someone. I had never needed to. Now, I did. It was after 9:00 a.m. in Jackson, after 9:00 p.m. in Kathmandu. Rinpoche seldom answered his phone in the evening. I dialed it anyway, and there was no answer. I called the monastery number. No answer.

I called Prativa. She answered right away. I asked her to call a friend who lived at the monastery to try to get in touch with Rinpoche—it was life and death.

I went back inside. The airplane pilot wasn't sure they could fly. The ER doctor thought we could wait another fifteen minutes, and then he would put Matthew in an ambulance for the almost two-hour drive to Idaho Falls. We both knew that might be too long.

My cell phone rang. It was Chokyi Nyima Rinpoche. I told him what was going on.

"I'll pray for him tonight. Tomorrow is a big puja at the monastery, and everyone will pray for him."

I had to ask. It would completely put him on the spot, but I had to ask.

"Will he be okay?"

"He'll be okay," he said, without hesitation. *I don't know everything,* he once told me, *but a few things I get a feeling.*

Back inside, the ER doctor said the plane was on its way. Jane volunteered to go with Matthew on the plane, and I would drive back to Kelly, get some clothes, and drive to Idaho Falls.

Matthew was in serious trouble. He was more likely than not going to be dead on arrival in Idaho Falls, no matter what method was used to get him there. I was familiar with a similar story. Natasha Richardson, the actress and wife of Liam Neeson, had taken a fall on a beginner's ski slope in Quebec. She hadn't been knocked unconscious, but they took her to the clinic at the ski area anyway. She refused further medical care because she felt okay, but two hours later in her room, she started to lose consciousness from her epidural hemorrhage. An ambulance was called that took her to the local hospital, and then she was further transferred about eighty miles to a hospital in Montreal. By the time she arrived, she was declared brain dead.

Back in the house, I tried to focus. What should I take? Extra clothes? Toiletries? How long would we be there? I went up to my home office, which housed all my statues and Buddhist books, and took some *nundrup* from a drawer, a precious medicine that you can put in the mouth of a person who has just died, giving tremendous blessing. I also had a special tiny booklet that you put on the chest of someone who has died, which contains blessing prayers. I took some *katas* in case we needed to put them on his body as a farewell gesture. Just in case.

I had skied with Matthew at the resort the day before, enjoying high-speed runs on groomed snow. There were no lift lines, and it was just him and me skiing together alone, the first time that had happened the entire season. I enjoyed riding up on the lifts with him. Matthew could converse about anything, often with profound insight: Dharma, medicine, politics, compassion, school, travel. And I enjoyed watching Matthew ski; he flowed down the mountain with a casual joy, able to ski forward or backward with equal ease.

Would that day be our last good time together, the culmination of our life together on Earth? What about the vision that I had when Matthew was conceived, that warm, overwhelmingly positive feeling that my relationship with my son would bring joy? Was it just going to end like this? Even as I tried to accept Chokyi Nyima Rinpoche's reassurance, I braced myself for the fact that Matthew might not make it, and I would just have to accept that.

The weather, densely foggy over Teton Pass, was crystal clear after I crested the pass and headed west. Jane texted their progress.

Matthew was in the ambulance at the Jackson airport.

They were waiting for the plane.

He was in the plane.

They were in the air.

The paramedics looked scared, she wrote.

"He'll be okay," Chokyi Nyima Rinpoche had said, but what else, really, could he say? He knew I was desperately looking for reassurance. Hadn't I said the same thing to Sarah's daughter in my clinic? But then, she had, in fact, ended up okay...

Jane texted that they had landed in Idaho Falls, racing with lights and siren in the ambulance, a high-speed, life-and-death dash to the emergency room where the neurosurgeon and his team were already lined up in a semicircle waiting to receive him. They took one look at him, grabbed his gurney, and started sprinting to the operating room. Jane texted me: "Very, very serious. Straight to OR. Eyes are starting to dilate."

I was still a half-hour from the hospital. He had arrived alive, but barely. He still had a chance. I found the hospital with my cell phone app. The last time I had gone there I had arrived by ambulance myself, and I wasn't exactly sure where it was.

Once I pulled in, I went upstairs to the waiting area for surgery and intensive care and reconnected with Jane, who had gone into a functional survival mode, not allowing herself to be emotional, not even exchanging a hug. A nurse had sent out word from the operating room that they had drained the blood out of his skull; they were still trying to stop the bleeding.

Another hour. The neurosurgeon arrived in the waiting area, bald head and white coat, in his late forties, with a sincere matter-of-fact manner. "I can't make any guarantees," he said. "But we stopped the bleeding, and his brain looked as good as it can look. Sometimes, after that amount of pressure, it swells up immediately after we drain off the blood, which is a bad sign, but in his case it looked normal."

I ran through the phrases in my head. *"I can't make any guarantees." "But it was as good as it could look."* He went on to say, "We'll keep him sedated tonight on the respirator, and tomorrow morning we'll get another CT scan. That will tell us whether there are any bruises in his brain or any other signs of brain damage. We'll know more then."

We waited while they admitted him to the ICU and set up his tubes and catheters and respirator. Then they let us in to see him, head wrapped in a beige, turban-like bandage, his arms laid out at his sides with IVs and monitors attached, a tube coming out of his mouth connected to the respirator. He was immobile, helpless, the machine triggering his breathing, large monitor screens tracing his EKG, blood pressure, and oxygenation. He was on propofol—*the anesthetic that killed Michael Jackson*, I couldn't help thinking—which kept him asleep, preventing him from thrashing around and re-starting the bleeding in his skull. We sat with him into the evening.

He had lived. Would he be okay? When would we know? The brain scan scheduled for the next morning was the next big milestone to get past. I thought about what my son's life might be like, what our lives might be like, if his brain was permanently damaged. "He'll be okay," Rinpoche had said.

What did that mean? Alive? Able to feed himself? Completely normal?

Standing at his bedside was painful. I suddenly had an overwhelming burst of compassion for all the parents who had suffered the loss or crippling of their children, about all they went through in first hearing about an accident, waiting for further news, dealing with the aftermath. I thought about the parents I knew in Nepal whose children had died, and the parents of trekkers who had died, their bodies unrecoverable in the mountains as if they had just vanished. I thought of the daily news, the domestic terror attacks, the stories that flowed in from war-torn parts of the world, the desert hovels being raided by marauders on horseback, the child soldiers in fetid jungles with AK-47s, the car bombings, murders, and rapes that are so common that we read about them with a vague numb awareness, unable to imagine the suffering involved in *every* individual injury or death. The suffering in these cases was truly unbearable to imagine, and now I didn't have to. I could feel it myself.

I stood at the foot of Matthew's bed as this realization flooded through me. The Buddha's first teaching, after he attained enlightenment, was, "Life is suffering." I suddenly understood these three words in a profound, new way. He wasn't just talking about the suffering of impermanence, the suffering of hope and fear, the vague suffering of never feeling completely content. The Buddha was talking about the unbearable suffering of the condition of sentient beings—the fact that it can never be okay, never come out right, the fact of old age, sickness, and death. If we're honest, life is suffused with the potential for unbearable suffering.

Of course, the Buddha hadn't left it at that—what would be the point of merely pointing out suffering if nothing could be done about it? He said that suffering had a cause: the ignorance that permeates our perception of the world, making us cling to our situation as real and solid, when it is actually dreamlike and fleeting. We form false concepts and cling to them as if they are the only reality, and then we suffer, unable to let go of those thoughts. The Buddha taught that there is a state of mind beyond suffering—the enlightened mind—and that there is a path of study and contemplation that can lead a motivated practitioner to escape the endless suffering of samsaric existence.

When I was lying in the snow on Teton Pass, shivering and unable to catch my breath, I was somehow able to focus on what lay ahead. I could let go of my attachment to this world, even my attachment to my wife and children. I could deal with moving on. The question I was now facing was whether I could deal with being left behind.

And then, surprisingly, as I stood there, the thoughts about suffering were replaced by a warm feeling in my chest, an open-hearted compassion for all sentient beings. I thought I had understood the need for compassion, but I had underestimated the depth of suffering we face, being forced to endure endless lifetimes of pain. "Samsaric existence is painful," my teachers had always said. "Aspire to achieve complete enlightenment for the benefit of all sentient beings." Profound suffering dictates the need for even more profound compassion. My heart attack had taught me about impermanence; Matthew's accident was now teaching me about compassion, about the *need* to help people achieve enlightenment, the only way to bring suffering to an end.

Matthew lay perfectly still in his bed, the respirator pushing and releasing, the monitors beeping. I sat down in an armchair, facing the bed, reflecting on what I had just experienced. The Buddha taught meditation not just to make our lives a little easier, to make our health a little better, or to achieve sharper focus at work. It was a method to decrease suffering, and to bring an end to the causes of suffering of all sentient beings.

Jane and I booked a hotel room a half-mile from the hospital. Around midnight, we drove there to sleep, returning at eight the next morning. Matthew was already downstairs getting his CT scan. He came back in a caravan of bed, IV poles, monitors, respirator, and attendants. We waited another hour until the neurosurgeon appeared to tell us that his brain looked nearly normal—no signs of bruising or swelling, but he still could give no guarantees. He would have a massive concussion, he said, and his recovery would be unpredictable.

That afternoon the nurse, a lovely caring woman named Michelle, briefed us on what would happen as they gradually weaned Matthew off the anesthetic and he started to wake up. He had to wake up enough to breathe on his own, and she said the first thing he would try to do is pull out the breathing tube, which they couldn't let him do. The weaning process took three hours, but they finally pulled the tube from his restless but still mostly-unaware body. It was his first chance to talk.

In his confused state, his hands pulled at his IVs, then his urinary catheter. We held his arms back with the cloth restraints around his wrists.

"Let me go," he said.

"We can't let you go right now, Matthew, you can't pull out all these tubes. You've had a seizure, and you fell and bled in your skull and had to have surgery."

"Let me go," he said. "This is a dream. If you let me go, I'll wake up."

Jane leaned in close. "Matthew, you need to listen to me. Don't you trust me?"

"I don't trust the dream you," he replied.

We couldn't connect with him, but Michelle said this was not unusual: his brain was trying to make sense of its confusing situation. She finally gave him a sedative, and he slept, and we went back to our hotel to sleep ourselves, still not knowing if we would ever recover the real Matthew.

The next morning, we went over fearing that we would have another day of attempting to orient Matthew to the world. When we arrived, he was sitting on the edge of his bed, listening to a physical therapist. He looked up at us. "What happened to me?" he asked. We told him. This time he heard us. "I don't remember any of that," he said, in his normal voice. He was Matthew! My throat choked up; tears welled into my eyes. He was back.

An hour later my phone rang. Chokyi Nyima Rinpoche was calling to ask how Matthew was doing. When I told him, he said, "This is the big obstacle in Matthew's life. Now it is finished. He'll be okay now. Don't worry."

The physical therapist stood him up and took him for a walk down the hall of the ICU. He could walk! Back in bed, we talked to him. He told us that he had met four people while he was unconscious, people he knew who had died. They were sitting in a room that looked like a monastery, and it was hot, with trees outside that looked like the area around Lumbini, the birthplace of the Buddha, which Matthew and I had visited when we were in Nepal ten months earlier. When he saw the people he said, "You guys are dead. Does this mean that I'm dead?"

One of them replied, "No, you are going back. We just have some messages that we would like to send back with you."

Matthew said he found some paper and wrote down the messages, "But when I woke up, I didn't have the paper." However, he still remembered the messages. Because the people he met have living friends and relatives, I'm not going to name them.

I've always been extremely interested in the stories that people tell surrounding near-death experiences. Are they dreams, are they real, do they tell us anything about the afterlife? I was pretty sure that Matthew's story was a kind of deep dream, but when I met Chokyi Nyima Rinpoche seven months later in California, he stunned me by telling me that Matthew's experience was real; he had actually met those people. They had somehow persisted in the intermediate state, but the fact that they said they were happy, and the setting looked like a monastery, meant that they were fine. Chokyi Nyima Rinpoche said that he could do a puja at his monastery that would help them move on.

Rinpoche told me that people who come close to death and meet other beings in the intermediate realms are called *Delog*, which literally means "going over and coming back." That night I suddenly had the thought: If these people are stranded in an intermediate realm, and can be rescued by Chokyi Nyima Rinpoche, how could we have known they were there if not for Matthew's accident?

The next morning, I asked Rinpoche, and he said, "Yes. That's true. Matthew has let us know that they are there."

Even for me, with all my exposure to Tibetans and Tibetan Buddhism, this was wild. Why was Matthew hurt? It seemed to be something that he needed to go through, and perhaps saved him from something worse, as my typhoid fever may have prevented my own more serious illness. But even more so, did his karmic connection with these beings mean that he needed to be put in a position to help them?

Back in the ICU, Matthew's personality proved to be completely unaffected. He managed to crack jokes; he thanked everyone who came in to help him, including the woman who was mopping the floor in his room.

Although his memory and personality were intact, he was still in severe pain and terribly nauseated, and they kept him in the ICU just to try to control his symptoms. However, just four days after he had surgery, he walked out of the ICU on his own legs, down the hall, and rode up the elevator four floors to the rehabilitation unit, where he would undergo further testing.

He took a short walk outside the hospital. With a hat on his head, he looked pale but normal, a big smile on his face at being allowed outside for the first time. Without a hat, he looked deranged—the right side of his scalp shaved and red and bruised, with a giant semi-circular scar pulled together with metal staples. The left side of his scalp still had longish blond hair. "I didn't have time to shave the other side of his head," the neurosurgeon told us. After four days in rehab, they told us we could go home.

What were the odds that Matthew would survive and have almost no signs of brain injury? As I looked it up in my textbooks, it seemed that the chances of surviving an epidural bleed with no brain damage when surgery is delayed for five hours are very slim. Matthew's evacuation had taken almost five hours from when he first hit his head. When he checked out of rehab, I asked his nurse, a veteran of eleven years on the rehab floor, whether she had ever seen anyone recover as quickly as Matthew. She didn't hesitate. "No, I haven't. Honestly, we're often celebrating if we eventually hear that one of our patients can hold down a simple job," she said.

What role did Chokyi Nyima Rinpoche play in all of this? Did he save Matthew with the prayers he said and the *pujas* that he arranged for him? Or did he just display a clairvoyant glimpse into Matthew's karma, knowing that he was destined to live despite this accident? Was it a little of both? Or did he just try to be encouraging, and turned out to be right?

When I met up with him after the accident, I asked him these questions.

He said that the *pujas* are very powerful, but his initial feeling when I asked him whether Matthew would be okay was that he would, in fact, be okay.

Chokyi Nyima Rinpoche's attendant later told me that after I talked to Rinpoche from the emergency room in Jackson, he woke up his most senior monks, and ten of them sat up well past midnight to perform a three-hour puja to help protect Matthew. These were the most critical three hours during which we were desperately trying to get Matthew to surgery in time to save his life.

The neurosurgeon showed me Matthew's scan from the Jackson emergency room. The bleeding had started in the usual place on the inside of his skull, an artery pumping blood into the space between the skull and the brain, pushing the brain away from the skull, squeezing the brain until the brain stem started being pushed down the hole at the base of the skull, compressing the most vital centers of the brain, shutting down respiration and stopping the heart. But in Matthew's case, the blood was somehow diverted before the brain stem was fatally damaged. The scan showed the blood traveling away from the brain stem through a small channel that had serendipitously formed at the time of the injury, allowing the blood to diffuse out over the surface of the brain, keeping the pressure in his skull low enough that he could survive the extra hours of his long evacuation. "The blood escaping through that little channel saved his life," he said. He held up his hand, fingers spread. "Five minutes. Five minutes longer and he wouldn't have survived."

"What do you mean? If he had gotten to the emergency room five minutes later, you wouldn't have been able to operate and save him?" I was incredulous.

"That's what I mean. His right pupil was dilating rapidly just as we met him, so we ran to the operating room. I drilled a hole blindly before we could even prep the scalp. That relieved the pressure."

"Would you consider this to be a miracle?" I asked him.

"I'm a neurosurgeon," he said. "I've seen a lot of different outcomes. You never know."

However, the neurosurgeon was not as matter-of-fact as he portrayed himself. When Matthew initially woke up, the doctor asked him, before hearing about his story, whether he had met with anyone while he was unconscious. I asked him why he raised this question, and he said, "People have a lot of strange experiences."

We all drove back to Kelly after eight days in Idaho Falls. Matthew was destined to be okay. Whether the experience would change him or not, it was too soon to say. But the experience had changed me. The fact of impermanence and the inevitability of suffering could not be clearer. I wanted to do all I could to try to ease suffering in the world. I needed to think: what more could I do?

FORTY-SIX

I am sitting alone in the highest retreat house in the Nepal Himalayas doing a personal retreat. Outside is an unbelievably spectacular view of mountains and valleys and clouds. I'm at 15,000 feet, on a ridge a thousand feet above the Pheriche Aid Post that first drew me to Nepal. At this altitude in early spring, the temperature in the unheated house is in the mid-thirties Fahrenheit, about the same as the inside of a refrigerator. I'm doing my practice, mimicking what it's like to be a full-time Himalayan practitioner— away from the world, in a place of natural beauty and isolation.

Why do Buddhist practitioners seek out these kinds of places? From the Buddhist point of view, there are three kinds of practitioners. The easiest way to practice is to be a wandering yogi, sleeping in caves, away from all other people. That way there is nothing between you and your mind, and you can progress rapidly, if you have the stamina for it.

The second kind of practitioner joins a monastery or nunnery. Surrounded by like-minded people, your daily activities are prescribed, and your life is devoted to Dharma practice and study. But you are still part of a community, with more distractions than if you went away completely.

The third kind of practitioner is a householder, a person living a normal life, but trying to incorporate Dharma practice as well. With the attachments of family, work, and recreation, it is harder to make progress. I was an example of a householder, but that's why it's good for me to go away at times and practice like a yogi in the mountains, just to get a taste of that life, and to give my practice a boost.

Many years ago, Tulku Urgyen Rinpoche told me that I should give up practicing medicine and practice Dharma full-time if I really wanted to help ease suffering in others. "People get sick," he said, "and sometimes you can make them better, but eventually they die, and then end up continuing to circle in painful samsaric existence, depending on their karma. If you could achieve enlightenment, you could help others end their suffering, not only in this lifetime, *but in all subsequent lifetimes.*"

At the time, I reacted with disbelief. Give up being a doctor? I had struggled hard to finish medical school. Becoming a doctor was how I got here, to Tulku Urgyen's side, to becoming his personal physician, to getting inside access to the world's highest Buddhist teachings. Not to mention helping thousands of patients, publishing research papers, and giving lectures at international conferences. However, even as I thought about those things, I couldn't deny that what he said was true. It was how Tulku Urgyen Rinpoche saw the world. He was right. I just didn't think I could do it. Cut all my ties and move into a cave? I wouldn't last a week.

I had overcome my uncertainty about becoming a doctor, and then found a highly satisfying practice. I came to believe what the young monk said to me: "Being a doctor is the best life you can live, because you get to make your living easing suffering in others." I had saved a lot of people's lives; I had eased a lot of suffering. Should I give up my career? In turmoil, I went to see Chokyi Nyima Rinpoche, who quickly reassured me. Although Tulku Urgyen Rinpoche was correct, he said, it was also true that I could help people as a doctor. It was still beneficial to ease people's suffering in this lifetime. I was grateful for his reassurance.

The next time I saw Tulku Urgyen Rinpoche, he also helped me be more comfortable with my decision. "It would be difficult," he said, "for you to abandon your family and become a full-time spiritual practitioner, and it wouldn't be fair to your family. Help get your family raised, and continue to work as a doctor, but don't lose sight of your goal. Keep up your Dharma practice, and when you can, spend more and more time on spiritual practice."

I hadn't lost sight of the goal.

When I'm at home, I do a combination of visualizations, recitations, and meditation that takes me about an hour and a half each day. I'm extremely diligent about my Dharma practice and haven't missed a day in more than thirty-two years.

It had been three years since my heart attack. During that time, my non-Dharma activities got busier for a while. I became president of the International Society of Travel Medicine, and my life involved traveling frequently around the world to attend meetings and conferences and helping to run the society.

I also went on tour with The Rolling Stones, as their tour doctor, traveling with them to Canada, the U.S., Japan, Macau, and Australia on four different tours. My musical life, as humble as it was in Kathmandu, had been resurrected, and I was living any serious fan's fantasy: flying on the plane with the band, staying in five-star hotels, and standing at the side of the stage while the world's best rock-and-roll band played to a screaming stadium full of fifty thousand fans. I was jumping into limousines and vans with the band and the entourage, racing away from the venue with a police escort at the end of the show before the fans could find their way backstage. My connection with the tour was through my close friend, Brad, whose phone call had saved Sarah's life. Our lives and the lives of our friends weave together in unpredictable ways. Touring with the Stones was something that one could never even fantasize about—how could it ever happen?—and yet it had. I thought it was amazing that I had entered the books that I read as a child; now I had entered the record albums I listened to as a young man.

Then, I decided to turn my attention to another fantasy that I had harbored for several years. I turned down a chance to tour with the Stones in Latin America and headed back to the Everest region to do the retreat on which I was currently embarked. The house is built under an overhang in a cliff halfway up a giant ridge. I first saw it thirty-seven years earlier when I hiked up to it during my first season at Pheriche. At the time, I couldn't believe why anyone would want to spend time alone in such an isolated place. My perspective had changed.

I spent seven days there alone. I arranged for a Sherpa to hike up each day with food, so I wouldn't have to think about preparing and cooking food while I was there. The retreat house was a single large room, with a shrine at the far end with a statue of Guru Rinpoche. The only window was small, and mostly opaque. The stones in the wall had not been mortared, and wind whistled through the chinks in the afternoon. The days dawned sunny and cold, with no wind, and I stepped outside and looked to my left to see the sun rising over the shoulder of Makalu, the fifth highest mountain in the world. Directly in front of me, dominating the view, was the north face of Ama Dablam, rising to a sharp triangular peak at 22,450 feet. The village of Dingboche was directly below me, a long line of lodges and houses along the river. The gentle rumbling of the river could just be heard when the air was still. Himalayan choughs—a black bird with a bright yellow beak—would land on the low rock wall and take food from my hand.

The spring season in the Khumbu brings frequent afternoon snowfall. By 10:00 or 11:00 a.m. each day, the first signs of a white mass of clouds started moving up the valley, obscuring the village below and eventually enveloping me in a white fog, out of which drifted a gentle powder snow that made a subtle swishing sound as it hit the rocks. The next morning, I'd awaken to a snowy landscape that would transform to dry dirt within a couple of hours, through the seeming magic of sublimation.

There was no bed, so I slept on the floor. I had a small table on which I kept my practice booklets. I bought the best down jacket I could find, and it kept me warm, wrapped as I was in ample quilts and a sleeping bag. Going to sleep by 8:30 or 9:00 p.m., I got up around 5:30 a.m. and started my practice. I spent two hours completing my normal daily practice. Then I would pause and eat breakfast and relax a bit before doing a one-hour meditation session. I did a second session before lunch, then spent some time outside, read books, and did more long sessions of meditation throughout the rest of the day. I could see trekkers taking day hikes on the ridge below me, but they were too far away to hear. I ate dinner, and then did one more session before bed.

According to the Sherpas who live in the village below the retreat house, I was the first Westerner to ever do a retreat there. I sat in a space that had housed a succession of serious retreatants for the past three hundred years. I could feel the spirit of practice that suffused the place, helping me to experience a patient calm throughout the day and night, despite the cold, the afternoon snow, and a vague nighttime eeriness.

The journey here had really started that day at Thyangboche Monastery when the strange longing to be taken inside had unexpectedly come over me. The monastery was just down the valley from where I sat, out of sight around a bend. This retreat house had served their monks and lamas.

While I was on retreat, I focused on compassion. Genuine compassion is the sense of deeply caring, of being patient, of conveying that you want to help—that you *will* help—no matter what it takes. Enlightened compassion is the desire to try to guide all beings beyond the suffering of constant rebirth. In medical practice, compassion allows a patient to relax and have trust that you will be there for them. It's the kind of compassion that my Buddhist teachers showed to me.

Despite all the attention paid in recent years in medical school to try to teach empathy and prevent burnout, there is still no training available in the West to increase one's *capacity* for compassion. Once I realized that my Dharma practice could help me experience and sustain a higher level of compassion in my work, I tried to figure out how I could share these insights with other medical professionals. Through the Medicine and Compassion conferences, the book that came from the conferences, giving lectures throughout the world, hosting retreats, producing a series of videos, and teaching a medical school elective, I have tried to show that compassion is something that can go beyond just a minimal reminder to be nice to the people that we care for to an inner quality that can become stable, vast, and effortless—words that are not even used in the West to describe compassion.

The Tibetan word for compassion is *ningje*, which means a feeling from the heart, or heartfelt. In the West, we think of our heart as the source of feelings, our mind as the source of thoughts. Ask a Westerner to point to their mind, and they'll point to their head; Tibetans will point to their heart. In their view, the mind is the source of feelings and is no different than the heart. The nature of compassion and the nature of mind are the same to them. To strive for compassion is to strive towards enlightenment. One of the greatest Tibetan Buddhist masters of this past century, Dilgo Khyentse Rinpoche, put it succinctly: *In an absolute sense, compassion is the awakened nature of the mind.*

How vast can compassion be? Are we to believe that Chokyi Nyima Rinpoche's compassion caused the rain to fall and put out all the fires when he arrived in Jackson Hole? Or was it just a coincidence? If I treat a patient for an illness when I'm not sure of the diagnosis and they get better, all I can honestly say is that their getting better *coincided* with the start of treatment. Just as Chokyi Nyima Rinpoche's ceremony seemed to magically bring a healing rain, modern medicine, when used in a culture without access to medical care, can also seem to be a form of magic.

It's possible to believe that Chokyi Nyima Rinpoche, through his compassion and skillful means, could have caused the rain, just as there is reason to believe that skillful diagnosis and good medicines can cure disease. If so, accepting that a great master may be able to manipulate the environment for the benefit of people and animals can expand our limited view of compassion.

Is the gentle rain of compassion just a metaphor, or something we can aspire toward? If compassion is capable of putting out the fires of anger in the world, how does that work? Rain is stronger than fire. But rain is not a unitary thing. It is the cumulative power of billions of raindrops, each one by itself incapable of affecting the fire, but overwhelming when working together with all the other raindrops. One could say that the teachers are the clouds that create the conditions for raindrops to form and help deliver them to where they are needed. Our efforts to train ourselves in compassion will contribute to a cumulative connection with compassionate people all over the world. We can't become rain, but we can each become a gentle raindrop of compassion, able to do our part, able to make it possible to overcome suffering. If we aim high, we can aspire to become clouds, and teach others ourselves. It's a slow but steady path; if you take up the practice of compassion, don't become frustrated or give up too soon.

I happen to be a doctor who learned about Buddhist teachings. As a doctor, I've learned how to diagnose illness and prescribe treatments. Buddhist teachings can also be seen as a prescription from a doctor. The doctor is the Buddha. The disease is suffering. To cure the disease, we need to find the cause of the disease. The cause of suffering is the fact that our minds form and cling to thoughts in a way that perpetuates our suffering. To be motivated to pursue treatment, we need to believe that there is a state of health, a state of mind that is beyond suffering. To be able to achieve that state of health, we need to follow a prescribed treatment. Wishing to be cured of a disease while doing nothing to treat the cause of the disease is not possible.

If we come to believe intellectually that there is a way to reduce suffering in ourselves and others, it will remain theoretical unless we apply it in our own lives. The basic approach to all Buddhist teachings is to first listen to or read the teachings. You need to make sure you understand what the words mean. Then you need to reflect on the deeper meaning, to try to decide whether what you heard is true or not. This requires an open mind, but not a gullible mind—you should analyze your doubts and try to determine what you think is true. If something isn't true, how can it be of value to you? If it is true, why would you ignore it? As you gain trust in the teachings, you then apply the instructions in practice, both in meditation and other practices that are meant to enhance our understanding. Even if you attained an encyclopedic, intellectual understanding of all the teachings, it would be of little value if you didn't apply them through practice, cultivating kindness and a calm mind.

I was fortunate enough to find my way to Nepal to receive these teachings from authentic teachers. I've had nearly forty years to reflect on them and apply them personally. Passing them on in this book is my best effort at repaying the kindness that I experienced from my teachers. My fondest wish is that all who read this book may be motivated to start exploring the path of compassion, or, if you are already on that path, to feel increased inspiration to practice.

You go through life getting glimpses of truths, unable to recognize them for what they actually are.

And then, suddenly, you can.

AFTERWORD

Although my memoir is now finished, my work is not. My goal is to try to establish a tradition of training in compassion in Western settings. Any profit that I make from this book will go towards achieving that goal. If my story has inspired you to explore training in compassion, I want to leave you with some resources that you can pursue.

Chökyi Nyima Rinpoche was the first Tibetan lama to introduce Tibetan Buddhist teachings on compassion to a Western professional audience. These teachings are captured in our book *Medicine and Compassion*, which remains the most definitive text on the subject, well worthy of study. The book is easy to read, but some of the concepts presented are very profound. A few words of guidance can be of value when reading these sections. In light of that, I've written t*he Medicine and Compassion Study Guide* that is available as an eBook on Amazon.

Chökyi Nyima Rinpoche is still teaching regularly around the world, with tens of thousands of students, and multiple retreat centers. His teaching activities can be explored through his website: https://shedrub.org.

I'm the president of Rinpoche's retreat center in the U.S., called Gomde California, which hosts Chökyi Nyima Rinpoche and several other great teachers every year (in non-pandemic times). The website is: https://gomdeca.org

Phakchok Rinpoche's teachings on compassion are profound, direct, and very accessible. A selection of videos of these teachings are available on my website: https://davidshlim.com

I've also created a course called "Training in Compassion" that is available on Phakchok Rinpoche's website: www.samyeinstitute.org.

Phakchok Rinpoche's main retreat center in the U.S. is in Cooperstown, NY: https://gomdecooperstown.org

My memoir ends in 2016. Since then, I established The Medicine and Compassion Projectâ whose main purpose is to provide materials that will allow individuals to enhance their own compassion, and eventually help to teach others. To review the courses, videos and additional materials that are available, go to: https://davidshlim.com

As an added incentive to visit the website, I've created a slide show of images from my life in Nepal that will give you a visual taste of what my life was like. And I've put up a recording of my song, "Peggy on the Train."

I would greatly value hearing from any of you who have read the book. I welcome your feedback, and in return, if I can answer any questions or offer you any guidance, I would be happy to try to do so. You can email me at: drshlim@medicineandcompassion.com

ACKNOWLEDGEMENTS

I began writing this memoir in 2004, just after my first book, *Medicine and Compassion*, was published. Many of the events depicted in *A Gentle Rain of Compassion* took place after I thought I had finished writing it, and had to be added in. A life is a work in progress, and so is a memoir; in my case, they ran parallel to each other for quite a few years. I owe a debt to many people who have helped make my life what it is, and to those who helped me write it down in a way that I hope will be entertaining and inspiring to others.

Chökyi Nyima Rinpoche took me into his world in a loving way and remains a close friend and teacher to this day, thirty-seven years later. He is responsible for completely transforming my life. His father, Tulku Urgyen Rinpoche showed me so much kindness and patience while sharing the most profound insights into meditation practice. I didn't realize how special it was, at first, to have stumbled into the most remarkable Tibetan Buddhist family on the planet. Although Chökyi Nyima Rinpoche can speak English, he gives teachings in Tibetan; his father spoke no English at all. Without translators, I would not have benefited very much from knowing them. Erik Pema Kunzang, who is Danish, came to Nepal as a nineteen-year-old, met the great masters, and taught himself Tibetan to be able to gain their teachings. He, along with his wife Marcia Schmidt, produced book after book that opened up the genuine teachings of Tibetan Buddhism to a wider world. A complete list of these remarkable books can be found at Rangjung Yeshe Publishing. Erik translated the teachings that became *Medicine and Compassion*. Most of the personal teachings that I received directly from Tulku Urgyen Rinpoche when I visited him at Nagi Gomp were translated for me by Andreas Kretschmar, who lived at Nagi Gompa for many years, and was always wonderfully kind and patient.

Phakchok Rinpoche has been a special friend and valued mentor. When The Medicine and Compassion Projectâ needed a boost, he offered to teach two Medicine and Compassion Retreats, at a time when his world-wide teaching obligations were vast. He and his wife, Norbu, have a special place in my heart.

I finished the first draft of my book in 2005, having worked nearly full time on it for a year. I found the courage to show it to my friend, Alexandra Fuller, whose memoirs of her remarkable and challenging life growing up in Africa have become bestsellers. I met her at a bagel shop in Jackson Hole to get her verdict on the draft, and she gently and skillfully suggested that I throw it away and start over. She said, "What you have written will be of interest to your friends. You need to write a book that will be of interest to anyone who picks it up." Sixteen years later, I'm hopeful that I have been able to do that in some way.

I received some valuable help along the way from two editors,

John Paine, and David Connor, whose kind insights help me shape the book.

I owe a special kind of gratitude to the first Jane, who appeared at the right moment in my life to help steer me onto the Dharma path. I've not been in touch with her since our final parting thirty-six years ago, but I often think of her and hope that her life has been happy and fulfilling. The second Jane, my wife, has been an adventurous, cheerful, loving, and supportive companion, and the best mother our children could have had. I've been blessed with a remarkably compatible family, who support my interest in Buddhism even if they don't all share my passion to the same degree. Having come within a razor's edge of losing them all when I almost died, and to losing my son when he almost died, my appreciation of them is never taken for granted for even an instant.

Initially, I wanted to name and thank all the friends I lived with in Nepal, and I started a list. But the list grew so long that I began to worry that I would leave someone out and inadvertently hurt their feelings. I made a choice, in writing the book, to keep the cast of characters to a minimum to not overwhelm the reader. I hope my friends will see this as a stylistic choice and in no way an indication that they were not important to me. There are dozens and dozens of friends who enriched my life in Nepal, and I love all of you. You know who you are.

To the many partners, nurses, and staff that shared the medical adventure of running the CIWEC Clinic: thanks for your help, your friendships, and the extra mile that you all walked many, many times to allow us to care for seriously ill patients with minimal resources. The stories of the patients we helped, and the way our staff pulled together to do that would fill another book. A special thanks to our laboratory technician, Ramachandra Rajah, who single-handedly, through his knowledge and skill, made our research program possible.

Lisa Choegyal makes several appearances throughout my book and that's because she has been a steadfast presence in my life ever since I moved to Nepal. She's the kind of woman who knows virtually every important person in the world. Through Lisa I not only met the first Jane, but also met and spent time with famous explorers, politicians, movie stars, and rock stars I would have never otherwise encountered. I have many nice memories of being with her at Tiger Tops, and dinner parties at her splendid house with the most interesting possible guests.

I want to thank David Peterson for both starting the CIWEC Clinic and inviting me to join it. Without either of those things, my life would have been completely different. And Peter Hackett, by appointing me to work at the Pheriche Aid Post, launched me on this incredible journey.

Prativa Pandey came along at just the right time to be in a position to take over the clinic when I left. She's the only doctor on the planet who could have guided it from the small outpatient clinic that it was when I left to the incredible hospital that she has since built with a wonderful staff that is appreciated by all the patients who go there. In addition, she and I share a remarkable amount of life experiences. She has been the only other Medical Director of The CIWEC Clinic since I left. She served as a volunteer at the Himalayan Rescue Association Aid Post at Pheriche, as I did. She was president of the International Society of Travel Medicine, as I was. And most recently she had a heart attack in the same part of her heart as I had. Even though her stories did not figure prominently in my memoir, my life would not have been the same if she had not been in it.

Although the book focuses on my education in Tibetan Buddhism and how I learned about training in compassion, my life was greatly enriched by close friends and mentors in travel medicine. It may appear, from my story, that I learned travel medicine on my own, but that is far from the truth. The friends I met through the conferences put on by the International Society of Travel Medicine shared their insights with me as our friendships grew over wine and dinners in exotic cities around the world, in Europe, Asia, and Africa. In addition to David Taylor, who is mentioned in the book, there is Charles Hoge, Alan Magill, Robert Steffen, Phyllis Kozarsky, Jay Keystone, Marty Cetron, Eli Schwartz, Nancy Jenks, Mary Wilson, David Freedman, David Hamer, Leo Visser, and many others.

A special thanks to Brad Connor, who not only shared the experiences I depicted in the book but provided me with the rare chance to tour with the world's best rock and roll band.

I want to especially thank Paula Wild, the executive director of The Medicine and Compassion Projectâ, who came to me through a referral from Kelsey Ripple, the invaluable media director of the project. It was through Paula that I connected with Di Angelo Publications.

And finally, my thanks to Sequoia Schmidt and the staff of Di Angelo Publications. As any author knows, getting a book published is no easy feat, especially these days when agents and publishers are looking mainly for instant bestsellers. After trying for years to find either a publisher or an agent who would want to represent this book, Sequoia and her staff immediately saw value in the manuscript and have helped me polish the book into its current form. I want to thank my old friend,

Eva Van Dam, who came out of semi-retirement to produce the portrait that graces the cover of my book.

Cody Wootten, along with Ashley Crantas, meticulously edited the manuscript, polishing up the language and asking for explanations that I'm sure will make for a more enjoyable read. I hope the book will live up to the faith they have placed in it, and that you, the reader, have something of value to take away from reading it.

ABOUT THE AUTHOR

David R. Shlim, M.D. is one of the most well-known and respected travel medicine physicians in the world. Drawn to the Himalayas to volunteer at a high-altitude rescue post, he later moved to Kathmandu where he ran the world's first destination travel medicine clinic for fifteen years. Early in his stay he offered free medical care at a Tibetan Buddhist monastery, befriending the head lama, Chokyi Nyima Rinpoche, and gradually discovering the benefits of Tibetan Buddhism, both personally and in his medical practice. His study of training in compassion led to collaborating with Chokyi Nyima Rinpoche on the first book that provided detailed Tibetan Buddhist insights into compassion for Western medical professionals, called *Medicine and Compassion*.

The research that he pioneered in travel medicine made his clinic the most famous travel clinic in the world. In 2013, he was elected president of the International Society of Travel Medicine, an organization with 4000 members in 100 countries. He also served ten years as the Medical Director of the Himalayan Rescue Association and was awarded a certificate for his lifetime contribution to rescue in Nepal by the Prime Minister of Nepal in 1998.

Dr. Shlim has given hundreds of lectures on travel medicine topics around the world and has also lectured widely on how it is possible to train in compassion. He recently created and taught a medical school course in compassion at the National University of Ireland, in Galway.

He currently lives in Jackson Hole, Wyoming where he practices travel medicine, teaches Tibetan Buddhism, and directs The Medicine and Compassion Project. He served as a tour doctor for The Rolling Stones for three years, traveling with the band to Canada, the U.S., Japan, China, and Australia.

VOYAGE

ABOUT THE PUBLISHER

Di Angelo Publications was founded in 2008 by Sequoia Schmidt—at the age of seventeen. The modernized publishing firm's creative headquarters is in Houston, Texas, with its distribution center located in Twin Falls, Idaho. The subsidiary rights department is based in Los Angeles, and Di Angelo Publications has recently grown to include branches in England, Australia, and Sequoia's home country of New Zealand. In 2020, Di Angelo Publications made a conscious decision to move all printing and production for domestic distribution of its books to the United States. The firm is comprised of ten imprints, and the featured imprint, Voyage, was inspired by the incredible power in our indiidual stories, reminding us that nothing is wasted and everything is a lesson in the journey.

DI ANGELO PUBLICATIONS
A Modernized Publishing Firm

Printed in the USA
CPSIA information can be obtained
at www.ICGtesting.com
JSHW012018140824
68134JS00033B/2761